PRAISE
BEYOND ENG

This is one of the most important books in leadership to have been written for a long time. It is one that needs to be read, not just by leaders but by everyone who works in an organisation of whatever kind. And why would this be?

Yetunde has taken a subject that at first sight appears to have little to do with work and shown how it is essential for the well-being of all and how for the more cynical it can translate into bottom line benefits. She has done this through using a series of quotes from senior leaders and building them into a clear and practical framework for applying love at work. The quotes by themselves are of immense value and offer inspiration and much to reflect on and use in the everyday difficulties of organisational life. However the author then builds on these and shows through chapters such as "Love and leadership team effectiveness", "Measuring the impact of love" and "Love and the future of work" exactly why we all need to work with love and the difference it will make to everyone. I have read hundreds of leadership books and this is one of the very few that deserves to be read, reflected on and applied. A truly brilliant combination of realistic observation with profound and far reaching ideas – and beautifully written.

Ralph Lewis

Programme Director, London Business School

Beyond Engagement is a wonderful book to read, from a perspective rarely ever discussed in senior echelons of corporations, the value of love-based leadership in organisations! It's all about being able to use our emotions and feelings at work to build a sustainable culture. This book is well-written, an eye-opener and important contribution to leadership literature on building a loving and compassionate culture at work—a must read!

Professor Sir Cary Cooper, CBE
50th Anniversary Professor of Organisational Psychology
and Health at the ALLIANCE Manchester Business School

Whether you love the concept of love in the workplace or hate it, we can all agree love typically brings out the best in us. What better aspiration can an organisation have for its teams and customers?

I love Yetunde's thesis, her passion, her crafted action points, and most of all, I love the deep conversation she has ignited.

Martin Butler
Author and Arsonist who enjoys lighting fires
in the minds of customer facing organisations

BEYOND ENGAGEMENT

THE VALUE OF LOVE-BASED LEADERSHIP IN ORGANISATIONS

YETUNDE Y HOFMANN

Published by Authors Place Press
9885 Wyecliff Drive, Suite 200
Highlands Ranch, CO 80126
AuthorsPlace.com

Manufactured in the United States of America.

ISBN: 978-1-62865-716-6

For
Akitunde and Yebo

CONTENTS

....

About the author

....

Yetunde is an internationally accredited Board level executive leadership coach and Managing Director of Synchrony Development Consulting.

Synchrony Development Consulting is an international leadership and change consultancy that partners individual leaders and leadership teams in the management of change, diversity and inclusion and the alignment of their teams and organisations behind them. It coaches leaders to be effective, leadership teams to be functional, and runs group-wide leadership and culture change programmes for companies looking to unlock the collective potential of their management and leadership.

She is the Founder of The Enjoyable Life Series - a community organisation designed to have men and women at all levels in business, education and community identify practical ways in which they can live more enjoyably in all that they do. In so doing, it supports their emotional, relational and mental wellbeing and contributes to the development of engagement and an inclusive culture in organisations.

The Tenets of her work are Love. Leadership. Results.

Before establishing a portfolio career, Yetunde built a successful, fast-paced career in FTSE 100 and Global companies like Unilever, Allied Domecq, Imperial Brands and Northern Foods. She began her career in Ibadan, Nigeria following the completion of her National Service at the International Institute of Tropical Agriculture (IITA) in Ibadan, Nigeria. Her last in-company role was as Global HR

Director for the commercial divisions of an FTSE 25 £30bn market cap business driving growth across 165 countries.

In addition to being a classically trained pianist, Conference Keynote Speaker and TEDx speaker, she is a Fellow of the Chartered Institute of Personnel and Development (CIPD), a Fellow of the Royal Society of Arts (RSA), a visiting Fellow at the University of Reading's Henley Business School and an associate of the Institute of Directors (IoD), United Kingdom.

As a Portfolio Non-Executive Board Director, she also sits on the Boards of a combination of commercial and charitable organisations and has been named one of the top 100 women to watch in the UK by the Cranfield University Female FTSE 100 Board Report.

She has a first degree (BA Hons) in Sociology and Economics from the University of East Anglia, Norwich UK and a Master's degree in Business Administration (MBA) from The University of Wales Institute of Science Technology (UWIST).

Beyond Engagement

The Value of Love-Based Leadership in Organisations

Learn, share and be inspired

To have the courage to do much more: for you; for me;
our people; our organisations; our communities; our society;
and indeed, our world!

Let's have the conversation

An introductory thought and reflection

....

THIS IS NOT NEW - indeed it is old. This notion that we live in a world of constant change. It is old and it will remain old. It will remain old because it will always be present, constant and true in every area and domain of life. Today the 4th industrial revolution is upon us and with it comes varying degrees of confusion and excitement; organised and unorganised chaos; certainty and uncertainty; hope and despair; all meshed into one.

There are winners and there are losers. As technology and artificial intelligence march onwards into the future, in the midst of all of this is the human being - the human being in organisation that also is community and also is society.

And yet since the beginning of the establishment of the human race, the greatest need and gift that provides security and belonging is love.

Why this book?

This book is designed to provoke thought, deliberation, reflection and, in hope, a call to action regarding the real key to unlocking the opportunity for extraordinary performance results in organisations. It dares to present the notion that the active and operational presence of love – the unconditional acceptance of oneself and thereby the unconditional acceptance of another – is real, though as yet unacknowledged as the key to high performance in business.

The world in which we live is increasingly volatile, uncertain, chaotic, complex, and ambiguous. Today's economic context is dominated by the knowledge worker buoyed up with rapidly advancing technology, artificial intelligence, combined intelligence and the replacement of highly skilled work by robots. The unrelenting competitive landscape, with unexpected disrupters to hitherto dependable business models, has made the fight for share of wallet, resources and talent, fierce; a desire to squeeze the highest margin out at minimum cost has become the underlying motive of business leaders. The resulting impact on the one most valuable asset that makes up organisation – the human being – is increasing levels of stress, the receipt of a deluge of initiatives on diversity, engagement, inclusion and wellbeing supported by various attempts by governmental and non-governmental bodies all over the world to introduce policies and programmes to increase the influence of employees or initiatives to increase productivity. Yet the simplest but potentially most impacting key – love – is one that is avoided or paid very little attention. Imagine if this were addressed. It would be a significant solution to unleashing consistently high productivity and performance in organisations. It would be the key to unleashing extraordinary results.

In fact, it would do more than that. It would give people in all walks of life and particularly in organisations, an environment in which they could connect with their own unique sense of purpose without fear of judgement, and therefore exist in the secure knowledge that all of who they are, every aspect of who they are, can be expressed.

This book makes a case for the head on and courageous exploration of the value of love in organisations and the difference it would make to people, to organisations, to community and to society.

It shares the contributions of experienced senior business leaders across a variety of industries, professions and walks of life. Leaders who were kind and generous with their time in exploring what it could mean for them, for their people, in organisation and society and who also willingly shared of their own personal experiences of love. Their contributions are a culmination of collected wisdom over their varied experiences in work and life, and a product of some of the most enjoyable and personally rewarding discussions.

What this book also does is provide ideas on how to introduce love in organisations as a way of being and how individual leaders may establish an environment in which people may love and be loved, thereby enabling true, genuine and sustained people engagement at all levels.

Finally, this book is for the Leader who wishes to be inspired to be courageous and to raise your head above the parapet because of the extraordinary potential that can be unleashed by the active and operational presence of love.

1. Defining Love

....

THE PROBLEM WITH THE L WORD

Love is many different things to many different people and herein lies the problem with the L Word. For some people it's all about emotion, for other people it's about personal sacrifice, and indeed for some, it's all about action. There are people who believe it's about faith and spirituality, and there are those people who believe it's about the physical and the romantic. As I engaged in discussion around it, what became clear to me is that through all these different perspectives on love, there is one clear divide: love is for personal life, it's for home life, it's for you and not at all for work or for the professional walk. In fact, when broached as a subject or even a word that can be explored at work, there's a raising of eyebrows, a chuckle or a furrowed brow swiftly followed by a variety of defences as to why love is not and cannot be a subject, a topic or a word to be raised at work. "It's too mushy"; "ah, it's not appropriate"; "it could give rise to sexual harassment"; "you don't want people to get the wrong idea"; "work is about results not love"; and so on.

In whatever way you examine the word love and in all its connotations, there is something special about it that generates a deep response and reaction emotionally, physically and mentally in the human being at work and at home. In fact, some may say that the demarcation between work and home is actually a root of the problem with love.

PERSPECTIVES

I want to start our discussion and exposition in this book with an understanding of the various perspectives and views of the senior leaders I interviewed.

In all their definitions was something special. They were personal to them - how they would as people, define love. Their definitions emerged in the context of self and how you feel, to the context of how you relate to another person and act towards them, be it family or friends and also to the context of how you feel about what you do. For some love is more of a deep feeling and for others, it is a matter of action and what you do. What I noticed that was contained in them, was an element of emotion, an element of the mental and an element of the physical and for some, an additional and overriding element of the spiritual.

The definitions had themes - some are in the context of self - how you feel about someone or something, some are in the context of others - as in what you do for them and others were in the context of the spiritual.

These definitions emerged out of reflection, how they challenged themselves and for some of them, a thoughtful admission that never before in their working lives to date, have they engaged in a discussion about love in the context of work and organisation.

Here is an example of one who defined love as centred around a passion and a deep enthusiasm for someone or something:

"A passion for a person, a culture and a way of life."

James Timpson

For others, love was predominantly about feeling and emotion:

"Love is about having a strong emotional attachment or a strong feeling towards another person and demonstrated in that you'd do anything for them, you'd put them before yourself, they matter more. This is how I would describe love."

Louise Fisher

"I look at love as an expression of affection. It is an emotional feeling. It is how you relate with people and how you express what you feel for them. Love is also an action - the things you do for people and it is what motivates what you do for people."

Sam Aiyere

For some love was defined in the context of others and relationship:

"Love for me is a feeling. And so, I ask myself: 'what does it feel like?' When I think about love, I think of my family, my children, my wife and my parents. In the recent past over the last two years I've lost my father and my father in law and what struck me in both situations is that at the end of it all, they all left possessions and family behind but what I remember the most from my dad, of what he left behind, was love."

Mark Scanlon

"Love is quite simple. It's about the compassion and consideration and thought that you have for another person. You may have love for an object - a piece of art for example - but the love you have for another human being is quite special. Love is about how you feel when you are with another person, and everything just makes you and them feel better."

Naomi Gillies

"Thinking about it from a personal and a professional perspective, they need to be the same. Love is the appreciation and mutual respect of another individual or group of individuals. It's a natural empathy and mutual understanding. Ultimately it comes down to respect. There is a connection and one that is usually an unwritten and unspoken one. It is a human connection which just says to you - 'I recognise you; I like and I love you' - if there's a deep appreciation."

Howard Kerr

"Love is used in so many different constructs. I believe that love is an unconditional acceptance of self and others. It can also be a passion about what you love doing and are enthusiastic about; it could also be about compassion and then you can take it much higher and say that God is love. There are many different constructs. When you come to the individual this can be a very deep sense where love can be described in a deeply emotional way which is the construct of human love."

Peter Cheese

"There is an unconditional and selfless component. A selfless care of or for someone that I deeply held. It doesn't mean that it is all sweetness and light because love can be painful and awkward but it has with it a profound respect for others. As with a lot of things it's not easy to describe but you will know it when you see it and you feel it."

Andy Mitchell

"To me, it's an indefinable term. Its manifestations are both subtle and infinite. Love is what we do, it's what we say. Sometimes it's what we do not say but it's what we show in our behaviours. It's both subtle and unsubtle. I think it's the most single and most powerful characteristic of human giving."

Ingrid Tennessee

And for others, love is seen in the context of relationship with oneself and then with others:

"I regard love as the care and attention that you place in yourself and in others and their relationships. It's important to elaborate for me that it is not putting others so far ahead that you don't care for yourself. You have to care for yourself before caring for others. When you're on an aeroplane you are taught how you should react when oxygen masks fall down - they give you a very clear instruction that you should put on the oxygen mask first yourself before helping others, so that you first reduce the burden that you could become on others and that secondly you are then well placed to help others. I do think there is a very interesting dilemma when you speak about love and putting other peoples' interests first, that it is not to the exclusion of placing enough attention and care to yourself so that you are able to be of benefit and to be of comfort or to be of support to others in the work place in particular."

Paul McNamara

"I thought about my wife who I've been married to for 21 years. I thought about her when I was thinking about answering this question which is very powerful. The first thing I wanted to say about love is this - when you love someone, it takes you to a place, a feeling; an outcome; a sense of being that is much greater than you as an individual and there is something very powerful about that."

Andrew Needham

"True love is to like someone so much that one is invested not only to embrace and fully accept them for who they are but to actually want them to progress and do as well as they possible can in their life, even if that means doing better than oneself. This includes tough love where personal growth has to be encouraged but also enforced. Love means to want someone else to succeed and be fulfilled. This is a very selfless act and it is in contrast to current values in society. The other problem is that people are not aligned in what that success means nor what fulfilment means."

Markus Hofmann

"Love is engagement and immersion. In the work context its' very different to the home context. There is romantic love and companionate love. The problem with love is that you also need an adverb for it. You have to describe what it means. It means to me the head and the heart and it also means respect. It's about the relationship between the two and how it affects how you see yourself. I believe that if you're not able to appreciate yourself in that way and to love yourself, it will be difficult to appreciate and love another person. It is an innate capability that should be built up within oneself. It is also about respect. Respect for yourself and respect for others. It can also be joy, fulfilment, inspiration faith, so many adjectives that you can use for it. It's therefore important that you define it in the way that it has meaning and makes sense for you and your organisation's context."

Charlie Wagstaff

The root of love being planted within the enclosure and relation of family and evolving with growth and maturity formed the basis of the definition of love for some:

"Love in our family has held so many meanings and because it's our family name; it's something that just cuts across so many different things. In the first place when I think of love I think of my family. We are the Love family. And then when I do think about what love really is, it actually is about family. It is the connection that you have to people that you feel strongly for. When I thought beyond my name and how that has influenced my definition, I saw a movie a while ago that triggered a very interesting perspective for me around love. It helped me to see love like a physical force; like gravity. For example, before Newton, we didn't really know what gravity was per se - although we knew it was there. The same in a way can be said about love. It is there and it is a force although we may not necessarily see it. We know that there is a connection that is established between people which is deep and fierce and it makes us do things and it makes us feel things. We don't really know what the equation is but we have a name for it and we feel it. It manifests in how we treat one another, how we feel connection with one another. I am married to a man whom I love deeply. I know that I love him. We are polar opposites and work extremely well together and I know that is love but I cannot equate it or put a number or an equation on it. This is what love is to me – you feel it, it's fierce, it's a force but you cannot really put an equation on it."

Charmian Love

"Love is first experienced in that loving cocoon of family. It is unconditional. My first experience of love was of unconditional love and of feeling therefore that I was of worth and I was supported and also disciplined and, in some ways, confined within rules. That's the first experience of love and to me it is the primary definition of love.

Then love in an adult sense has this very strong element of reciprocity and you learn that as you emerge from immaturity to maturity and you learn that it's not all about what you're receiving from others, it's also about what you're giving in return.

Love in terms of a lifelong partnership or marriage has this unconditional element - you make a commitment which is unconditional because you've chosen to share your life with somebody and that sense that they will be there for you and you will be there for them in sickness and in health as in the Christian marriage service which still speaks very deeply to me. That is love.

Love can then be stretched to a sense of international compassion and indeed loving my neighbour is all about loving somebody I've never met before."

Mark Goyder

"This is about how you view relationships. So if it's a zero sum game then someone wins someone loses. There has to be a win-win so you've got to have an attitude in relating with people so that both of you in that relationship should win; both parties would benefit in some way.

Because life is not just about loving your family, loving your parents - that would be narrow - but if you have the right attitude in you, then you have the ability to love anybody and everybody."

Richard Eu

"Love is about unconditionally giving of yourself for the benefit of other people. It's about compassion and it's about putting somebody else's needs above your own. It's also about joy - the kind of joy that lifts your spirit to high levels - for example, when you look at your children and it fills you with a warmth that nothing else can really achieve."

Norman Pickavance

And for others, love goes beyond emotion, relationship and feeling and into action as an act of service:

"I would define love as unconditional and sacrificial giving of oneself in terms of goodwill, benevolence, and kindness to another, without expecting anything in return and with a desire to put that person in a better place than they were before you met them. So for me, love is an act of will and not a feeling.

When you look at Scripture, the Bible talks of all kind of love. To me the highest expression of love is what Christians refer to as agape love, which is measured in terms of what it does. Love is always shown by what it does. It talks about God who is rich in mercy and God so loved the world. We have that beautiful description of it in 1st Corinthians 13 which talks about the different qualities of agape love and ultimately that love never fails."

Emmanuel Mbakwe

"At its core, love is about your subjugating your own ego and a degree of selflessness about the needs of other people and your ability to sort of ratify what you need. It is your ability to not always think about what you need ahead or what others need from you. There is a healthy balance in all relationships of course but it is a sense at its core that there is something more important than you, something greater than you and that you can be a part of that but not on your own."

Tracey Killen

The world of literature, the arts, film and music is also littered with various definitions, plot and perspectives on love and I would be committing a huge oversight if I did not acknowledge William Shakespeare's own perspective which in my view sees love in a variety of ways. His sonnets define love as passion and emotion, as unconditional as in Sonnet 130 and also as an action to endure and one that if real, proves resilience and stands the test of time - as indicated in his sonnet 116:

> Let me not to the marriage of true minds
>
> Admit impediments. Love is not love
>
> Which alters when it alteration finds,
>
> Or bends with the remover to remove.
>
> O no! It is an ever-fixed mark
>
> That looks on tempests and is never shaken;
>
> It is the star to every wand'ring bark,
>
> Whose worth's unknown, although his height be taken.
>
> Love's not Time's fool, though rosy lips and cheeks
>
> Within his bending sickle's compass come;
>
> Love alters not with his brief hours and weeks,
>
> But bears it out even to the edge of doom.
>
> If this be error and upon me prov'd,
>
> I never writ, nor no man ever lov'd.
>
> **William Shakespeare**

Then there are definitions provided by academic researchers and other authors too. For example, Barbara L. Frederickson in her *Handbook of Emotions (1996)*, concludes that *'love, then, is not simply another positive emotion. Rather, it is the momentary phenomenon through which we feel and become part of something larger than ourselves'.*

Writers and researchers Lewis, Amini and Lanon, in their own definition of love, separate being 'in love' from love by defining it as a form of mutual interdependence as a result of a deep knowledge and understanding of another. For them, love is therefore a consistent, mutual and willing interdependence that is sustained over a period of time. It is one where each person takes care of another, driven by a strong attachment to each other. The benefit of this mutual interdependence is that both thrive and are resilient to the peaks and troughs of life. (Lewis, Amini, & Lanon, 2000). I find this an amazing definition of love.

Cam Caldwell and Rolf D. Dixon, in their 2009 paper on *Love, Forgiveness and Trust: Critical Values of the Modern Leader,* define love as the 'unconditional acts of respect, caring and kindness that communicate the worth of others and that promote welfare, growth and wholeness'.

And then, of course, there is the spiritual angle - the one presented by Christianity. Here we find love presented and described in four different ways 1) Eros as depicted in the Songs of Solomon in the Old Testament; 2) Storge love which is about brotherly or sisterly love; 3) Phileo love, which is about deep friendship and companionship and lastly 4) Agape love which is unconditional love. They all have a place and a purpose. The one however that underpins them all is the fourth - Agape love. Unconditional love.

CS Lewis in his book *The Four Loves* - presents a definition of love in four parts - Affection, Friendship, Romantic, and Charity, where affection is both the need of one person for love and the gift of love that can be bestowed on another by a person. Friendship love is a strong bond that can grow between people who have shared values, outlook, interests and even a common purpose. It can be as strong as the love between brothers or sisters. Romantic love is the feeling of being in love or being loved - the closest to Eros in the Bible. And Charity love, which is about selflessness and unconditional love; a love that stands the winds of time and changing circumstances.

James Autry in his book *Love and Profit*, writes that good management is 'largely a matter of love' (p.17). For Autry, the expression of love was integral to leadership and because leadership is relational, in this context, love cannot be expressed or defined without it being in relationship to another.

Finally, in the Hofmann and Money discussion paper *'Can the study of love help business build more trusting relationships with society?'* we offer a definition of love as a 'positive emotional state focussed on another person or entity that has its foundation in the unconditional acceptance of the self and others'.

NOW WHAT

I could write reams and reams of pages on the various definitions of love and the perspectives that different people, cultures, writers and authors have about it. This has got to be one of the reasons why it's been a challenge to introduce love into organisations or indeed to freely talk about it. The decision on what definition to work with would always be a ready distraction. Where would you start? How should it be defined? This, however, is no reason to avoid it. Instead, we should, in our organisations, take a courageous and bold step towards the introduction of it into business and our work. A genuine introduction would have significant vicarious benefits because it would impact the organisation, its work, the lives of its people and the lives of the people that its people, in turn, impact.

The notion of engagement is dead in my view and the various well-meaning initiatives around the world in organisations on happiness, well-being, diversity and inclusion, and the various manifestations of it, are wearing thin. It's time to focus now on love and what I offer you is a definition that can work in organisation, and in all domains of life. It is a definition that goes one step further than the one earlier offered in my discussion paper. It is this:

Love is an unconditional acceptance of all of who I am as a human being and an unconditional acceptance of all of who you are - who others are. It is therefore the ability to value myself and others, for the beautiful human beings that we are and in so doing, enable myself and others to operate at our very best in the world. Love is therefore, an action, a behaviour, a capability. It is beyond an emotional state even though it can provoke and evoke emotion. What this definition allows and enables, which no other does, is the separation of the individual from their behaviour. It enables compassion, care, respect for all of who an individual is without making excuses for a behaviour or way of being that may be unacceptable. It encourages and enables the ability and desire to act in love irrespective of emotion. And for the individual, what it enables is a development and an instilling of a level of resilience that enables a withstanding of challenge and adversity, no matter the source and/or a readiness to bounce back that no other attribute can bring. It seems impossible doesn't it? It isn't. There is no limit to what we can do or become as human beings. The only thing it requires is a decision to act and a will to follow through.

2. Applying love in an organisation

....

YOU MUST BE KIDDING!

Defining love and what it means is nothing without expression or application. What is clear is that love in action when genuinely and authentically demonstrated can be the most powerful key to the unlocking of performance and potential in organisation. If your people feel genuinely loved - and it is easy to tell if actions are not genuine – what they become capable of is inexplicable. We know that the human potential – the maximum level of what a human being can do has not been reached. We have not even scratched the surface. The study of neuroscience underlines the potential of the human being to do so much more creatively for the organisation and indeed for self, the more psychologically safe he or she feels. This is because the part of the brain in which we solve problems and where the most work is done intellectually thrives the most when the distractions of insecurity, judgement, fear, exclusion are eradicated or minimised. Love enables and allows the presence of security and safety so the possibility of what can be done innovatively, and the speed with which day to day problems of whatever size are solved, can therefore be accelerated when love is present.

Yet the use of the word love in organisation is met with varying responses – from outright derision to strenuous attempts to qualify what it means. Very few organisations use it in their vocabulary. You might say that the use of the word doesn't matter. I believe it does.

There is the power of words and thoughts leading to action. Every action begins with a thought and the expression of that thought in words enables understanding. The idea of introducing a culture of love is one that is more often met with a little chuckle or raised eyebrows rather than with a ready willingness to explore what it could bring. How is it that the concept of love in organisations is one that is not immediately embraced? Why is this? How is it that the most powerful yet simple key to unlocking performance and potential is one that is met with such resistance? My own view is that love is seen as one of those 'soft' words that doesn't fit – 'it's not what we are about'. Talking about love is playful and has no home in the serious business of making money, delivering shareholder value, creating results for high paying consulting clients.

My senior leaders had their take on why this was. One felt that it may be too precious an expression to be used in the workplace:

> "I find the use of the word difficult in business because I worry about devaluing the term for those more intense relationships where it is as it were at home. In the relationship of marriage or in the parent-child relationship or in a sibling relationship there is a kind of lifelong continuity which may at times happen in business though you can't, in the same way, expect it to and so love in the context of those deep and lasting and lifelong commitments is one thing. To me a value chain relationship between a parts manufacturer and a car manufacturer, for example, can have a long term shared destiny relationship, you can develop deep levels of trust with each other and it may well be that quite legitimately and without anything unethical you may decide commercially to terminate the relationship and to me that's different to love."
>
> **Mark Goyder**

Another felt that the reason may be down to culture and the systems that have been created in organisations:

> "I think this might be cultural. In Britain, we are not used to talking about our emotions and love. If you watch American programmes on TV when family members are talking to each other they're constantly saying love you at the end of their calls - this is highly unlikely in my experience in the UK."

Louise Fisher

A third one believes the DNA of the organisation must be such that it enables an opportunity for love.

> "One thing is the DNA of an organisation. Does it enable the flow of love? The DNA of a conventional business is designed in such a way that you have to be selfish to be successful. It is only through culture and good practices that we can exercise the flow of love. If we don't design business in such a way that all the interests are balanced, and not only shareholders' interests, then automatically we are forced to put a hierarchy on whom we will take care for. Instead, if we adopt a legal structure where we can expand the fiduciary duties to all stakeholders in the short and the long term, we enable an equilibrium of love towards all possible parties."

Pedro Tarak

What I, however, took heart in and found most encouraging, is that none of the senior leaders I interviewed believed it impossible to apply love in organisation.

THERE'S LIGHT AHEAD

Can love therefore be applied in organisation? Can one overcome the challenges of definition and have it be present?

"It really can apply in organisation. It can apply through values, beliefs, principles, behaviours. Definitely. If you start by defining what love means in your organisation and what values, principles and behaviours go with it, it can certainly apply in an organisation."

Andrew Needham

"Thinking about it from a personal and a professional perspective, they need to be the same. Love is the appreciation and mutual respect of another individual or group of individuals. It's a natural empathy and mutual understanding. Ultimately it comes down to respect. There is a connection and one that is usually an unwritten and unspoken one. It is a human connection which just says to you - I recognise you, I like and I love you - if there's a deep appreciation."

Howard Kerr

"From a values-based perspective and a values-based organisation perspective, this can be a principle that determines how we describe how we are with each other and how it supports the work that we do. It could fit into organisational purpose and then be translated in terms of organisation and individual behaviours – i.e. the culture and the environment you want to create and how you want to shape the organisation."

Sam Allen

"When you come to the notion of love in organisation, I would define it in relation to the acceptance of others and the presence of compassion and caring for one another. You could also use love in the context of a passion about something or a purpose or a process and so love in this construct is not always about a human or a personal relationship it can be about having a passion about something to do with your work."

Peter Cheese

"If you are talking about unconditional care and if you're talking about a real respect for another person and for people as individuals, there's an awful lot of similarity with what we try to do and aim for here at Tideway. When you think of your children and the unconditional care and love you have for them, this is entirely possible in a work context, without that any sense of being weird. You've got to work with people and we all need advice, help and correction, and love involves being truthful in those actions. This is not just happy clappy stuff, if you really care about someone, it should show in the way that you relate to and with them."

Andy Mitchell

"In a business context where half of our waking hours are at work, what we do has to be more than just a functional effort. I'm in a context where I like what I'm doing, I'm happy with what I'm doing and what I'm learning and also with those that I share this mission with. It is in this that I would allow the concept of love to come in. You are sharing so much time with colleagues that some of the aspects of love must come in. If you love someone, you're rooting for them, if you love someone you wish the best for them, if you love someone you inspire them and they inspire you. So it may be a big and heavy word to some people but many of the attributes are so relevant. Winning teams - are often mad about each other. They enjoy their colleagues; they stay late and longer not because any boss has asked them to, they stay longer but because they want to."

John Mangan

"Love can be reflected in the value statements of corporations. These statements should reflect the concept of love being an act of will. Then it should be built into policies and processes. For example, the reward systems should be built to reward those who exhibit those values in the course of delivering corporate objectives. If the reward system promotes individualism - i.e. 'I win, you lose' - as opposed to 'we win together' then there's a problem."

Emmanuel Mbakwe

"In organisation, if we can love our customers that's where it can be so powerful. You can love your job - for example, I was exploring the possibility of a new role with my boss - and when I really thought about it, I didn't find anything in that new role that I would love doing as much as I am doing now and so it was an easy decision for me. I said no. There are many things in my job now that get me out of bed and eager to get into work. I think that the more you can get people in organisation loving what they do the more successful the organisation can be."

Naomi Gillies

"It can't not exist in organisation. It's important. I think it holds the key to the difference between the engagement and the emotion and sometimes the line that some people cross and find difficult. But when you put this aside, it is also very interesting to find how many people find true love through work. For example, my wife, I met through work and so work also does have a social element to it. But let's not confuse it with the line that can be crossed sometimes that steps into the unwanted and unacceptable as we see reported in the media. There is also in work the companionate and the compassionate type of love which is about the head and heart and how we've got to use emotional engagement and get to learn the power of that a lot more as an entrepreneur where you love what you do and are able to create an opportunity for other people to also love what they do.

Interestingly and which is a good thing, I am seeing the word love used more and more too. People are using the word love more as we move away from a world of heroic leadership in organisation, which is all about one individual and more towards an environment which is about the why and love is the why. It's all about the why."

Charlie Wagstaff

"First of all, you've got to love and appreciate yourself and that allows you to appreciate others. Is it a romantic, parental or friendship type of love? Love can fall into all of these brackets. I think all of them would work because I've got a romantic love and connection for my workplace. I've been here for 16 years and like with any relationship where you have your lows and your highs, I've had that here too. It's the love that keeps you going as it's not every day that's an easy day. Parental love also works here for me because I started off in my career here as being a child and being taught and guided on what was important; on morals and on expectations and now in my current role I'm doing the same for others, giving them guidance and supporting our leadership programmes. In terms of friendship, I've created different types of friendship both personal and professional ones whilst here and all of them though different are all underpinned by love. So I think all the different types of love I can think off can work in organisation.

In organisation, I think the friendship type of love is one that is probably the easiest for people to apply although as I think of it, the most effective is parental love. It is the one that also comes closest to unconditional love."

Alan Price

There is light at the end of the tunnel. This is because increasingly, senior leaders are calling on the attributes of love in the consideration of the culture they would like to introduce into their organisations. This is being helped along with the increasing levels of uncertainty in the context – all aspects of that context in which organisations need to operate in order to survive let alone be successful.

WHAT YOU DO WITH THE LIGHT

How then could love be applied in organisation? Well, the first thing that you do is define what love means to you and to your own organisation; what it means in your organisation for your people. Giving your people the opportunity to participate in its definition will also contribute to removing it as a taboo or from a concept that is seen as taboo in organisation. The co-definition process can itself be an expression of love in action. One way of showing love is the act of including the opinions and the contributions of others in the decisions you make for your organisation and the concepts you want to bring in particularly when there is or will be an expectation of adherence to and honouring of the new way. The emphatic point here is about your people feeling like they have been heard. Feeling listened to. Genuinely. Even if what they have contributed is not included, feeling heard and genuinely so is what is most critical. It means that you can demonstrate love in the way that you go about defining it in your organisation; in the process that you employ in reaching the definition of what it is in your own organisation and how it can be made present. That alone in itself can be a demonstration of love.

Love can, therefore, be applied and enabled to show up in what you ask your people to do and the behaviours you ask of yourself and of them to demonstrate.

> "My definition of love in an organisation will come down to the personal attributes of love. So, for a person to be loved by the organisation it is feeling secure, allowed to express oneself and have an opinion, to try something out, not do so well and learn from it. On the other hand, there is also chastisement. So, if you're not doing right, at least you point it out. An organisation just can't be fantastic and saying you're all wonderful and everything is fantastic and beautiful. It has to be balanced. An organisation if it's going to love somebody must be able to make them relaxed, get the best out of the individuals within it to ensure that they're content and also have the level of security but you also have to give that guidance - the shepherding - correcting in a kind way."
>
> **Mark Scanlon**

Love can be applied in what you enable your people to do and the permission you give them to try new things freely without reproach; it can be applied in the way you help them understand that each and every person in the organisation is part of the whole.

"It is about having people do a lot of things, trying different things and making mistakes, and encouraging that. It is allowing a culture of total openness where people can be themselves. This is what love in organisation looks like."

Andre Angel

"In organisations we build relationships. Leaders with those working with them and leaders to leaders. I believe we can bring the concept of love into organisation when we are open; we are honest; we are compassionate, and we actually understand the feelings of others and deal with them on the basis of that - as humans."

Sam Aiyere

"Therefore, love is about recognising that people are in a company and in certain positions in that company for a reason and hopefully for merit and motivation. The organisation functions because of everybody, not because of one person and certainly not because of only the Chief Executive."

Howard Kerr

"What we are trying to do is something about how we educate people and to get the message about how we can help people understand the consequences of the decisions that they make for themselves every day - and this is not about throwing a campaign out at them. -e.g. - eat 5 a day, exercise x number of times a week and so on - this is about helping our people think carefully about how their decisions may affect their personal health before taking the decision. I talk about this regularly and encourage my team and their people to do so and in this way, the business will start to embed it."

Steve Fox

"In a retail context, you want your teams and employees to love their customers and sometimes that can be hard because some customers can be difficult but I do believe that partners in our branches, genuinely love our customers and will go above and beyond what you would expect them to do. We have some amazing stories, one example being where we've had customers who've shopped with us for over 40 years, who've always come in as a couple and sadly when one of them has died and they come in alone again, our partners would walk around the shop with them to keep them company as they shop or they would go and have a cup of coffee with them. Our partners do this because they love their job and they love their customer. The power of getting more people to do what they love shouldn't be underestimated."

Naomi Gillies

"One of the principles of love is that it's not a zero-sum game. The more I put in the more I get out. It is an abundance quality and I guess this is what the best businesses have. You can almost sense it the moment you walk into their reception. You have this sense of abundance and a sense that "we're here to do something important and we value each other in our common quest to do something; we love our work in the course of loving our work, we love each other.""

Mark Goyder

Love can be applied in the environment you create for your people to operate in and to live their working lives in, physically and virtually.

"Demonstrating love in work is when you are able to create an environment in which your people do not feel like they need to wear a mask when they come into work. How can you be at your best if you've got to come to work and put a mask on? That doesn't sound like a right organisation. For people to be at their best, they need to be able to be who they are."

Andy Mitchell

"Companies have a role to play in creating a spirit of enjoyment of each other, valorising and promoting helpers and enablers; they have a role to play in consciously showing the world that we promote generous people. We promote people who think beyond themselves and who clearly look out for others. If this is done once, then 10 times and then a 100 times, people who come into the business will see and experience what values really matter and will then self-select themselves in or out."

John Mangan

"The next thing is about making sure that it is embedded into the organisation culture. Culture is the way we do things around here and people do what people value. So, if the reward system is designed so that it drives individualism and grates against working together, then there's another issue. When we look back in terms of how the principles of love and the gospel are seen in action, we can go back to the 1800s - during the industrial revolution where the likes of the 'Chocolate trinity - i.e. the Cadbury, Rowntree's, and Frys - were driven by Christian principles and values. They built libraries, houses, had pension and health plans. Some may say that their actions were that of enlightened capitalism. I beg to differ. I believe what drove them were the principles of caring for your neighbour which Jesus not only enunciated but demonstrated through His death on the Cross."

Emmanuel Mbakwe

Love can be applied in the behaviours of your leaders at all levels of the organisation and what you ask them to role model; water only trickles downwards and the behaviours of your leaders will impact the lives of the people for whom they are responsible; in fact the behaviour of a leader can be the single most impactful differentiator in the performance and affection of your people towards their organisation and the people who lead it.

"Values and principles should drive your behaviours. Values really help define who you are who you want to be, what's important to you, where you want to go in your life - all this comes from understanding your values. Love can come alive through the values that you want to hold up in the mirror so that you as a person, as a leader, can look in that mirror every day. I'm always struck by leaders that I've read and really loved what they've written about leadership only to find out later that the values that they've espoused in their books on leadership are not values they live or lived in their personal lives. I'm really struck too, by leaders who do and can go on public platforms; and they talk about principles and values to do with leadership and yet do nothing like that in their private lives. That's false and when you look at it through the lens of love, you would say - if you really love someone, you wouldn't sleep with another woman; you wouldn't betray your people, your colleagues. I've been really disappointed by leaders in public life who are not the person they say they are; who don't live values they say they have in their private lives or in their work lives. And for me as an entrepreneur, everything that I want to be judged for in my work life, are so interrelated to my personal life that if I did anything in my personal life that betrayed who I am in my work life I've ultimately betrayed who I am. You can't have a value set at work and then have a different value set in your personal life."

Andrew Needham

"By having people that love each other and people that are rooting for each other - there is a base and a concept - that if I'm obsessed with rooting for you and I'm out there trying to make things work for you and you in parallel are also trying to make things work for me; If everyone is focused on trying to make things work not for themselves but for the others in the team and it creates this positive spiral it can be a powerful thing. The French have an expression - 'Entraide' - it means helping each other out. But a spirit of Entraide is a spirit of not just cooperation. It is much more generous than cooperation. It is about each of us helping each other out because I'm there for you and you're there for me. This spirit comes when people learn to appreciate each other and therefore in leadership in organisation, the role of the leader is to create the right climate and overseeing and checking and just being sure that the climate of cooperation, the climate of Entraide is present - 'Do people have the opportunities to get to know each other?'; 'Have they been given workloads that are fair and that don't create conflict?' And so on."

John Mangan

"When you look at people that you hire, you don't see them as hired hands, you see them as hired hearts. There is a moral meaning and requirement. A leader must do the right thing and with the right heart and for the right reasons. I believe this with my own heart and soul. I think that servant leadership expounds on this and it talks about the connection between leaders and followers. It is not only deep but it is very strong. I hope and I aspire to offer this in all aspects of

my being as a leader and I would really like my leaders in my
own organisation to share this, emulate this and accept and
understand that in order to have really true connections with
the people that we serve is that they must love and they must
come from that place as seeing people as hired hearts and not
hands."

Ingrid Tennessee

Whether you like it or not, a boss or leader has a big impact on
your life and if you are not as resilient and life proof as you would
like; if you are not as self-accepting of yourself as you should be and
as loving of yourself as you really should be, the bigger the impact
on you by your boss's or leader's behaviour will be. Positively or
negatively. The negative impact of course, lasts longer.

Love can be applied in the rules of engagement you ask your
people to adhere to and that you model in the various touch points in
your organisation's lives. The most common touch points being the
ones where you gather together for decisions, process and progress
checks, creating new ways, problem solving and so on. Meetings
that you convene at all times and for all reasons and with all kinds
of people can build or bring down unity; a glance sent across the
room with disapproval, a mutter under your breath, can set the
tone for the day and for the mood; it can send an aroma across the
organisation that signifies sweet or bitter; a contribution, decision or
comment made from a place of 'me' versus from a place of 'us' can
have a ripple effect, the consequences of which may last much longer
than the time taken to convene and will impact people and lives far
beyond the geographical boundaries in which those contributions,
decisions and comments were made.

When you and your people deal with each other in love, and
relate to each other in and with love, it impacts how they feel in

organisation and indeed how they may feel in life, because an organisation's responsibility should not be only to the individual at work, it should be to the individual at home. Your people are whole persons. They take all of themselves from home to work and back again - the concept of work/life balance in my view is dead and unreal.

> "If I go back to the childhood experience of love, it is this feeling of being valued. I think most of us have been fortunate enough and over a career lasting several decades to have had at least one boss who you felt valued you above and beyond anything about your role and what they were going to get out of you. They simply valued you and wanted the best for you. There is a kind of unconditional love element to that. It can be in the early stages of one's career."
>
> **Mark Goyder**

> "In Spanish there are two expressions to be moved with emotions. 'Conmovido' (moved with others) and 'Emocionado' (moved oneself). Your love can affect other people. This is energy. So the flow of emotions can have a positive impact in the culture of an organisation because when one person feels it, another may as well. And that can keep roving to the rest of the people."
>
> **Pedro Tarak**

> "I have no problem in business finding the cash or the ideas. The difficulty is in finding the people. When you then get the people, you've got to take care of them. They remember you not for the pay cheques and bonuses, even though that is welcome, what they remember you for is how you treated them. Nobody can remember what bonuses were paid to

them in 2012 but they can remember whether I was good or bad with them. That's what people remember. How did I treat them?"

Mark Scanlon

The age and nature of your organisation may influence how love is applied. Organisations established relatively more recently may have it easier. For example, Patagonia or some of the organisations listed in the Frederick Laloux book – *Reinventing Organisations*. There is evidence that also says that age may not be the reason why some organisations may find it easier. South West Airlines, a long established organisation, is often cited by academics and non-academics about their application of love in what they do and in how they serve their customers and their people. It is an organisation that has been around a long time and survived the fiercely competitive airline industry. Martin Butler in his book – *It's Not About Us, It's All About Them* describes the culture in Southwest Airlines as one in which love is present.

In the UK, organisations like Timpson's who operate in an industry which, given the developments in technology and the big shifts in the world of the consumer and routes to consumer channels, should be struggling, have not struggled. Instead, they have thrived and continue to do so. Timpson's has not found it difficult to apply love in its organisation.

"In business, you would use love in business when you love working with your colleagues, you admire your colleagues and you love the mission and purpose of the business you're associated with and are working in.

Love would show up in the way people behave to one another and to those connected with the business whether it is customers or suppliers. It will show up in peoples' behaviours and commitment outside of work, to work and it is how they talk about it in the pub or to their family. If there is a crisis in the business, if people are passionate about the business, then they will pull out all the stops, whether they are on holiday or a day off but if they're not passionate about the business they won't."

James Timpson

Regardless of the age of your organisation or industry in which you operate, love can be applied up and down your supply chain and in the behaviours you demonstrate in these channels to your clients, your suppliers, whatever size they may be, to your consumers and to your customers. As a customer of Timpson's, I've experienced care and love in the way that I've been treated; in my doctor's surgery, I've experienced care and love in the way that I've been treated - depending on the doctor of course; and as the owner of a boutique consultancy, I've experienced care and love in the way that I've been treated and have certainly recognised and experienced the opposite. What I have discovered in every way is that it's all about people. It's all about the interaction with people and people behaving in their organisation in the way that their leaders either model or have made possible through the decisions that they make.

The opportunities for the introduction and application of love in organisation are therefore immense and easy to spot. Making this happen is within our gift and the gift of the leaders who run different parts and aspects of the organisation. We simply just need to get on with it.

LET'S GET ON WITH IT

How then can love be applied? Having a purpose that is beyond the day to day and one that is infused with a genuine and fundamental intent to make a difference to human kind, or the environment in which that human lives, or the society that the human impacts, or the community for whom the human is responsible - a purpose that has an intent to make a difference would be a great place to start. This is because it is impossible to have such a purpose without at its fundamental base, a platform of love.

The perspective of senior leaders in how you may apply love varies but all have the following characteristics and themes: – it is important to incorporate the application of love into your organisation's values. Even if you do not use the word itself, though I think we should, you can incorporate its attributes and core essence into your values.

> "People may not say the word love. But how many people say I love my job, or I love it here? What do they mean by that? I think it's the attributes of love that people are identifying with when they say that; attributes like security, being relaxed, perhaps being accepted, being at ease, being content, and having that feeling of the world around you being reliable; you're in a place of safety."
>
> **Mark Scanlon**

The application of love in organisations starts with the definition of what love means to you. Your organisation's role in society and community and to your people. To do this, it means the genuine inclusion of the views and perspectives of all of your people or certainly of the representatives of all of your people. It would mean understanding what it means to them to be loved. How they would experience it, when they would experience it and from whom they would experience it? It would mean, also, understanding and defining what love is not.

The application of love in organisation would mean talking about it and with a sense of seriousness. This is serious business after all. We are talking about the greatest need of the human and the greatest gift that an organisation can make possible for its people. It is an acknowledgement that if a big proportion of our lives is spent working and therefore in engagement with other people, then it is a human right that those years and experiences should be some of the most enriching and fulfilling.

The application of love would invite a question around what love would look and feel like right through our supply chain - upwards and downwards. How would we treat our suppliers, our clients, our consumers and how would we encourage our suppliers to treat their suppliers? How would we expect to be treated and to feel in all of our dealings with all of our stakeholders? My time spent to date as an independent entrepreneur has helped me understand the challenges of being a supplier, albeit a boutique one. Currently, there have been times when I've felt like a spare part and felt dehumanised in the interactions I have had with potential clients. There's been a very clear message of, 'you matter less'. I remember once, being sent to an office in one part of a country when the meeting location had changed to another part of the country. The first time it happened I put it down to work pressure, the symptoms of busyness and therefore a simple mistake. The third time it happened I got the message - 'You don't matter to us' and 'your time is of less importance than ours'. Therefore, when you apply love in organisation, you would ask about the impact you want to have on all those people whose lives and working lives depend on the decisions that you make and on what your organisation does.

In the application of love in organisation, you would explore what it would look like and feel like in the execution of your processes and policies and adapt and modify them to allow for the expression of love to come through.

NOW ABOUT THOSE PROCESSES

The increasing eradication of performance ratings in organisation coupled with a focus on strengths is an indication of a move in this direction. When you do however surface the notion of love and the definition that underpins it; that acceptance of the individual as a human being; what it would further enable are questions that ask: 'how do I demonstrate that I see the real person and human being in all that I do?'; "How do I demonstrate that I see the heart beneath the role and the job title, appreciating that this human being is more than a means to an end; and how do I ensure that they see me - the real me, the human heart beneath and behind the status?'.

I believe that the real key lies in seeing and being seen. Despite an increasing focus on strengths in organisation, the emergence of supportive evidence-based neuroscience, and the emerging eradication of performance ratings and labels, plus the introduction of equality, diversity and wellbeing initiatives, engagement levels in organisations across the world and in some of the most affluent countries, are still inconsistent. They are inconsistent because at some level, the majority of these initiatives are implemented because the primary driver is self, and the material acquisition for self and shareholder and not the love and appreciation for other people and society.

> "As I grew up I began to appreciate the words from the play by Alan Bennett - The History Man - where he's a flawed character and a teacher but his great quality is the way he challenges and treats the pupils in his care and his great line is 'pass it on boys, pass it on' - that sense of passing on what you understand, passing on experience and getting others to recognise that they have potential - I think that would be a flourishing of love in business."
>
> **Mark Goyder**

"There is a Latin expression which says, 'Nemo dat quod non habet', which simply translated means you cannot give what you do not have. So there must be a particular care that you have for yourself which you are then able to pass on to someone else."

Emmanuel Mbakwe

LAYING DOWN ROOTS

Love will be applied in organisation through the way that roles and vacancies are filled. Be they filled through external means or through an internal process. If you say that to get a particular job there is an open application process, then there should be an open application process. Not that one thing should be said and another thing done. If there will be a combined process of interviewing both internal and external applicants, then the methodology must have integrity and not just being done to tick the right box. If your preferred candidate is internal, then your case as to the reasons why, should be made and made without condition or expectation of the candidate, or with an intention to prove the decision-makers and gatekeepers wrong, should they reject your proposal and insist you go through a structured process with both internal and external candidates.

The recruitment process can be one of two experiences. Either, one in which the candidate is treated and feels like a commodity and a product at the mercy of the recruitment agency or platform, or one in which it feels like a mutual journey of discovery and appreciation of one's strengths and skills and capabilities that can be leveraged for the benefit of others in the organisation, then or later. It would be a process which confirms for the candidate what they have in their hand to offer the world, regardless of the outcome.

FIRST THE FOUNDATION

Love can be applied in every aspect and domain of an individual's life. If it can be applied in every domain of their lives, it, therefore, can be applied in every domain of an organisation's life. It can be applied even in the simplest of things. If love were present and applied; if this were the starting point, even in the smallest of actions, it can potentially have the biggest impact and ripple effect. For example when your people and team members are on a training workshop, you would give them the space to be fully present at that training workshop and you would resist the temptation to request that some piece of work be done urgently, because of course the world would end if it weren't done. If love can be applied, it would be in every single process - from how you define what and who you need, to incorporating this into the whole life cycle of your people and all that they experience; their recruitment, on boarding, resources given, resource allocation, performance management and development, resources to do the job, training and development, promotions, travel to do the job, relocation, bereavement support, decisions around pay all the way through to process of departure and parting for whatever reason, in small or big numbers and so on. All of them, will start from a place of love. They would start from an intention of acceptance of the human being and to see the human for who they are first, and only from that place get on with what needs to be done.

> "It's a great reminder that at the end of the day, performance and progress relies on human interaction and human trust. So if there is a culture, a set of behaviours, a set of values which puts at its heart the wellbeing of individuals in the organisation and those who are interacting with the organisation, then it's a much more powerful place to be, it's a much more productive environment, it's an environment where there is greater levels

of trust because there is a set of established norms which place the individual much more at the centre of what is going on."

Paul McNamara

"I think that love is not an add on and is not about enhancing productivity, it is a fundamental necessity of any organisation particularly with the changes that we're facing, technologically, societally, and so on; we have to be a resilient organisation with resilient people and this comes from being fundamentally healthy - all the elements and component parts of the organisation have to be healthy - and that most critically means its people."

Andy Mitchell

"Organisations are the institutions that humanity have created to enable humanity to do the things that you cannot do on our own. Organisations are the greatest human invention. That capacity to collaborate towards common goals and in so doing achieve more than you could ever achieve on our own.

So organisations are created to really help society to solve the problems that it faces and I think organisations at their best are the ones who are helping to solve those problems. So going back to the love definition, where there is suffering, organisations can help to relieve the suffering, where there is need, organisations can help to fulfil those needs but they can also help people to realise joy and happiness and great times too and when organisations stop serving the needs of society, one has to question what it is they are there for."

Norman Pickavance

The starting point, of course, is therefore the definition of love. If it were a definition that incorporates an unconditional acceptance of yourself and who you are it will in turn instil in you a robustness and an assuredness of who you are. It will instil in you an unconditional acceptance of others and because of this, the great and positive experiences of your people at work would be even greater. In addition, the bad and negative experiences of your people would be less bad and less negative. Their memory bank of unpleasant experiences in life would have a much shorter lifespan. When you start from a place of love, of which the core component is acceptance, the attributes of compassion, respect, trust, responsibility, and speed will flow. And out of these would flow the human expressions of forgiveness, grace, fairness and mercy - the every day to day terms that are core to our humanity. These are terms that are not devolved from who we are. They are terms that connect us as human beings regardless of our context but suppressed and denied a surfacing in organisations.

It is therefore not at all impossible to apply love in organisations. There is absolutely no area of an organisation in which love cannot be applied. It is in the gift and hands of the people in it and of those who lead and care for them to do so.

Yet there are barriers - seen and unseen, deliberate and not deliberate. In order to overcome them, we must first examine what these barriers are.

3. BARRIERS TO THE PRESENCE OF LOVE IN AN ORGANISATION

....

THE BARRIERS TO THE active presence of love are many and can be seen and unseen. They also are a product of our conscious and unconscious doings as human beings. But whatever they are, we are able to deal with them and the starting point is naming them.

WHAT'S WORK TO DO WITH BALANCE?

Many a barrier can be laid at the feet of our upbringing. I can see your nodding head in agreement. Those early years at home with family and parents form our behaviours, our values and what we believe to be important in life and for life. The friends we make along the way starting from kindergarten age and right through to adult life will have an influence. The adults and people whose actions impact us and vice versa will have influence on our attitude and understanding of love as well as our ability to give and receive love too. The teachers that we have in our formative years and as we get older and transition into adulthood, those who encourage and those who stifle, will contribute to our outlook on life. The groups, gangs and tribes we join and enrol in overtly or covertly, and the communities and subsections of community we identify with, will enable or lead to the formation of barriers of all sizes, seen and unseen, conscious and unconscious, to the presence of love in our lives and therefore in organisation.

As children the words of encouragement or limitation spoken over and to us by those whom we love and spend most of our time with, can contribute to feelings and thoughts of self-acceptance and self-worth or beliefs about success and achievement, confidence and fear that may serve or limit us. The various figures of authority in our lives who have played prominent roles in our formative years will have contributed too - intentionally or unintentionally to our outlook in life.

What we do not appreciate enough, although there is an emerging realisation of this, is that life and work are not separated. They are one and the same. But therein lies a barrier which exists today - a continuous belief in organisation, and by the people who lead organisations, that life and work are separate. Even though the world of technology has led to a physical blurring of those separations and an acceleration of the fusion of the two worlds of home and work, the internal separations within us have yet to catch up.

It is this separation of life and work that forms the first and most fundamental barrier. It prevents us from taking our whole selves to work and reserves the workplace wherever that may be, for a place where only the professional, the well behaved, the preferred and well-crafted image is allowed to emerge. Depending on the industry or the context, it reserves work for a place where in the past it was pin striped suits and today it's the jeans with holes as the only outerwear allowed. The separation of life and work has established the work life as a place where your deepest beliefs of self, orientation, faith, views are left outside the door and wait to be picked up on the way out as life returns to home life.

"The reason why people may not be so readily open in organisation is determined I believe by their belief system and their value system inculcated from a very young age. We probably have to blame the parents! When you look at a young child - I don't think you're born with your value systems it comes with the environment in which we grow up and the influence of parents. Instilled from very early life."

Richard Eu

"I observe many people bringing in many personalities to the workplace other than their true personality. People wear a mask or a face or adopt a professional demeanour in a professional environment because they are expected to play a role which is not necessarily 100% who they are as individuals. So, there is often a façade or a disconnect between how people think of themselves in their life compared to how they play their role in an organisation.

Part of this is explained by history because there have been hierarchical master/servant roles and behaviours in most organisations for many years. The division of labour, which was great for productivity in many ways, has however pigeon-holed people into specific and limiting descriptions of their authority, the boundaries of their influence; the degrees of freedom they have to interact with others and where decisions get made. This has acted against colleagues in a workplace bringing all that they can to their organisation. If there is more focus on roles rather than people, then there's a risk that individuals feel less cared for, less appreciated, less loved."

Paul McNamara

"Love is not talked about in organisations today because, unfortunately, we have developed a system which is quite binary. For example, by how we think about profit on one side and purpose on the other, or male and female or good and bad, or work and life. I really hate the concept of work/life balance. We shouldn't be balancing because it's assuming that we are trading off one thing for another and there shouldn't be a trade-off. We should be who we are. All the time. Rather than balancing, you should be blending things. Maybe one reason why we don't have an open discourse in organisation, because love is seen to be something in your life and not in your work."

Charmian Love

"A barrier also is the comfort that some people have in organisation to the use of the word love. They see it in the personal context. They see that the parental, friendship or even romantic type of love doesn't apply in the workplace. There is a disconnect. There's empathy rather than sympathy; there's a barrier that says they've got to be able to make difficult decisions and love would stop that happening. But in the personal context, you've got to make difficult decisions particularly from the parental point of view, regardless of how much you may love your children, or your mum or your dad. My dad has had health issues and it's about saying to him, you must go to the hospital or you die. And of course he doesn't want to go, but you've got to make that difficult decision and insist that he does. You've got to help him. The same happens in the employment relationship where love doesn't mean you avoid a difficult decision, sometimes because of love, you face that difficult decision head on and make it."

Alan Price

I had a conversation with a colleague once as we were getting ready to attend our company's global leadership conference. As we mused over the various presentation and experiences we would have, he turned around to me and said - 'you're going to have a great time because you're outgoing and able to talk to anyone.' I smiled and told him that to the contrary, I dreaded large company events where everyone would be vying for the attention of the chief executive and playing to various audiences. He was surprised. I continued on to say that I knew that because we worked in an alpha male culture, he would fit right in. He was also running a big part of the business, was well respected and always sought after at company events. He burst out laughing and told me that he also dreaded those types of events and experiences because he was always under supreme pressure to ensure he said the right thing, cracked the right jokes, was on top of the latest golfing, football and rugby stories, when what he really wanted to do, was talk about poetry, art, his most recent visit to the theatre and time spent with his grandchildren. As he finished his story, we both sat down. In silence. We looked at each other and smiled. Nothing more needed to be said.

The consequences of the separation of work and life and not bringing your whole self to work can range from the profound realisation and quiet admission of pretence or carefully manicured self-image between two colleagues, all the way to a life of stress, mental and emotional breakdowns and outburst, illness and in worst case scenarios, suicide. The scary thing is that we may not even know the depths of despair our colleagues experience or the severity of the personal challenges they may face. There may be no signs at all until a family member or loved one rings in to inform colleagues. This is how deep seated the desire is in some of us to keep our real selves hidden in work. The consequences can also deprive organisations of the benefit of the best and most novel ideas, the competitive advantage of the first mover, and the resilience that comes from the joy of knowing that all of who you are, is present at home and at work and at anywhere else you may find yourself.

For some senior leaders, the issue is not about living a separate life at work to home, it is more a matter of the difference in the application and experience of love at work versus home.

"In my instance for a business to function fully and properly there has to be a disconnect eventually. It is work. There is a stopping point. There comes a time when there is a reciprocal relationship between remuneration. People will know where the line is and where the stepping off point is. Where chastisement becomes an issue of underperformance, which becomes an issue for the host, and as a leader in organisation you will have to deal with that underperformance and that may not be experienced as love.

In addition, in the context of organisation and business, I may need to change a person or swap one out for another because things are not working; performance may not be what it's meant to be, but I could never contemplate swapping out a family member, but as a manager of a business for the good of the business and everybody else, I may need to swap a person out. This is the point where the two worlds - love at home and love at work - do live apart for me."

Mark Scanlon

And it is this that might actually make it challenging to use the language of love in organisation - the fact that it is individual and personal to each human and what one intends as love towards another, to the recipient it may not be experienced as such. At least not in the moment.

PLEASE DON'T MENTION THE L WORD!

One of the consequences of the separation of work from life is the lack of mention of the word 'love' in organisation. It's just not talked about, it's hardly mentioned and when it is mentioned, it's often accompanied by a giggle, a quick joke said in embarrassment or a hurried attempt to explain oneself.

"The first is the fear of the word love in the work context. Just even the idea that anyone would use that word would elicit fear. And if your boss started talking about love at work, he or she would get some strange looks - so the fear of the word love would be the first barrier without a shadow of a doubt!"

Peter Cheese

"The word love is not commonly used in business because it is not very macho. People don't really associate love with business. A lot of people in business just follow what other people say and people, certainly the British, are not exactly the first to embrace words like love."

James Timpson

"It is also not a language that you typically have in the workplace, so if you've had your career develop in a certain way and you've adopted different behaviours, it's easy to have the same expectations of people behind you. So in order to move forward, we may need to have something much different and that something different would lie in the caring of your people, the valuing of your people, valuing their contribution, recognising them for it, rewarding them for it - but it is different and difference is not easy to adopt."

Louise Fisher

"We don't often use the 'L' word. I think historically people have separated work and life and seen them as two different things and this in itself is a barrier to the presence of love or to the use of the word 'Love' in the workplace. There is a lot of preconceptions around work. There is a formality - you've got to be serious and this is business and a whole bunch of different language and vocabulary is wrapped around what work is meant to be and it's never really explained to us that the product of an organisation is a by-product of it being a good and efficient organisation made up of people - thinking, feeling people."

Andy Mitchell

I am thankful though that the mention of it actually is on the increase and that in some organisations the expression of emotion is seen as an advantage. When this happens in an organisation like Tideway where the possibility of folding up and its people having to find alternative sources of income once their work is completely done, is a reality, it can be inspiring.

"We're lucky that we stumbled on the 'rekindling a love affair' concept in our work here at Tideway because it allowed us to bring emotional language into our work vocabulary and narrative and this helped us and gave us a different set of words to the standard corporate language and love is one of the things we talk about. Freely."

Andy Mitchell

Talk about love in organisation and what it would bring to us as humans and to our communities as well as societies is not growing as fast and as deeply as it should be. This is because when love is not talked about or mentioned, it minimises the opportunity for its expression and the contribution it can make in the success of an organisation and its people. If self-acceptance enables self-expression, which it does in my view, and self-expression facilitates creativity, a willingness to speak up and speak to, a readiness to try and to dream plus the courage to pursue, then an absence of an ability to talk about love and with a degree of seriousness must mean a limitation to the potential contribution that an organisation's people can make to its success.

I therefore wonder why an attribute and a word that is so all encompassing and fundamental to the human being is not a ready part of vocabulary in organisation and the world of work. The fact that the definition and experience of it is individual to each person should make it all the more a subject of discussion and a way of understanding what motivates, drives and makes each person tick. One reason may be the history of organisation and the world of work - a world where facts and data are the only currency welcome.

> "Traditionally the way organisations are set up, particularly those that are commercially driven, the idea of feelings or emotions, whilst we see them day to day, is non-existent; they tend to be more fact or data driven. They are essentially set up to make profit and so anything that may conflict with that, is relegated and not considered. Love comes at a cost. A sacrificial cost. The way things are set up currently - a dog eat dog approach to things, a focus on the short term - does not lend itself to this."
>
> **Sam Aiyere**

> "Part of the barriers is also the general discomfort. It's a sensitive word with its own nomenclature that people are more or less and often less comfortable with. It is intangible and so how you can bring it in is not easy to impose - it would take some very careful thought."
>
> **John Mangan**

> "Corporate speak in organisation is a very big barrier, People talk about innovation inspiration, in corporate language; but in real life, nobody talks to each other like that. You and I would

not have a conversation using those terms. It's important to take into consideration how people talk to each other on a day to day basis. Language like that doesn't really help because it corporatises language and it also corporatises feelings and it sets the parameters within which people feel they can behave and be."

Tracey Killen

And in some organisations where corporate speak has a life of its own and the focus is data and evidence, facts and figures, the opportunity for the expression of emotion is rare and even when it's talked about, to talk about a word that can evoke a level of emotion that demonstrates vulnerability, can be a challenge.

"Another barrier is that love in the workplace is seen as slushy. Some people say - why would you want to have love in an organisation? Isn't that something that is just reserved for marriage? But what is interesting is that when I look at the NHS and how my grandmother who was admitted to hospital there was treated by the staff - they genuinely just showed her love. There was no worry about how they were perceived or the nurses feeling self-conscious about how they were treating her; in that organisation and in that situation, it is acceptable to show love and I guess you would have the same in Macmillan. In the corporate world in general, I do think there's something in this whole compliance and litigation world that lead some people in the workplace to believe that love should be confined to your relationships at home and must therefore be left at the door as you come into work."

Naomi Gillies

"A lot of company values are not designed for people to identify with or to embrace; they're designed to speak to investors, to markets and for public affairs purposes. And therein lies a disconnect."

Tracey Killen

The concept of emotion and emotional intelligence is however not new. These are subjects that have been around a long time. Daniel Goleman, in his books *Emotional Intelligence and Working with Emotional Intelligence*, illustrated the importance of being aware of your emotions and being able to understand them and that of others, as key to being an effective leader in organisation. Self-assessment questionnaires have been designed and used in many an organisation to support people in their leadership development in this regard. In recent years, social intelligence has emerged as an additional attribute and capability that supports leader success in organisation. None have, however, paved the way for the easy flow of discussion of love in organisation.

The good news is that the world of work is evolving and there is an increasing focus on the human being and what it means to be a human in organisation which means that it should become easier to talk about love and the difference it would make, but is it?

"We are now in a world in which there is a focus on the humanistic nature of work, so why wouldn't love be part of that - why shouldn't it be a part of how we talk about work and in this context the other barriers would be choosing and understanding - i.e. - in what construct are you using that word? Help me understand it. This means that the other barriers would be the ability to put it in the right context and in the right construct."

Peter Cheese

"However, it is interesting to see that many organisations are now moving back towards what was previously more organic and human-centred interactions, much more devolved decision making, much more empowered organisations where individuals can take more rounded views on how they can interact. I think the next generation is also demanding this based on the much broader social interactions that they regard as normal before entering the workforce."

Paul McNamara

SAFETY IN NUMBERS

A lack of diversity and a tendency for organisation and the world of work to be dominated by one gender can be a barrier to the presence of love. In many organisations, this dominant gender has been the male human. Men talking about love in the workplace, or even acknowledging that it can be present, is not common, although I have met several men for whom a discussion about love and its place in organisation has not been an issue. However, for the odd one, none included in my interviewees I must add, it did take some persuading. When an organisation has the dominant presence of a particular gender, especially if that gender is male and is in majority of the leadership positions and positions of influence, ego can get in the way of the presence of love. Where ego is predominant, love has no place - at least not on the surface - because it reveals vulnerability, and vulnerability and ego do not live side by side.

"Possibly because most of our organisations are led by men. Leadership teams tend to be male dominated and white – this is a huge generalisation - and therefore you tend not to get the softer skills, the emotional intelligence displayed by those types of leadership teams as much as you would from a more diverse team whether it be diverse in gender, race, age or other characteristics that enable diversity. So I think it is the leaders and their types. I also think that there are organisations that just don't have demonstrable respect for their people - the employee is still much lower down the food chain in some organisations - 'I pay your wages, I expect you to turn up, that's it - that's our two-way relationship sorted.' Whereas in an organisation where you expect love to be flourishing, you'd expect much more respect for the individual - their rights, their values, their feelings - you'd expect the people aspects that you take into account into your decision making to be as equal as other things that you may factor in when making decisions."

Louise Fisher

"Work has been synonymous with fight. With battles. The market share battles. Screwing the competition, annihilating them, taking them out and winning the competition war. Business has been dominated by men, and men before business were conquering land with swords. This is the culture that was used to establish organisations in the past and is the legacy we are still dealing with today."

John Mangan

"Barriers at senior levels - there are just too many men and what that does is that it causes big business to have quite a narrow and binary view of what is required from people in the workplace. So, the truth of it is that a lot of organisations espouse diversity and inclusion, but they don't really actively seek to build inclusive cultures where people feel, completely, they can be themselves and can bring their whole selves to work. Those cultures are very narrow and very specific and are very driven by the financial value that organisations need to drive."

Tracey Killen

"Gender can be a barrier too. Women may find it easier to use the expression and express it easier than men can. I think in addition, things have been made a little more difficult because of the 'MeToo' campaign, when you observe what's been going on. You may have men who are unable to cope with the 'MeToo' campaign, let alone expressing love. It's a shame in some way because I think men are beginning to express themselves better, so this is a setback, although this is an extremely important issue. So the lines which have been blurred by some very bad behaviour have made it so that some people have an inability to cope with the difference between romantic love and the respectful and companionate love. It also means that there are some organisations in which the men are unable to cope with where to draw the line between hugging a colleague because you genuinely care for them or wanting more than that colleague finds acceptable. The sad thing is that hugs are key to wellbeing and a few people have made it more difficult for the majority to be genuinely loving at work. Now, of course, there are cultures and faiths that may not permit hugs and these must be respected. Respecting that is also showing love at work."

Charlie Wagstaff

"Mostly it's ego. I may not have recognised this had I not been successful. We always try to do so much more. As humans we love to compete as males, we love to compete. Competitiveness in human DNA is there. Males exhibit competitiveness I guess in a different way to females. But in general, we want to compete, we want to be the best, to be successful, to beat everybody else - that's nature. Even a baby lion would want to be closest to its Dad. So it's innate. The question then is how do you tame that? And I think that it's the recognition that you can't do it alone and in some of the lectures that I give, I say that 'no matter how smart you are, no matter how badass you think you are, you're never going to be able to do it alone! So, you better go out and get yourself a great team."

Andre Angel

There are however exceptions. Not all men are one way, just like not all women or indeed black women for that matter are the same. I have come across many a man and indeed some who may describe themselves as supposedly alpha male, who have championed and are championing the power of diversity and the promotion of women in organisation. I have been a recipient of this championing, and from the most unlikely of quarters.

THAT'S NOT HOW WE DO THINGS HERE

Organisation culture is another barrier to the active presence of love - 'the way we do things here' or 'the way we've always done things here' can prevent the contribution that love can bring or indeed stifle it, should it try to break through. If your organisation is one where challenging the boss in public is frowned upon, love cannot show up. If you work in an environment in which it's important to be seen and be physically present at work, no matter the number of initiatives on working from home, childcare arrangements, paternity and maternity leave and so on, love will not show up. If you have a leadership group who clearly has membership clubs, the terms of membership for which you have no clue, then love cannot show up.

When your organisation convenes conferences, key strategic meetings, away days, special sessions with the C-Suite and Chief Executive on site or off-site, the participation in which there are no clear rationale, then love cannot show up. If you work in an organisation in which hardly anyone shows up at the various corporate events and celebrations, like the Christmas party, love is not present.

When you have your town hall meetings and nobody responds to the invitation to ask questions or challenge openly with an independent view, love cannot be there. When your business unit, department, or local market spends months preparing for a half day visit of a senior leader from headquarters or corporate, love may not be present. When all your colleagues do, (and that may include you) is spend time managing upwards in order to climb the greasy poles of power and promotion and sometimes at the expense of other colleagues, intentionally or unintentionally, love cannot be present. When members of your team dial into a virtual meeting and go to great lengths to pretend they are not at home and keep silent the uncontrolled cry of a child, then love certainly will not be present. When your people strive and go to great lengths to hide their sexual orientation from the glare of others, love is not present. When you or your people feel consistently excluded from meetings and events that you know you can contribute effectively to, there is little or no love.

If after a team meeting where all have agreed to a way forward and a line of action, the next meeting convenes with the same people around the water cooler and undermines all that was said in there, then there can be no love. When the boss confirms a line of action and immediately goes into the office of his or her own boss and delivers a contradictory message on behalf of the team, there is no love. When many pre meetings beyond the norm take place over and over again with the same stakeholders that are actually going to be in the room for a meeting in which you're looking for a decision or an opinion there never can be love in that organisation.

When feedback is given dishonestly to a sub-division or local unit leadership team at the end of their presentation requesting additional investment and resources in their work; a presentation that took blood, sweat, sleepless nights and late night rehearsals to prepare, then there absolutely can be no love in that organisation. What are your own examples? I could go on.

Once upon a time, I observed a company board leadership meeting where a country general manager and his team had travelled 5 hours to present their investment plan for approval. They had rehearsed for days. Their boss had coached them and assured them that with his feedback and visible endorsement in the room, they would have no problem. They arrived at the board meeting at 1.30pm for their 3pm slot on the agenda. At 5.30pm they were rushed in and told to reduce their presentation time by half. They took courage and did their best. After all, it's not uncommon to be put back and delayed for your slot on the meeting agenda of your very busy bosses. At the end of their presentation, the CEO turned around to the team's boss and asks: "What is your view? Are you supportive of this?" Their boss nodded from side to side avoiding eye contact with the general manager or his team and remained silent. The CEO turned to the country general manager and his team, thanked them for an excellent and well-presented case and said, "We'll come back to you. But well done!" As soon as they left the room, the postmortem went like this: "wasn't that presentation terrible? Ill-prepared? Illogical?" "They clearly are not on top of their numbers." "They're clearly going to have to do this all over again!" Their boss nodded in agreement, saying nothing at all to support them.

The senior leaders I interviewed share their examples and perspectives too.

"A lot of this is not written down it is what you pick up when you get there. It's like someone saying to you, you shouldn't be socialising with frontline staff, you're a manager or saying to you, you're a graduate, you should be socialising more with senior management and so on. Those unspoken requests for ways of behaving that actually are not said but overtime can create barriers to the presence of love in organisation."

Sally Cabrini

"Leadership style - power versus engagement or prescription versus persuasion or 'I am right you are wrong' or point scoring or overestimating your position versus quiet support or indeed employing clever people with potential and then instructing and telling them what to do."

Lewis Doyle

"Also, where human relationships and those informal interactions don't take place, people fill the gaps and misinformation emerges because there is nothing better to take its place - e.g. 'I don't like the way the boss did x' - well actually the boss did nothing but in the absence of not really knowing the boss or spending time with him or her then individuals fill in the gaps and not always with the positive. So what helps and works best is where the team gets together and spends informal time together knowing each other."

Richard Gillies

"We live also in a very competitive world and many things are about win-lose - see the sports world for example. So many things in life are about wanting to be champion; in school we want to be top of the class and so on. So, if you want to progress you always feel that you must progress at the expense of other people - Ranking of universities, for example. Also, people measure how much you're worth, how much you earn, the material goods that you have - people take comfort in self -worth by material and other forms of measurement."

Richard Eu

"If the definition of love is that you have an environment where people are content and are happy and are able to give of their best, then lots of things can get in the way. A person's ego can get in the way; an organisation's structure can get in the way; a tradition can get in the way; a way of doing things that's historic, an absence of permission and so on. Then when it comes to the person, the person may not take the time to understand how people work, how people feel, how the teams work, how we communicate to the rest of the organisation; also the person may have an aversion to failure even though failure is not always a bad thing. So one barrier may be the function of the organisation and the other will be in the person themselves.

One example of the person themselves is a colleague who joined my team and would always start a sentence with 'I might be wrong' ...It made me smile because actually, you might be right and right a lot of the time! So preconceptions and ways of working in the past in other organisations may cause barriers within the person to experience love in the workplace when they join a new organisation."

Mark Scanlon

"Because society is not about love, at its best it is about acceptance, but it is only about the individual not the community. Furthermore, well-being and success are two areas that are constantly shifting in their meaning and therefore it is difficult to define with longevity and consistency."

Markus Hofmann

Meetings of all kinds, and in particular, those in which there are high stakes and a degree of personal risk, are a great place to observe and experience an organisation's culture and to experience at first hand, the presence, or not, of love. Your own self-reflective responses following a meeting to the question - 'what would have been different if love were present in that meeting?' - would also be a great way of sensing the culture of love in your organisation. If you find yourself with many reasons and ideas, then it's likely that love is not there. When you think about it, the barriers to the presence of love are really very easy to identify.

The culture of relationship and the way you do relationship with your suppliers, and particularly the small, boutique ones, will be an indication of the presence of love in your organisation. When a supplier is taken through an arduous process that is constantly updated in order to get onto your organisation's database, love is not present. When that supplier then at times turns up at meetings only to find that the meeting is cancelled without notification, there can be no love present. And then when that supplier has to wait a lifetime for the payment of an invoice for work already done and carried out to the satisfaction of the client organisation, that is not a demonstration of love.

> "The same happens in commercial deals. With a quid pro quo transactional type of relationship in the market, our natural selfishness fully prospers. But we miss the opportunity of the infinite potential that a human based commercial deal has when you enable the flow of love. We have actually emptied out the emotions, the values, the belonging to a community... all elements that we have in other spheres of life like family, religion, football clubs, NGOs and even politics. In the marketplace all that has been cleared up. Given that today the market is the most dominant place of daily interactions, the lack of humanity is paramount.
>
> For example, you have huge companies delaying the payments to small entrepreneurs who barely make a living, e.g. 120 days

to pay small suppliers who suddenly realize that payment is deferred putting under risk their existence. That's lack of love! That´s not being able to put yourself in their space or place and feeling for them. But that is also not developing the muscle of empathy and consciousness. It may be legally okay for the large and powerful but may affect negatively the possibility of survival for the many small."

Pedro Tarak

IT'S ALL ABOUT ME

This leads on to another barrier to the presence of love in organisation. The greed and self-centredness that pervades many a human being in organisation and particularly some of those in positions of influence, authority and power. When decisions that impact others are made almost exclusively from a place of self-service, no matter how eloquently packaged and full of corporate speak the reasons or excuses, it presents a barrier to the presence and contribution of love. Greed, however, is one of those words that evokes discomfort in people. No one likes to be called greedy and very few people would admit a tendency to be greedy. At least not to others and in some cases not even to themselves. But if leadership is relational which it is and what you do, say, share, decide or not impacts someone else, when those actions are done because the driver and motive is self and at times greed, it can be the furthest away from allowing a presence of love.

"Greedy leaders are not very good. It's like a salesman - they are generally overpaid. They're good at selling themselves. A lot of change management people are brought in and are over-promoted and this is where it all goes wrong. Greed is a terrible thing for a business and it destroys its core. When they turn up at the top of an organisation, they really are interested only what they can get out of it as opposed to what they can contribute."

James Timpson

"Greed - that monster of absolutely zero consideration for anyone else than me, myself and I and where the only KPI is size and profit not about your team or their wellbeing, that notion of the bigger number the bigger profit and so on. Greed that is a barrier. It has been around a long time and in organisations and that culture has had its impact of creating too many winners and champions and solo players and I would argue, too many men!"

John Mangan

"Barriers are Leaders who are focusing on what is more important to them than focusing on what is important to others. A barrier is also the fear of being seen as soft or as weak - that notion of a leader having to know everything and always reminding people of who is boss. A typical greeting or response from such a leader and I've had this before, would be 'do you know who I am? I am the CEO, don't speak to me like that! You're just an officer, I make the rules around here. You follow my instructions if you know what's right for you.' I think those are real barriers to the presence of love. They see leadership as a given and there's no place for love in that."

Ingrid Tennessee

WHERE IS YOUR FOCUS?

Greed is, however, fed and nurtured, and it is the conditions that feed and enable it to manifest that also present a barrier. Incentives and rewards, targets and objectives and how they are formed - all this contribute to the feeding of greed and self-service. Even if greed were not the driver, the way many organisations are owned and their people rewarded and incentivised, makes it challenging for love to truly flourish. This may well be one of the reasons endless attempts both novel and varied, to improve productivity and engagement, have achieved inconsistent results. If principal stakeholders operate from a position of self service, or require quick and high returns on their investments, it is difficult to pay attention to what it means to love your colleagues and to work for the greater good of them and the communities in which your organisation resides.

If you want to focus on the demonstration of love and its attributes because you believe and know the contribution it can genuinely make, but your stakeholders and the gatekeepers to your success have as their priority short term, financial gain, the rapid acquisition of share of market, the growth of the bottom line and the eradication of the competitor, it becomes difficult to site your focus on love and the benefits you know it will have for your people which will be a healthier return on investment in the long term as your reason for not delivering in the short term.

> "What I observe in the PLC world are organisations that don't know how to deal with shareholders' influence and don't have the strength to stand up to them. Many organisations say they do stuff but don't do what they say. The incentives that are given are not aligned and are all around the wrong things - so this is quite a barrier. We also see targets and performance indicators in all sorts of walks of life, and the problem with them is that they have good intentions but drive the wrong behaviours. Behaviours that respond to the indicator that is being measured and this is a problem with a lot of organisations because they all operate the same way and what they do is they drive and

incentivise, usually financially, senior employees to deliver those things that they measure and this is a flawed way."

Steve Fox

"This can be an incentive - performance management. The incentives that can incentivise individualistic behaviours and individualistic behaviours can result in friction in an organisation."

Lawrence Hutter

"Another barrier is that the wrong things get measured in business, or we are not measuring the right things. If we are not measuring the types of outcomes that focus on how leaders operate within their organisations, the cultures they create in their business, how they relate to their people and their customers, how they think of their organisation's responsibility to the communities in which they exist and serve - unless we measure and focus on these things differently - we won't create and sustain the shift that is beginning to take place in the world of work."

Peter Cheese

"I do think that scale is vital. Take Facebook. The original idea of Facebook was that it enabled people to connect and share. The unintended consequences of the Facebook business model as its scale has grown, I believe, has been that it's opened itself up to all sort of manipulation to and of people that want to share. This will not have been a serious problem had it not been for its huge scale. This is combined with the fact that it's a listed company which has made ambitious promises to the capital markets and thereby created a relentless pressure on itself for quarterly results, with less concern for how those results are achieved. In a world where we made devolution and decentralisation an absolute priority - in that world, it would be more possible for love to flourish."

Mark Goyder

"Numerous barriers exist. Short-termism is one - the focus on that year's results, that quarter's results above all else drives a certain behaviour and a certain pressure being applied and perhaps individuals and teams needs are put aside in the pursuit of the goals. So there ends up being a misalignment between what the company needs and what the people within it need. Constant change of direction, constant change of emphasis, constant change of strategy leaves people feeling confused, disillusioned, disengaged; political environments don't lend themselves to love – a place where it's about self-promotion, pushing yourself ahead of other people - that isn't an environment where love is flourishing; also leadership style, the quality of leadership. If a leadership style is about command and control and do what I say, it doesn't create that environment where people feel I've got a voice and I'm valued. I suppose the pressure comes from companies not performing in line with expectations and how organisations deal with that can go with one of two ways. It can become about being more inclusive and saying to their people 'what do you think is going on? What do you think we should do?' and therefore creating a sense of love -or it could go completely the other way which is 'you're not doing what is needed, you're not performing well enough and I'm going to put more pressure on you."

Neil Wilson

MY JOB COULD BE BETTER

Greed, the wrong focus, and the demands of stakeholders could be one thing, but if your people are stuck in jobs that give them little or no joy, it's difficult to experience giving and receiving love and the difference it would make to performance. Sometimes, we join organisations for the wrong reasons, which at the time of joining may have felt like the right thing to do, only to find a few years later that 'this is not the company I joined'. And we may stay on in spite of this realisation for different reasons. Some honourable and part of a long-term plan to sacrifice what you have now for what you will become and have and be able to do in the long term. Other reasons are purely to do with the material gain and the money that could be earned by staying put in an organisation that operates in an environment and in a way that is not aligned with your values, with a team in which there is mistrust and dysfunction and for leaders who want nothing more than to line their pockets. And when the reason is purely for the financial gain and hardly more, it will be a barrier to the operational presence of love at any level in organisation. There is hope, though, in enabling your people to do jobs that they love and actively introducing ways of working, resourcing and role fulfilling that maximise the likelihood of them finding themselves doing jobs they love and that bring the best out of them. This again would require a demonstration of love and care for your people and a belief that an emphasis on joy and self-fulfilment in a job is a key to high performance. The reality, however, is that the opposite is what occurs in many organisations, and where there is instead an emphasis on the skills and competencies than on the intention to facilitate the placement of your people in jobs they truly love, it becomes another barrier to the presence of love.

"The other one is about how much importance an organisation places on how much people should be doing roles that they enjoy. How much does an organisation think that someone's happiness is as important as their competency? Someone could be very competent and actually unhappy in their role. It's important to have a balance between the two but some organisations would focus on competency alone."

Naomi Gillies

As the life span of the human race continues to increase and we therefore live longer, and because of this, work longer, it would be a very sad thing indeed if the number of years we spend working are not some of our most enjoyable and love filled years of our lives.

RULES, PROCESSES AND LEGALITIES - HUGS NOT ALLOWED

"We've also created processes that get in the way - for example - the performance management process and the whole forced ranking part of it. This is the process that gets in the way and it does really damage the trust relationship because you're always thinking what is the real truth here? How do I know my manager is telling me the truth when he/she says I would have rated you a 4 or a 5 but I wasn't allowed to. I was forced by my boss to rate you a 3!"

Peter Cheese

Once upon a time, I had a boss who had already rated my performance a 2 on a scale of 1 - 5,where 1 was very poor and 5 was outstanding. That boss had actually evaluated my performance before my appraisal discussion. However, the boss sent me an email asking me to prepare for the discussion and asked that I be sure to include my own personal evaluation of my overall performance; how I thought I'd delivered against the agreed objectives of the year before, what I believed I had done well and where I believed I could improve. You can imagine that with this sort of heartfelt preparation, my expectation was that my contribution and views would be taken into consideration when being awarded a performance rating.

What I experienced during the meeting, and that raised a small alarm bell in my ear, was a rigorous counter argument against every point I made or another piece of evidence that contradicted my own evidence for what I had done well, no matter how weak it was. And in moments of determined desperation, reference was made to feedback given on me by third parties, never before shared but was important in that moment to the appraisal. You can imagine the way my heart both sank and the desire for escape I felt by the end of the meeting.

When I later discovered my rating had been decided and submitted much earlier in advance of the meeting, I felt a rather perverse sense of relief too. The final straw was then finding out about the pre-submitted rating from a member of my own team whose responsibility included performance management who shared this with me innocently and unaware of my recent experience. Now think about this. If love were present in that organisation, even if it did still have a policy and way of working, ignorant though it may be, where ratings were decided and submitted in advance of the appraisal discussion, the experience would have been different.

If love had been present, an admission on the frailty of the process would have been made, a directness in the communication of the decision would have been given, and a clarity in the reason for the decision would have been shared along with evidence that supported it, and the reasons those pieces of evidence had been selected. You see, very few people including me, no matter how bitter a pill the news may be to swallow, would have found it a little easier to draw a little solace then or later from the appreciation that the person was honest. When a tough message is given from place of an appreciation and acceptance of the human that you are, the intention will be felt, because coupled with the communication, will be a genuine desire to listen. She would have demonstrated a seeing of the heartbeat beneath the recipient of her message and I will have seen the heart beneath the giver and transmitter of the decision. At some level and at some time, much sooner than there is today, the sting of the experience would have passed and been replaced by an appreciation of the human connection and the appreciation of the human that she also is, an appreciation ahead of the job and the role requirement. But it may not have been within her gift. I wonder.

Being stuck in a job you don't love is one barrier as we've learned the other massive barrier are the rules, laws, and processes that we've invented in organisation some of them not only stifling and minimising of humanity, they also stand in the way of simply getting the job done. The erosion and abuse of trust in organisations has contributed to more rules being introduced, with penalties, some of them livelihood threatening and severe for breaking them. The sad thing is that movements like 'MeToo', which gained momentum rapidly across the world through highlighting the perverse behaviours, and rightly so, of certain people in some industries, have led to the suffering of the many for the bad behaviours of the few. There are many more people who shouldn't have to be overly cautious in their interactions with each other as human beings. A hug which is one of the simplest and warmest demonstrations of care, compassion and indeed love, with the exception of instances where a respect for religious belief prevents it, is an act that is at risk of being seen as perverse because of the breakdown of trust in organisation. And where there is no trust, there can hardly be love.

"Rules and regulations constrain us, not in our small groups, but in the widest work relationships or the whole employee group. We have rules and policies that provide a framework for us around a minority of challenging relationships or difficult situations and we then take those things and extend the 'rules' and approach to everybody except perhaps the closest group. I think this would create a barrier. We can worry about doing the wrong thing, worry about being criticised, about doing or saying certain things rather than being more relaxed about relationships or focussing on being friendly with people. It's borne out of a good place of - I don't want to do or say the wrong thing - but it can be a barrier. If I reflect over my career, I worried more about showing my private or personal side at work when I first started at work than I worry about it now. I'm more inclined now to be more open, to share more, certainly ask more and probably be less formal with everyone – not just those in a small circle of colleagues."

Sally Cabrini

"When I think of barriers, I'm immediately drawn to employment issues and to legal issues; to a lack of trust - in the workplace. When trust breaks down you then find yourself as an organisation or as a business having to behave in a certain way because the law dictates or there are certain protocols that dictate the way you have to behave - and these force you to be less human and personal as your actions are now determined more by legal protocol.

What comes to mind are the people in some of my businesses that have worked for me and have not been happy. They're in the wrong job. And you should be able to tell someone that they're not in the right job because every day they are working in a job that doesn't make them happy is a day they could be working in another job that fulfils them. I feel a responsibility to tell them. However, because of the law, you just can't do that. If someone's been working in your company for a number of years, you can't just sit down and go "look, we've been working together for a while now, we've had 121s and I can see that you're not happy in your job."

Andrew Needham

"The rules of work have not been conducive. You have to set up your shop right and for the way you want your people to behave. What you reward gets done and so another barrier will be the types of rules and the types of rewards organisations have in place - if they're not conducive to the presence of love, it will not be present."

John Mangan

"It is a lack of purpose and direction; the lack of clearly defined strategy - even in the short term - so that the people know where they are going in the next six to 18 months - this provides a sense of security which is key to the presence of love. The other barrier is the lack of leadership and a leadership that doesn't provide direction and doesn't create trust within the teams. Managers who lead by dividing, managers who lead and derive their power from knowledge that they have and others don't - this is unlikely to create a sense of trust between individuals within their teams."

Richard Gillies

I sat with a colleague once who had just been expatriated from the UK to Brazil with his family. The organisation had very generous expatriation packages at the time, one of which was the provision of two business class return flights a year for my colleague and his family on a select group of partner airlines. Now this colleague had elderly parents and a wife who wanted the opportunity to visit her own parents more regularly than twice a year. And so, in their effort to stay within the financial limits of the two business class flights, they did their research and discovered that for the same money they could buy 5 economy class return flights a year which means that they could visit home twice as many times and at no extra cost to the company. Excited at the opportunity of a win-win, he made the request to his boss for a change in the relevant terms of his expatriation package. The response was 'no'. The expatriate policy allowed for two business class return flights a year and nothing else. It was not negotiable.

THIS PRECIOUS THING CALLED TIME

Time and the pace of change in life and in the environments organisations find themselves can sadly be a barrier to the presence of love. The scarcity of time can stop an organisation and its people from breathing and the pressures of delivery expectations that have us be busy, busy, busy whether you're a leader at the top of the organisation or one at the bottom end, means that time becomes a scarcity and the more tasks to be fulfilled, the less time there is to relate and connect as human. The risk, of course, is that the human is then treated, though unintentionally sometimes, as a means to an end and by the way, that also includes how we treat our own selves too.

I learned of a Managing Director who would allow only 15-minute meetings for her people and anyone who wanted to meet with her regardless of how far they travelled or how important it was to them to have this special time with her. About 10 minutes into the meeting starting, her Personal Assistant would dutifully knock, put her head around the door and say that her next meeting will be starting in 5 minutes and with a very important person for an equally important matter and so she should round up her meeting.

The Managing Director would then turn around to her guest and say 'don't worry, we have five more minutes' and of course 5 minutes later, her PA would again return to the room and stand at the door so that the meeting would finish and an apologising Managing Director would usher her guest out of her office with a promise to reconvene at a future date.

Now what this Managing Director did not realise was that her people talked about it and shared notes of their experiences and about how small this behaviour made them feel. These feelings were made all the more worse when various people observed her spending much longer time - hours and hours, some said - with a select few of her people who were perceived to be her favourites. The reality of the situation is that the Managing Director will most certainly not have intended to have that kind of impact on any of her people. What it does, however, demonstrate is the importance that we place on time and the message time spent with each other sends.

> "Always time. Time. We are so time pressured. Pressure is good but you need to create space to have quality conversations with people. I'm not as good as I should be with my people. I still don't create enough space to have those quality conversations. There is always something more important and something more pressing. You could and should argue that there is nothing more pressing than having open conversations with your people, but the reality is that there is something that is always more pressing than that."
>
> **Howard Kerr**

> "One of the wider societal challenges is the rapidity of change. The degree to which the workplace is being disrupted for everybody. We are all being moved at such a pace that in some ways, businesses have less control than they have had for a long time. And so it gets harder and harder in the midst of that to say that I'm going to consciously think of my organisation

really holistically and genuinely ask about my people - how are they? Are they well? Are they happy? Are they scared? Is the pressure of the work where people and social media means you have little respite getting to my people? It gets very hard to create the time to think about what really matters. Also and let's be honest, shareholders don't really value it."

Tracey Killen

And yet our time and personal space is increasingly invaded by technology and artificial intelligence, cookies and bots. The internet is now where many humans live. It connects us, transforming the world into a global village and a place where connections and tribes comprising people from different geographies and time zones can be formed. The opportunities for learning and economic survival and the levelling of opportunity of access to education for the digitally fluent are amazing. Yet, the dark side it affords in the sense of increased media scrutiny, a propensity for comparison, the intoxication with the superficial and the facility it provides for bad leader behaviour in organisation means that the opportunity for the activation of Love in the individual and its presence in organisation may seem a more distant proposition.

The consequence of course is the prevalence of stress and anxiety in the midst of increasing innovative and frenzied drives for productivity - more, faster, cheaper, earlier - through the introduction of wellbeing and happiness initiatives. But the pace of change is not going to slow down. The competitive world will become even more so and new players will enter into it all the time and players that we never before imagined; players that compete even on platforms that until now were thought to be the singular domain of the human, platforms like coaching, care and companionship. And so the demands and pressure to stay ahead of the game add to the continued demand for our time and the time of those around us whose lives impact our own and whose lives we impact.

Yet, time filled with genuine human connection and the energy that comes from a genuine smile, and the meeting of minds as one can in turn produce the most extraordinary of results beyond the financial. This is because time infused with this sort of energy will help you to solve that critical problem, make that breakthrough, win that ever evasive contract; include the supporting glance from a colleague across a meeting room that says it's okay, you're going to do just fine; it is time spent together with company that says 'we matter more than the 'what'.

AND THERE IS MORE

The master of all barriers, however, lies within us as human beings. Our attitude to ourselves, to each other, to our communities, and our environment. This attitude can prevent us from establishing and allowing a presence of love at home, let alone in organisation. We are constantly judging, comparing, competing, suspecting, evaluating each other and this is instilled into us right from our childhoods through education and of course at work. Many a leader today will have joined his or her organisation, current or past, at a time when recruiters told you that the hiring decision is made within the first few minutes of entering the room. And now we have technology supporting the hiring decision in the early stages, it still does not negate the experience of the first impression. It may just come a little further down the chain of interactions and exchanges. Once that impression is formed, there is pressure to maintain it no matter what happens and goes on outside the organisation walls and in our lives. The masks may be taken off as we walk out the door physical or virtual but it's put back on the following day. The image designed must be carefully managed and of course in managing our own images and masks, we enable and encourage our colleagues to do the same. Sometimes we get so skilled at managing and maintaining our images that it becomes challenging to express who the real person is behind them.

The inability to fully express who we are as humans is a barrier too and that may lie in the lack of purpose we may have in life. If you are unable to answer the question 'why do you exist?' or 'why are you here?', it is unlikely that you are able to help others in answering the same question for themselves. Additionally, if you are unable to answer the question 'who are you?' without attaching labels to yourself, then it is unlikely you will be able to help another person with answering the same question for themselves.

A human being without purpose is one who is less likely to be resilient and able to withstand the challenges of life and work that come their way. A human being who doesn't know who he or she is other than the labels and the roles they play in life is one that is easily swept up by the winds of change or the credible sounding voice of another whose opinion should matter less. Without purpose, the beautiful currency of feedback in organisation becomes a tool of manipulation, ingratiation or of one-upmanship. Without purpose, it is difficult to create an environment of love in which you flourish and enable the people around you to flourish too. When leaders have no purpose in themselves, it becomes difficult to establish an organisation with purpose and challenging still to align your teams and people behind that purpose too.

The consequences of a purposeless organisation and purposeless leadership is the existence of teams that are susceptible to dysfunction, the loss of talent and at times the disengagement over time of the talent that remains. When your organisation and leadership have no purpose, you leave no anchor on which your people can hang their own purpose even if it be for a season or a period of time in their journey of life.

The barriers to the presence of love are many, and diverse. They are such that when examined, you wonder whether there can actually be any room for love in organisation. What is even more worrying is the potential and long-term impact of what we lose by not encouraging the active and operational presence of love in our organisations.

"Firstly, it's not talked about. Secondly, it's difficult to articulate and pin down. Thirdly, organisations are focused on shareholder value. It's only recently that the concept of Corporate Social Responsibility (CSR) has come to the fore. Up until recent times, corporations just exploited the people and the environment, almost with impunity. Think of the oil spills and the degradation of the Niger Delta in Nigeria, the devastation of the Amazon rain forest. These things were little spoken about, save for the increasing voices of environmentalists and other pressure groups. It is only of recent that we are starting to get a conversation around certain things that have to do with corporate social responsibility, which is a values-based approach to doing business. Fourthly, it is the fact that our education and societal systems are built on competition. If you build something that is fundamentally competitive rather than collaborative and cooperative, there is an issue."

Emmanuel Mbakwe

"If the definition of love is that you have an environment where people are content and are happy and are able to give of their best, then lots of things can get in the way. A person's ego can get in the way; an organisation's structure can get in the way; a tradition can get in the way; a way of doing things that's historic, an absence of permission and so on. Then when it comes to the person, the person may not take the time to understand how people work, how people feel, how the teams work, how we communicate to the rest of the organisation; also the person may have an aversion to failure even though failure is not always a bad thing. So one barrier may be the function of the organisation and the other will be in the person themselves."

Mark Scanlon

"One of the most important topics that we need to examine and must accept is that there is something that we are doing in the modern workplace that is not helping people's mental wellbeing. The mental illness crisis that is emerging should worry every organisation leader. It really should. Because it's only going to get worse. It is an epidemic which is incapacitating people. We talk about things like presenteeism, and this is nothing compared to peoples' inability to really contribute with mental health issues. The issue too is that we don't really understand it. We don't really understand why it is that it's going on. My own view and what I would say is that it's because we stopped loving in our workplaces. There's an absence of love. One of the dimensions is that is not great from a perspective of mental wellbeing is that you're doing work that is not attached to you. You have to do it, you take it home, you're on the device, you're always available and there's no opportunity to refresh, to recharge and to do other things in your life that will bring richness. So for example, no longer having staff canteens where people go out to the shop and take it back to their desks. We discourage, maybe not verbally, not to be at their desks not working and so people work on being seen to be working. And this is not an environment of love. It is not fear in terms of an angry boss looking at you, it's fear in terms of big brother, people watching you to see if you're logged on or not and they can see whether you've put that report in exactly when you said. So unconsciously, we've created environments that are not good for the human spirit."

Norman Pickavance

4. Breaking down the barriers

....

IF YOU CAN NAME THE BARRIERS, you can delete them. All the barriers to the presence of love in organisation are erected by human beings. That means people like you and me who have done so consciously or unconsciously. Some of them may seem impossible to break down because of who has erected them and how, but each one can be taken down one brick at a time until hardly any exist if we only really truly wanted to.

FIRST DECIDE

Any action and any step towards change or the delivery of progress comes with a thought and a willingness to see what can be possible. It also comes deciding not to keep the thought to yourself, and a desire and willingness to share and to engage others in the discussion and conversation. What if a barrier or the barriers to the presence of love were to come down? What difference would it make to you and to me? What difference would it make to our organisation, the people we serve and whom they serve? Imagine this - what difference would the presence of love in our organisation make to our communities, to our societies and even the world?

Building a huge monument starts with the laying down of only one brick, and before that, it started with the coming together of people with shared goals, leveraging each other's capabilities, skills, wishes and ambitions and before the gathering of people. It started with a thought, that led to an imagination that in turn led to a motivation to do something. If this can happen with ornaments and buildings and constructions of beauty and legacy, it can happen too with obstacles and barriers seen and unseen that if in themselves were broken down, would enable the creation of breakthroughs and achievements for the human race that we never before thought were possible.

So the first thing is to decide. To break down the barriers to the presence of love in organisation is to decide to do so. How hungry are you and how hungry am I? What would it really take from you and me to break down the barriers to the presence of what can be the most incredible gift to each other as human beings and that if present can enable the achievement of the most extraordinary of goals? In deciding to do something about it, we will engage in conversations of courage. I say conversations of courage because to talk about what love may mean and what it can mean in organisation will require a conviction to face the implications of this. It would take courage to face up to the vulnerabilities it may reveal and the discomfort that may emerge as we venture into the type of conversational territory that we have never before ventured into.

> "Despite a world that is changing, we've still got a huge number of leaders and bosses and managers who would run a mile from this kind of conversation. There are huge swathes of people - leaders, managers and bosses amongst them that can't talk about love in their personal lives, let alone having to talk about it at work! And some of these people will be working in the most liberal of organisations. So a key step forward would be through education and encouraging dialogue around it at work."

> **Peter Cheese**

Indeed, to talk about love at the deepest level and how it would impact us would require an emotional and psychological nakedness that many people, and that may include you and I, no matter how strong, have experienced. If there were compelling reasons to do so, then it may just make it easier to decide and the compelling reason may at first be more than the tangible. That compelling reason may lie in the reason why - the reason why you and I exist.

When organisations, their leaders, and the people within them pay attention to the reasons why they exist and what they are here to do for humankind directly or indirectly, that attention will form the basis of a motivation to do what may not immediately come naturally but will do it in service of that purpose.

"There has to be a sense of purpose. In our case it started with a sense of purpose with my great grandfather's business and even though the number of businesses grew over the years, this ethos has been carried out through the generations and we do this by storytelling.

In my company, my great grandfather started it as a social mission and so we tried to inculcate this with everybody who joins. The name of the company Eu Yan Sang - our surname is Eu but my great grandfather when he founded the business, he called it Yan Sang. This is nobody's name; this is the mission of the company. The mission - in English - means caring for mankind. It is about benevolence towards humanity. This is really what it means. He started this business as an antidote to opium. In the 19th century, the British Empire largely grew on opium trade. My grandfather was a Tin Miner and he saw that the workers out in the fields had no healthcare, so they resorted to opium for their pain management and to find relief and as a result, they got addicted and sadly less able to work. The result, of course, is that they never were able to earn enough money to send home to their families which is why they were there in the first place. My grandfather decided to break the cycle and started to bring in medicinal herbs to help cure the addiction even though he was not himself a physician or a herbalist. He was just a businessman. He brought in these herbs and apart from giving it to his workers, he after a while also started selling them. This is how the business developed. So it is very much in the DNA of the business to think about trying to help people."

Richard Eu

"Love engenders in us something that is greater than us and to have a sense of purpose should deliver the same thing. When you have a sense of purpose you are driven something that is greater than you and so love based leadership means that you are driven by a sense of purpose of something greater than you."

Andrew Needham

"When you introduce the discussion on legacy or long-term footprint in organisations, you also enable an atmosphere for love. Legacy seems to be the expression of love beyond lifetime. It is about creating and establishing something that the future will benefit from."

Pedro Tarak

Deciding to do something about the barriers to the presence of love, which will gain energy and momentum in courageous conversations, can have compulsion, if wrapped around legacy and purpose. The absence of love in operation will prohibit the realisation of purpose, assuming that purpose is honourable. Purpose and legacy that come for the examination of your reason why, will be the compelling case for action to decide. And for those organisations that may believe and say they have a purpose, my challenge to them is this - how much more would you be able to do for mankind, for the world and starting with your people if you would allow and facilitate conversations about love and its attributes and the difference it would make if it were actively present in your organisations? If we exist in a world in which there is poverty, inequality, discrimination, war, waste and so much more, which we do, even organisations of purpose with lofty and admirable visions and actions are not doing enough.

For an organisation of any size to have purpose it starts with the individual, the one person who alone, or together with others, establishes the organisation. Let's remember that any organisation is the people within it. No matter its size, it is living and breathing. And when you end up in leadership at the top of the organisation, the question 'why?' for you is one that you must answer. Who are you and why are you here? To really get the best out of all of your people and to create an environment in which they are able to feel safe and at their best, you must be able to say why you do what you do and have them be able to do the same. And when your combined 'why' is one that has mankind and the human race at the heart of it then at its most fundamental and deepest core, your organisation's actions must be borne out of and executed in and with love.

YES IT STARTS AT THE TOP

When you lead with purpose it becomes easier to lead with love and when that purpose is in service of a much greater good and a world beyond your walls and the boundaries that you can see or touch then the only place from where you will come, is love. I would argue that if in your leadership, you are impacting people directly or indirectly, the only place from where you should lead is love.

Whether we like it or not, anyone in organisations who is in a position of influence, no matter at what level, or who indeed is able to influence because of their innate gifts and talent, is someone who can be a role model. You will be in the spotlight and many people will take their cues and leads from you and so with great status, great influence also comes great responsibility. For the barriers to the presence of love to be broken down, the way you behave is key. What you say, how you say it and of course when you start talking about love, what it means, how it can be defined, the difference it could make to you, to your people to the work you do and what you are trying to create together, the domino effect occurs. Soon it becomes less taboo to talk about it and all the substitute words and stand-ins that are used and are really an indication of our unwillingness to be vulnerable at the deepest level, soon start to disappear and make way for the fundamental need and solution to our wellbeing, creativity, prosperity, joy and productivity.

Yet, it can be the most challenging and fearful of topics to broach in leadership groups. One reason may be because historically these groups have comprised more men than women. But in my experience, I have found that in general, more men than women have been willing to explore the notion of love in organisation in conversation with me. But what it could actually mean more is that in order to attain senior levels of leadership, the individuals who eventually did make it had to fight, compete, work in ways that they never want to again, deny themselves of their dreams and childhood hopes and ambitions and many a time suppress emotion and the language of human for the language of corporate and manicured image.

But when a leader at any level or place in organisation steps out of his or her place of comfort and chooses to make a start with one conversation at a time, out of there will birth a wave that will create a new language, new ways of thinking and new ways of being. These will be new ways of being that can only be for the common good of the people in the organisation, their families, the communities in which they reside and serve, for society and, as the ripple and butterfly effect come into operation, for the good of the world.

"Leadership is a strong way of overcoming the barriers to the presence of love in work. It is having constant vigilance. It is not published like our mission; it is more like how you nurture love in your own life with your family and your friends. It's the call to check in, the time given without expectation and spontaneously; the giving without expecting always something in return; the small gestures and actions of generosity around the organisation - these are key to establishing a culture of love and overcoming the barriers to its presence."

John Mangan

"I think Leadership is really important. Having role models. What leadership pays attention too is really key. Using the evidence base is crucial particularly the evidence based around employee engagement. Around healthcare it is also from the customer's perspective. Bringing the voice of the customer – the voice of the patient, the voice of the career, the family. The acts of kindness. That empathy, that human connection. The stories are some of the best ways of talking some of these barriers. You do also need a board and a leadership that's signed up to this in a very authentic way otherwise people will see through it."

Sam Allen

"You overcome those barriers by your actions. The people in a company will look at the CEO and they will say - how does he behave? It is not how he behaves when he gets up and gives the key company update or key speech, it will be how does he behave when he comes to my desk, when I'm with him in a 121, that behaviour I think, those actions - that is how you do it."

Andrew Needham

"You overcome the barriers by being willing to compromise. Compromise is important. Facilitating the opportunity for someone to have a frank and open discussion about what is agreed or disagreed upon. Also praising people. Everybody likes to be praised and everybody likes to be encouraged. In my organisation we learn from our mistakes we don't blame. We overcome our problems and challenges by working together; encouraging responsibility and not defensiveness. In overcoming these barriers, a leader who is working hard to promote love and ensuring that love is the key driver in organisation is one who can enable the barriers to love to be overcome."

Ingrid Tennessee

And for James Timpson, the barriers to the presence of love in organisation can be brought down simply with this: *"By leadership that acts in a way that it's easy for people to love what they do and who they work with."*

Having the courage to talk about love, its attributes and the difference it would make is one thing and a great start to breaking down the barriers. It, however, shouldn't stop there. It is also about encouraging and enabling the people you lead, your teams, your colleagues and others in the organisation to talk about it and to demonstrate it in the handling of difficult, challenging and sensitive topics of conversation. It is about enabling them to set examples for themselves and others in what they say, how they say and how they are as humans in the exchange of those conversations - whether those conversations be in person or in writing.

One of the fastest ways to breaking down the barriers to the presence of love in organisation is in what feedback is given on and how that feedback is delivered. When you focus on the great things, the strengths and the beauty of others; when you walk in your feedback with the evident assumption that the recipient in his or her actions wanted nothing more but the best for their team and for their organisation, it not only lowers the walls to receiving the feedback, it also maximises the likelihood of the exchange being a sharing of perspective, a clearing of the air of misunderstanding and a powerful way forward underpinned by trust and a shared purpose in the context of the organisation.

BE A TURKEY, VOTE FOR CHRISTMAS

Enabling an environment in which love can be present would require a level of sacrifice from your people and particularly us as leaders that is against the norm in most organisations. It would require a genuine focus on the longer term. An analogy comes to mind. It would mean seeing the oak tree when you plant the acorn and at the same time, retaining a sense of expectation and hope at the time of planting. It would mean seeing the full bridge or the entire mansion at the time the first brick is laid knowing that the outcome will be great no matter what because each detail, day by day, will be attended to and the needs and wishes and wellbeing of the eventual occupiers of the mansion or travellers on the bridge would be the most important driver. A prioritisation of the needs of our consumers, our clients, our people and the communities in which they live and impact directly or in-directly would create the opportunity to relate with one another in ways that allow a creativity and a diversity of thought and ideas that never before then had been able to surface. Purpose and outcome would supersede rules and processes. Skills and capabilities that are most needed for the job at hand will be tapped into and the lengths and widths of the organisation will be searched in order to uncover those talents best suited to the project, the work and the objectives at hand. Status would hardly rule. There would be no room for judging or making ill based assumptions about each other on any basis at all because there would be no time for that as the ultimate focus of all will be on the good of the organisation and what it wants to do in the world.

> "The concept of unconditional acceptance is very strong and if brought into the workplace would have a massive impact. It is about encouraging people to be non-judgemental but it would be a challenging concept to make happen because of what it would demand from people."
>
> **Sally Cabrini**

> "If you have a passion for what you do and for what you believe in and you have to apply love in organisations, you must listen and hear what people are saying. You mustn't just listen and let got, but you must take it on and try to interpret also what is not said. What is behind what the person is saying? Really trying to understand so that if I have not been doing the right thing, in the right way and for the right reasons, that I then work really hard to make sure that I do and of course to let my team know that I also am human and I make mistakes."
>
> **Ingrid Tennessee**

It would, however, require drastic and, maybe for some, heart rending changes. Our systems and processes in the main, plus the demands of powerful stakeholders, and I daresay, for some organisations, the investor community, means that we are wired and ingrained to focus on the short term. A quick and high return on investment and money spent, is required and is a major demonstration of success. The higher the return for the smallest of investment even better still. The monitoring of progress by analysts and media provides the added pressure to demonstrate a delivery against set expectations or well-crafted and managed communication should the actual result fall that little bit short. A laser focus on cost and the delivery of profit margins of eye watering proportions are often applauded by the investor and the analysts that support them, as a demonstration of entrepreneurial prowess and commercial acumen. All this and more will need to change if the potential of what love can do were allowed to come forth. The attitude to what is seen as cost effectiveness would need to evolve too - because in many ways, cost effectiveness today operates in a fashion that creates what may be a win-lose. In order to maximise profit and margin, organisations negotiating terms with suppliers that may be in the longer term detrimental to the prosperity of the supplier and at the other end, accepting negotiated terms with clients that risk the wellbeing of their people and the livelihood and wellbeing of those whom their people impact.

And yet if on these terms, there were hardly any wastage of resources in the world today. I guess we could say there was a great reason and purpose behind this focus on cost. But when we live in a world, which we currently do, in which the amount of waste in all resources, be it food, clothing, minerals are at epic proportions, I believe that a shift in focus and a leaning towards love would actually enable a more effective allocation of resources and a cost effectiveness in organisation that delivered what it actually is meant to deliver and for a greater good.

"So changing the purpose of companies from profit to societal solutions is crucial. You introduce the purpose into the mission statements of the articles of incorporation and express it in every decision and behaviour. Naturally, the opportunity for love starts to emerge. Rather than maximising profit for only shareholders you start maximising purpose for all stakeholders. Of course, a new competitiveness emerges driven from integrated value creation for all parts."

Pedro Tarak

"It would be great if there was an increase of focus on the return of value organisations make beyond shareholder value. Let's pick up the links between what we value, how we behave i.e. focusing on our behaviour and link it absolutely to the commercial performance of the business; the more regulatory bodies and government think that way, it would really help towards breaking down barriers."

Tracey Killen

Some processes and ways of working simply need to be removed completely in order to enable the presence of love. One such process or way of working is in the payment terms that organisations have with their suppliers and those with whom they partner in order to deliver their products and services. When you think about it, payment for work done or a service provided should be made on receipt of the benefit of that work and an agreement that the work has been carried out in line with expectations and what was agreed. And yet today, in many countries of the world, we experience practices and transactions that don't see the human behind the invoice but instead see an opportunity to enable short term cash flow, maximise interest payments in banks and make more money. We see practices and policies of paying suppliers even of the smallest sizes, a minimum of 90 days on receipt of invoice for services and goods and when as it at times happens, that invoice is misplaced or disappears in a black hole because of some coding error, the number of days between receipt of invoice and payment could be longer still and can easily double.

To break down the barriers to the operational presence of love would require a complete shift in mindset in the corridors of power of investors and government, a willingness to do a root and branch review of the supply chain system and a willingness to go back to basics on the role and purpose of organisation in society. It may mean changing the legislative rules of engagement that may get in the way of the fulfilment of this genuine purpose. It seems almost impossible and you may even think a fantasy. But when you dare to dream and dare to imagine what can be possible should the biggest barriers to the presence of love in organisation be brought down, those same biggest barriers to the presence of the most significant gift and need to humanity, you can also dare to say that where there is a will, there is a way. And if by reading this book, it starts one conversation in one place that leads to another, and then another that ultimately takes decisive action in the required direction, then we can dare to believe that what at first may seem impossible can be made possible. It's like the oak tree that is seen at the time the acorn is planted.

> "These barriers remain a big issue because of how our world and global economies are organised. Being built on a competitive model, there are certain elements and dimensions that are measured. If you look at shareholders, they are all about ensuring that there is a return on their investment and that the capital invested is not put at undue risk. If this is under threat, significant changes are made. So it's about making sure that all those who are involved in the value chain and in the overall economic and value creation process are really anchored in the new set of values and will stand strong and tall and say `I don't have to make 30% net margin, I can live with 20% because that is what helps the collective rather than the individual."
>
> **Emmanuel Mbakwe**

"Mindset shifts. It is not about a mindset shift in this particular case of working life. I think it's much bigger. I think it's a mindset shift in everything we do and it's much bigger. I'm interested in the concept of quantum and the level of shift we need to make in life is a quantum sized shift of mindset. This is because the mindset shift needed is significantly bigger than organisations but will impact organisations. This is because quantum will go beyond the binary. The shift needed is about how we do things across the board. It is not about how we adapt to technology for example, it is about how we run our businesses in general; it's not about how we make money on one side, it's about making an impact and how those impacts can and should be experienced."

Charmian Love

A change in mindset in the corridors of power is one thing, another is a willingness of leaders themselves to let go of the desire for incentives that drive short term behaviours. I admit it. This issue may lie more in publicly listed organisations who may feel themselves encumbered by the requirements of their boards to win the perceived competition for the talent to lead them; a desire fuelled by the outputs of reports of consultancies hired to conduct external reward and benchmark surveys and studies of other organisations deemed to be peers and competitors. And whilst certainly in the UK, there is a movement towards incentives for organisational leaders and leadership teams of listed companies that encourage a focus on the long term, a realisation of purpose and the wellbeing of environment and community, the move is not fast enough and a great proportion of compensation packages, still predominantly comprise a reward for delivery against short term goals.

"It is redefining what should actually be the core of an organisation; what should drive it and what should be at its forefront, whether it's commercial or non-commercial. Individuals within an organisation - their well-being - I think is critical. Their development I believe is critical and if we pursue this, I believe that the objective of profit will essentially be met in a reasonable time. Rearranging our priorities as leaders and as organisations should help us to overcome the barriers."

Sam Aiyere

"Money is a problem. Peoples' obsession with money is a problem. So one way is to change incentive structures fundamentally and incentivise things intelligently or do away with them and just reward people on overall performance. This is a very politically incorrect notion when you look at the way the whole corporate world works. If you look even at the stock exchange - the value of a company goes up and down so frequently - and this is driven by a money focused mindset."

Steve Fox

Breaking down the barriers to the presence of love in organisation may lie in our education. What I mean is the way we educate our leaders right from the earliest of years, from kindergarten and nursery school all the way to higher levels of education.

The root of insecurity, fear, competition, envy, vindictiveness and so many evil behaviours may reside in some of our educational institutions and this is where they may be nurtured and fed. In my experience, the boarding school is a particular hive of activity.

I went to one of the top boarding schools of its time in Lagos, Nigeria. I transferred there after a year spent at another boarding school - which was a school my mother had attended and was so proud that her youngest daughter was to go there. My father, however, believed that his children had to have the best education he could afford them and although this was a wonderful school, it was not the best school. At the earliest opportunity, he transferred me to his chosen school. This was a school that had so many of the best attributes of top-class secondary school education of the time. It was also a school in which I had some of the saddest and darkest years of my life. I was bullied by some classmates, whilst over stretched staff turned a blind eye; I was made to carry out chores akin to slavery in the name of boarding school rituals and excluded from membership of some of the most sought after 'clubs' in the school run by the most popular girls.

The topic of love was never broached and neither were its attributes encouraged, discussed or demonstrated. A veiled attempt at introducing the notion of acceptance came up in the guise of a government introduction of a quota system in the nation which meant schools had to provide places for a minimum number of girls from diverse ethnic groups. The other veiled attempt at introducing the notion of acceptance was in the teaching classes on faith and religion which were taught in some of the most boring ways you can ever imagine and by teachers who couldn't wait themselves for the end of class bells to ring.

I've often wondered back to those days and reflected on my belief that if love were in itself a true subject of education, its implications, its attributes how they can and should be demonstrated, would be prevalent. Tutors would demonstrate and act in love and with love to each other, to their students and to the families of their students and then we could dare to imagine that maybe, just maybe, there would be a reduction in teenage and young adult suicide and a more prevalent occurrence of self-assurance and confidence in the person who arrives in organisation.

The other type of education lies in the nature of management development and learning practices in organisations. These too can be addressed in order to bring down the barriers to the presence of love. They can enable a shift in the balance of focus to the human from the hard or data and numbers. They can enable a shift to the focus on the human face of the impact of actions taken in the context of executing strategy and organisation goals from a focus on profit and market share gains. And they can enable a shift to the focus on the wellbeing and emotion of people in the delivery and requirement of change during the merging and integration of acquired organisations away from the focus on how to maximise synergies, cost reductions and profits. When we shift the focus of our education, management and leadership development practices we have every opportunity to break down the barriers to the presence of love in our organisations and enable the difference, it can make to flourish.

The irony though is that in order for our educational institutions and those who provide education and learning interventions to feel at liberty to introduce the topic of love and all that it represents, they themselves must be organisations and a people who allow love and all of its attributes to flow through who they are and what they represent.

> "Since we have grown up in a world where work and life were two rather separate ideas, and that work was about turning up and getting paid to do a job that you're told to do and when you go back to Milton Friedman's quote in 1970 that said that the sole purpose of business was to make money for the shareholder - and that has driven a lot of thinking about the purpose of work and the purpose of work is to maximise profitability and to reduce cost and there isn't much room for humanity in any of that so another way of bringing down

these barriers again lies at the root of education - that we have to go back into all the ways in which we teach leadership and management and what business schools talk about - encouraging them to include talks about corporate culture and behaviour and what motivates people, instead of focusing exclusively on strategy and financial engineering and such like."

Peter Cheese

"We'd need to go back to fundamentals. First, you build it into the education system from nursery, to the primary school, to secondary school, to University and beyond. You've got to start from scratch. It is also important to articulate and display in the workplace and training programmes - the values that are important to support a loving working culture. If you have a set of standards and values, they need to be visible; they need to be enacted and be seen being enacted, and that begins with leadership. If you have good practice, they have to be promoted. Finally, it is about making sure the reward system is aligned to the behaviour you want to see. If there are examples of good practice, then promote and it socialise them."

Emmanuel Mbakwe

"So it may mean better education and better training for our leaders and for our managers around psychology, what makes people tick, emotional intelligence, cultural sensitivity, unconscious bias - all those things that get in the way of having good relationships with your colleagues and people at work."

Louise Fisher

"Another way of breaking down the barriers is through the learning and development in organisation and teaching from a love-based approach. So offering opportunities such as mindfulness in the workplace, open dialogue and other varied self-awareness approaches through which this can be brought in can help break down the barriers. Involving staff and work colleagues in workshops and promoting opportunities for external support to facilitate and taking time out of busy schedules and offering techniques like meditation and also having a laugh and other innovative initiatives can reduce stress and promote bonding and a collegial approach."

Ingrid Tennessee

HUGS AT HOME

The root of education however starts right in the home, where we are born and where our children are born. The Bible says that if we teach a child the way that he should go, when he is old he will not depart from it. I find this is true. The values and beliefs that are instilled in us and in the people we love and eventually work with in their youth and early years, are the values and beliefs that in the main remain throughout life and into our working lives. How parents address and speak to their children is key and instrumental. It contributes not only to our mental, physical and emotional wellbeing, it makes a significant difference to our attitude to others and in all areas of our lives.

The voices we hear as children can sometimes be the voices that we hear in our heads and when the inner critics come to play. The experience we have of love and how love is influences our perception of love as adults and how we demonstrate love. Breaking down the barriers to the presence of love in organisation can therefore start in the home and years before we venture into the world of work, organisation and relationship. It means taking a long-term view as parents and governments and governmental agencies across the world exploring ways of supporting parents of all kinds in the nurture of their children, not only physically and mentally but also emotionally and all with an eye on the future.

In the interviews I conducted in the research for my book, I learned that many of the senior leaders came from successful childhoods, childhoods in which there was love and security and it did not matter whether that childhood was one with money or not, high, middle or low class, the common theme was a presence and demonstration of love within their families. I believe that this contributed to their ready willingness to explore the topic of love in organisation with me.

> "I am very loved. I grew up in a very loving family that gave me everything. Not a lot of money but gave me everything from travel to piano lessons to food and shelter and a lot of encouragement and love. I don't remember going out to eat in restaurants as a kid, but there was a lot of love and support and every time there was a problem that I'd got myself into, there were so many people that jumped in to support. There was accountability too - I come from a background that is very demanding of firstborns, which I am. So there was a lot of demand but there was also a lot of support and love. This has been one of the biggest influences in my life."
>
> **Andre Angel**

> "I think the other way that barriers can be brought down at work is what happens at home. How is love expressed in the home? I have an extremely good relationship with my brother and I say I love him and he says he loves me. I also say the same to my son and he also expresses that love to me. This is where the home environment is important. With my father, he does

also say he loves me - not always verbally. He does it in different ways too. He is in his 80s and is not great at expressing himself in the way that he would like to and therefore it is important to notice the signals and to be mindful of saying there is no love just because a person doesn't express it directly. Many people express it indirectly. But in the context of barriers, when love is absent at home it is difficult for it to be present at work."

Charlie Wagstaff

"I'm very lucky because that adage - the greatest thing is to have loved and to be loved in return - is fantastic and I've experienced love in all my relationships - all my employment relationships. I feel I've got friends that love me. My wife loves me. My kids love me. My mum and dad love me. My brother loves me. My sister loves me. I feel that a lot of people at HeadBox love working here. I think there is lots more we can do of course. I feel really lucky. I feel that I've experienced the positive feelings that being loved and loving someone can bring - because it's a two-way thing - you get as much joy out of being loved as you do as loving someone."

Andrew Needham

"I like to think that I'm a person who likes love and is not afraid of it. My mother who sadly died a couple of years ago, was well known for being a very loving person and you sort of become that. It is part of who you are."

James Timpson

Children who experience loving hugs from those they love become adults who have no issue with the expression and demonstration of love. There is even scientific evidence that hugs contribute to the physical and emotional wellbeing of people and therefore will contribute to the physical and emotional wellbeing of people in organisation. Neuroscience research tells us that hugs are one way of increasing the neuro chemical oxytocin which affects positively the emotional parts of the human brain and increased levels of oxytocin increase the feelings of contentment we feel and strengthens the social bonds we have with each other. Hugs are also meant to increase the neurochemicals of dopamine and serotonin which along with oxytocin make us feel good about ourselves. When we feel good in ourselves and about ourselves, we are likely to be less stressed and anxious and more able to focus on what matters in our organisations and in life in general which then allows us to feel great about other people too and create environments in which those other people can feel great about themselves around us.

The power of physical touch, too, cannot be underestimated. Photos of people both famous and not famous hugging, evoke positive emotions. They demonstrate care. Science has also uncovered the power of physical touch on the emotional security and wellbeing of children, you just need to observe the response of a crying baby when held close to the skin of his or her mother, who then of course turn into adults in all walks of life, many of them in organisation and with the power and influence to impact the lives of others.

In addition, it is of course important to respect the requirements of the personal wishes, faith and religious beliefs of colleagues. This is also a demonstration of love. It is very sad that in recent years and in many forms of organisation and industry, particularly the glamourous industries across the world, the unwanted and harassing behaviours of people in influential positions has led to the raising of barriers more than the breaking down of them and for the guilty, justice will be carried out.

But when we focus on the greater good and the positive aspects of hugs, when you are in an organisation where a big hug from colleagues is a welcome greeting, a congratulation or a celebration of success, it can be one step to the removal of the barriers to the presence of love.

THE ART OF THE POSSIBLE

Redesigning the whole aspect of governance, ownership controls and the entire education system of the world may take some doing but we need not even look that far to start the breaking down of barriers to the presence of love in ourselves and in our organisations. You'll notice that I say 'in ourselves'. This is because it starts with us. With you and with me. We must at first confront it and then enable it in the relationships we cultivate and nurture in our environments in our families and in our organisations. I mentioned talking about it earlier on in the book but it goes even further than that. It is being role models as leaders and as human beings, knowing that others will follow when they see the good in us and in what we do. It is also in organisations, finding and enabling reason for people to talk about love so that it is wrapped around a subject or a purpose or a direction that serves beyond the bottom line.

"Finding a reason that people can connect with as to why using that kind of language as part of the working day because it's important and we take it seriously, is important. It's not just a loving thing that we do to tick a box, it's got to be part of where to start and if you get the start right, the rest of it and breaking down any other barriers becomes much easier.

It's got to be around open and honest conversations. We are lucky here at Tideway because we had a subject and a purpose around which we could use that kind of language. We have the love affair with the river. If you just sat down with your people and said 'right we're going to talk about love in our business' it wouldn't really make sense. You've got to have a context;

you've got to find a story that relates to what you're doing. A story that adds a greater meaning to what you're doing."

Andy Mitchell

"Have a love policy. Define your culture and beliefs. Question yourself as to why love isn't one of those fundamental things you require from your people in the way that they behave."

Alan Price

It is also as leaders finding opportunities to connect in a human way in every interaction that forms part of an organisation's operation. Business meetings of all kinds are an easy way and place to start. Beginning meetings first with attention to the human beings in the room and taking the lead in role modelling the desired behaviour is a great way to start the breakdown of barriers. Allowing for meetings between peers and colleagues to have a space to connect as human beings will also help. It's amazing how much it happens today that colleagues and fellow travellers in organisation could work together for years and at the end of their journey have as little knowledge about each other as they did at the very start; the loss of many a missed opportunity to really create and produce something beautiful for their organisation gone with the non-tapping into the latent talents of each other which will have been discovered and utilised had a connection on a more human level been made.

"If there was one silver bullet it is an honest conversation. Creating the space for an honest conversation. I always remember when I was a kid being told, treat people as you would like to be treated yourself. This is in fact wrong. I believe that you should treat people how they would like to be treated. This is important. And to do that, you must understand how that person wants to be treated."

Mark Scanlon

"Better conversations too in organisations. Sometimes accountability isn't really understood on either side. You can say that leadership isn't creating the right environment but it's a two way thing. Trust and respect is a two way relationship. If people are trusted to get on with it and they're empowered to do what is needed and then don't do it, that's problematic. So the quality of conversation between people where there is an equal level of challenge and support is a great help. We can't falsely tell everyone "isn't everything fantastic, aren't you great", if it actually isn't. There has to be a focus on 'are we doing what we said we would do, are we achieving what we said we wanted to achieve and if not, what are we going to do?' Let's have that conversation if it's not going well. Sometimes it's the tough conversation that leads you in the right direction."

Neil Wilson

"In our business - not saying that we are perfect - in our business, our leaders' jobs is to know their colleagues. To really know them. To know for example, where they last went on holiday if they have kids, how many kids they've got, what are their kids names, what their favourite hobby is, what their football team is - to know them as individuals. When you encourage a culture where your leaders know their team members individually and care about them, genuinely care, then you create a culture where love is embraced."

James Timpson

"You also demonstrate this as a leader in your action - to be kind and gracious. A kind and loving leader is gracious in saying no; in saying yes; and also gracious in saying how else can I be of service to you and in acknowledging when you haven't done things right and being willing to work very hard with your team to get those things right. That's how you demonstrate love in organisation."

Ingrid Tennessee

And in a world in which technology has allowed for virtual meeting room spaces, meetings and conferences, we should not underestimate the power of the physical human connection in contributing to the breaking down of barriers.

"You could spend more time doing reviews and having conversations with your people, but the mutual respect may not be there. If you had love in the organisation, you would certainly get more engagement with people. We don't spend enough time on what really matters and you see it and realise this when you have your people around you. Last year I brought all of my management team from across the world together for a leadership conference - and when you have all your people in a room you can see for yourself and hear for yourself how they feel and what is going on for them. The money spent is nothing compared to what you experience in the room. I think a lot of our success is down to people starting the year feeling very connected and feeling very motivated. People across the organisation as a result of our conference at the start of the year are now connecting spontaneously because they've met in person. There is no substitute for human connection. In a world where devices are predominantly the medium through which we connect when we connect in person, it can make a significant difference."

Howard Kerr

The small acts of kindness that you demonstrate as leaders and encourage those around you to do will also lead to the breaking down of barriers. Because when you focus on the person, the human being behind the label, the job title and the status, it makes it easier to value and accept them for who they are. In those acts of kindness, what you are role modelling and communicating, is that you as a human being matter beyond the bottom line, as do I.

"There are two things that are really important to understand. One - it is to know that it is not just a colleague that you are trying to inspire in a business it is their family as well and we believe that's really important. We have holiday homes - 20 of them currently - where colleagues can go on a free holiday with their family and their friends it doesn't cost them anything - of course they have to pay for their own food and drink but we pay for the accommodation, pay their tax, pay for the cleaning of the accommodation, and things like that are really important. You get an extra day off for your kid's first day at school, you get a day off for your birthday, you get a birthday card and a present from the company every time you have your birthday. So the colleague, the individual is important but also so is their family. The other is understanding when things happen in peoples' lives, you can step in and help. For example, a colleague who's worked with us for about 3 years - a guy. He fell on his way to work, and he's been in hospital about a month, and will be off for another six months. His biggest concern was his wife - he's just had a baby - and how he's going to pay the bills. So I phoned up his wife and I said to her, 'just to let you know, we're going to make sure he's paid full pay all the way through his time off don't need any sick notes and if he needs to take another month or two off work, then that's fine. What is important is his health'. Something like this, done genuinely is a huge way for someone to buy into our company. It is a two-way thing, it is not just giving someone money in return for their labour, it is about doing something more."

James Timpson

"Another example is when a person leaves a company and maybe things hadn't worked out right - how do you let that person leave the company? How do you demonstrate who the person means to you? It doesn't matter that things didn't work out - but how you behave in those circumstances. If that person hasn't given everything to HeadBox, you don't say get lost, you should still get behind the person and demonstrate that they are human and it says that it's okay that people disagree with you. It is important to engender this idea that you can disagree with me - we have this very robust, very direct - we call it wrestling or hustling - conversations and this is good because people should think, 'I can say what I think and I'm not going to be shouted down.'"

Andrew Needham

"Demonstrating quiet support, showing small steps of kindness, for example, passing a yellow sticky with a tick and a small note that says well done to a colleague in a board meeting can speak volumes, acknowledging performance with personal letters those types of actions can go a long way."

Lewis Doyle

ORGANISATION IS HUMAN

Remembering that without humans you have no organisation is a great way to break down the barriers to the presence of love. When we appreciate and act in the belief and knowledge that who we are in head, heart and gut is who we are in organisation. Often, we talk about organisations like they are devoid and separate from us. They are not. How we think, what we do, how we feel, the moods we experience and create for others and the conditions both seen and unseen that we establish within which we and the people around us work, can create barriers and significant ones to the presence of love in organisation. When we are sick and stressed, our brains do not function as well as they should and we learn from the world of neuroscience that the part of our brains in which problem solving takes place, creativity, innovation, the outputs of invention, are the same parts that thrive the most when we feel safe and feel taken care off. Therefore, if in organisation, we placed more attention to the wellbeing and health, the genuine health of our people physically, mentally and emotionally, we will have all the opportunity to break down the barriers to the presence of love. There's no point talking about love to colleagues who do not feel or believe that their wellbeing is at the heart of their organisation's existence and purpose.

"We need to be bold and define personal well-being (Body, Soul, Spirit) and what it takes to cover these needs (e.g. to have peace of mind it takes financial security, for development training and education are key, for health a form of healthcare is needed, then there is community). Success is something that is very personal but has to be defined as a long-term goal. We have to allow for mistakes but map personal progress to make the advancement tangible. There are peace of mind goals and there are progression goals."

Markus Hofmann

"One of the great ways to break down the barriers to the presence of love and care is really improving the causal link between people's wellbeing at work and their contribution and the success of the business and this is important to us here at John Lewis/Waitrose."

Tracey Killen

"I think that all of these things are interconnected. We are talking about the principles of an effective, decent and human workplace. We are however talking about it in an environment today where it is very hard to be shielded from pressure; where it appears to be considered by many people to be normal to continually look at your emails everyday whilst you're on holiday and so the application of the principles of love, fellowship, respect, that we recognise that you are a whole human being and we want you to bring your whole self to work and the corollary of that is that we want you to have sacred spaces of time which were truly yours and able to feel relieved from the stresses of your work would enable help break down barriers."

Mark Goyder

Because organisation is human, we should not underestimate the power of role models and the fact that the higher up you are in the organisational food chain, the louder your whisper is as a leader. And so, it is important that leaders up the hierarchy appreciate the value of love and if you believe in it, which hopefully you do because it's a critical leadership capability. The act of courage in role modelling what it is to love and be loving and to incentivise loving behaviour is one of the fastest ways of toppling down the barriers to the presence of love in organisation. It means leaving your ego firmly at the door and abandoning it at the door as you leave once again to go home; it means being willing to take one for the team in service of all of your people, yours and their communities, the communities whom you serve and of course society. It is the willingness to speak your truth in all circumstances and with love and depending on which side of the table you are sitting on, making self-preservation a lower priority than the delivery of good work for your organisation and for those in it. It is also about creating an environment in which self-preservation is lower down the priority of those who report into you and who believe that your every decision can impact their livelihood in the short or long term.

"I think this is something to do with the way power operates. I think there's something to do with those around powerful people that wants them to be insulated. In a way as a powerful person you almost want to be insulated because it's very hard doing what you're doing, you're under lots of pressure and you're struggling and perhaps people want to ease your struggle, so they consciously take away problems that you shouldn't need to be bothered with and in doing that, the layers and insulation start to build up. I don't think it's a conscious thing on anybody's part, although we all know about instances where boards aren't given the harsh realities - because when company executives report to their board on the performance of the organisation, there will be a sense of self-preservation and a presenting of a view that enables them to influence the board and to a certain extent manage their responses. They don't want to demonstrate that they're not in control. And then of course the same thing happens with regards to the people that work for these executives too!"

Norman Pickavance

"Leadership courage! Leaders have to be prepared to lead by example. Encouraging leadership values of honesty which breeds trust; Integrity too and also humility because this demonstrates a willingness to learn, will contribute to the breakdown of the barriers."

Steve Fox

"I am super self-critical. I see my own successes and failings but focus on my failings much more. I am constantly looking for things I could do better. I'm always in a hurry and I'm impatient. I do believe that I go out of my way to ask about people, their personal lives but I guess I could also be doing more. The challenge as a Chief Executive is recognising that other people have different needs to yourself."

Howard Kerr

You could argue that a lot is being done in the world of work and organisation today and much more than has been done to date, that if added up is leading to the bringing down of the barriers to the presence of love. Yet the barriers still remain and are very evident. The senior leaders I interviewed have a perspective on this.

"In modern society we have seen a series of cycles. After the First World War, we talked about homes for heroes. There was something about that war experience that brought out our essential humanity and made us feel we have to do better than this - in the love we express for our neighbour. That implies setting government to work to provide things better Then gradually over a period of time, we forget that mood and other things crept in - so after the 2nd world war in the U.K. there was again a real flood of concern and compassion and for the disadvantaged, a sense of concern and compassion for those who had sacrificed their lives and a sense of shame of the quality of provision that we had and we had a government who brought in the health service and introduced compulsory education and the welfare state came along.

But then - and this is where the human nature trips in – what one generation provides; the next generation feels entitled to. And then in a democracy, what begins to happen is that we say we're entitled to all these things but we don't want to pay for them; each generation wants to do better than its parents but it's not putting the money into the public sector, it won't pay the taxes. Government lets the private sector rip. There is the pressure to keep up and live at a certain standard. So all of these things come together - the entitlement mentality of the citizen, wanting all the services but not prepared to vote for a government that would raise taxes, expecting my own standard of living to be higher than that of my parents and assuming a lifestyle that means there will be two of us in full time work. Add to that the feeling that everything is so visible where you can see on your smart phone the life of your 'neighbour' who may have many things that you don't have. This heightens the sense of deprivation real or unreal. All of this together is what leads to the failure of the barriers coming down."

Mark Goyder

"However I think there still is a 'them and us' in most organisations. In most organisations, leaders are not in it with their people. In many organisations, a restructuring would happen bottom first instead of top first. One senior leader could replace 10 employees and yet we take the 10 employees out. So I think we often look at the solutions in perhaps the wrong way. We should turn the pyramid upside down."

Louise Fisher

BABY STEPS ARE FINE

If the barriers to the presence of love in organisation were easy to break down, they probably would have all come down by now. They are most certainly not easy to break and when you spend time thinking about them, the amount of courage it would take and the personal risk and vulnerability that may be called for, attempting to do anything fundamental may seem overwhelming.

The most important thing, however, is to take the first step. Start. The world can be changed with one conversation at a time. The butterfly effect is real and so is the domino effect. One tiny little domino at the start of a chain can, by the end of the chain, have knocked down a domino the size of you and me. When you take that baby step, what at first seems foreign and different will soon become familiar and the norm. But it's a step certainly worth taking when we give ourselves the permission to think about the potential impact on the world and on humanity of more love in organisation. The very purpose of what organisation is shaped for will come to life.

The level of effort that is currently put into producing and production, plus the focus of nations and governments on what we need to do to maximise the productivity and production capabilities of our workforce, will be much reduced. With that small baby step, the end of the journey and certainly one of the milestone stops will be a destination and place in which stress and mental health is confined to rarity, engagement initiatives the norm, diversity and inclusion a subject of interest for the history books.

"Also talking about love in the right context and people may use different words - the idea of compassion and compassionate management for example - these could be alternatives to the word. It may not be the full sense of love but it is one of the most important aspects and of the meaning of love and a product of it and so, in the world of work starting here could be a good way to overcome the barrier to talking about love."

Peter Cheese

"Finding a reason that people can connect with as to why using that kind of language as part of the working day because it's important and we take it seriously is important - it's not just a loving thing that we do to tick a box, it's got to be part of where to start and if you get the start right, the rest of it and breaking down any other barriers becomes much easier."

Andy Mitchell

"Even if you believe in it, it's difficult. I guess it takes courage and bravery if you're going to put love on the agenda.

One thing I hate is the corporate bandwagon where everybody jumps on the latest initiative. But true leadership is being brave and courageous about what you do believe in. It means a few brave leaders starting to talk about love and in 6 - 12 months' time it becomes more familiar and common place; you'll have a lot more leaders talking about it - because others have set the tone and the pace.

Love is about attachment and it is about trust. It is about the extent to which people may express their emotions and feelings at work ... and maybe that's not such a bad thing."

Howard Kerr

"Using the language of love - using the word itself - wouldn't it be lovely to do that? It feels it's so open to misinterpretation. But if you found a way of framing it in line with your organisation's values I think the use of the word would be fantastic. To be able to say to people we love our employees and say what we mean by that, could be a really powerful thing."

Neil Wilson

At the end of the day it doesn't matter where you start, what matters is that you do start and that when you do. It is with a purpose and a real belief in the return on investment of a love filled organisation; and that no matter how soft or slushy it may feel or seem, or how risky it may be to stick your neck out and embark on the journey, you can hold out and stay strong in the knowledge of the benefits and the difference it will make to you, your people, your organisation and therefore to your communities, to society and indeed the world.

Love - that unconditional acceptance of all of who you are as human and the unconditional acceptance of another for who they are as human is not at all slushy. It actually is hard. Very hard.

> "Some people may say that love is a nebulous concept but it's only nebulous when we talk about it. But you can see it at work. When you experience acts of humanity, acts of kindness, acts of friendship that we see on a day-to-day basis, that's not nebulous, that's real and practical."
>
> **Emmanuel Mbakwe**

5. THE DIFFERENCE LOVE
MAKES

....

IF THE BARRIERS TO THE Active and operational presence of love in organisation were broken down, what difference would it then make? What would happen? What can we dare to imagine and dare to dream would take place? Love at its very basic level is the unconditional acceptance of self and others. That unconditional acceptance of all I am and the unconditional acceptance of all you are, so that in giving space to all of who we both are to emerge, we have the greatest of opportunity to create the most extraordinary of results that impact our lives and the lives of those we impact near and far most positively. This however is not about accepting or tolerating or indeed turning a blind eye to behaviour that is bad or not in line with our values and agreed ways of working. It isn't. In fact, to the contrary, when we are able to see and value who we are as humans it makes the challenge of bad behaviour or the challenge of having those potentially difficult conversations a lot easier because we should be able to separate the individual from their behaviours. Let's imagine what difference love would make if it were present in organisation - the type of love that I am advocating, talking about and inviting us all to embrace. I asked the leaders I interviewed what they thought of the difference the presence of love would make in organisation.

> "I would hope that the difference it would make is that employees
> would feel that people are worried about their hearts and their

minds and that as a result of that, I would run over the cliff with these people if I had to. I would care about all the things that my organisation cared about because I felt cared about too. I would feel trusted, respected that the organisation was sharing the gains and the pains with me. That I would go that extra mile and I would feel equal as a participant in the organisation, that there was fairness and that the leaders were role models and demonstrated all these things in the actions that they took."

Louise Fisher

"Real love does not see colour; It doesn't see gender; it doesn't see status; love is love. If an organisation is run on a basis of love you would see a very stable employee. You would see engagement; less grievances and if there were grievances, they would be open and they would be resolved; over time, productivity and performance would be positive. There would be growth."

Sam Aiyere

"Love in an organisation will be seen and felt; it would be potent and powerful. People would exude an aura of warmth, of graciousness of genuineness. There would be everything in the touch, the feel, the sound - everything about our organisation; employee engagement would be high and there would be full buy in to the organisation's aims and objectives; there would be a real commitment from the teams and team working to achieve all of our goals."

Ingrid Tennessee

"I think it could be massive. But again it does come with its challenges because love brings emotion and that needs to be channelled in the right way because it can lead to disappointment and upset. So I think it can have a massive positive impact but there will be some downsides too. Because love can have a negative side as well as a positive and if you love someone and there's a breakup or a difference of views or expectation which can happen between individual or individuals and organisation, it can have a negative effect too. But that's no reason why you shouldn't actively look to have love show up in your business."

Alan Price

"One is it makes you more commercially successful, I'm convinced. Secondly it reduces colleague turnover, it reduces colleague sickness and time off and it makes your business more equal - I feel - where everyone is treated as an equal. Love has no hierarchy. Just because someone works in a warehouse doesn't mean that they get treated and made to feel any different to someone who works in finance."

James Timpson

"The problem we have in organisation is that people get in the way. Different people will have different attitudes and different value systems. You can't tell when you hire them what their value systems are. In my business, we are headquartered in Singapore with operations in South East Asia and Greater China and most of our staff are ethnic Chinese. We do have other races obviously but primarily it is still Chinese. However, that racial homogeneousness doesn't mean that there are no differences. Perhaps the idea of having the presence of love in the organisation will enable everyone to see through their differences and be able to work with each other instead of for oneself only."

Richard Eu

"I think it would have positive impact in organisations because if you think about the ultimate example of love in action - Jesus - and look at the transformative impact that His life singular act of love has had on the history of the nations, and if you think about the Gospel and the Gospel values and the Christian values and you think about the impact and influence that it has had on societies around the world - those things are immeasurable. For example, whilst some may deny it, Western society is built on the values of love – doing good before God and to your fellow man. My view therefore is that the practical visible presence of love would improve organisations. It would benefit not just the organisation but the wider society."

Emmanuel Mbakwe

ALL OF YOU, IS WELCOME

Right from the start of an individual's working life, if love were present in the organisation in which that person would be working, the whole recruitment and hiring process would be a joy. It would be rewarding every step of the way. The first encounter, whatever its medium, the internet, a call from a recruiter, a post on a social platform professional or personal, a referral from a friend - would be one that communicated to you, that all you are is welcome.

The hiring process would confirm it and whatever the outcome, both parties will have experienced a sharing of perspectives, an understanding of wishes, hopes and ambitions and an appreciation of purpose, choices and decisions made in a way that enriches and in some way leaves both as better humans than before they met. Potential candidates would not have a need to hide parts of who they are and will be open about how they see themselves today and tomorrow without fear of retribution or discrimination; without the fear of being declined at the door and turned away, depriving the organisation and society of the talent and potential of what could have been created.

It's disappointing the number of people of all ages who today still hide who they truly are in order to get over the threshold of employment and into organisation. The opportunities presented by technology and the advancement in AI are immense and indeed the world is fast becoming a global village as a result. However, no matter how digitally fluent a user may be and no matter how easy the access to opportunity of employment may become, at the end of the day, it is the freedom of expression to be all of who we are that really matters and that freedom can only come from a demonstration of love in action - that unconditional acceptance of the human for who he or she is - is what will enable a genuine exploration of fit for both individual and organisation. When hiring into senior levels of status in organisation, head hunters and executive search firms will be motivated by the opportunity to place a great candidate with all the potential that the client needs and in so doing, be willing to challenge with confidence, the bias both conscious and unconscious of the client, and whilst I appreciate we've all got economic needs and need to eat, they would be motivated less by the need to secure the ongoing contracts and retainers with the client as the recruiter of choice. This is because they would have at their helm and in their teams, leaders who took their responsibility seriously and had a purpose beyond earning a fee and commission. In their dealings with the candidates there would be trust and integrity and an honesty in communication of the outcome of the process.

Time would be invested to share with the candidate the real reasons why the client and/or they decided not to go forward in this instance. Timely updates would be provided to candidates anxious to learn their fate, discussions around expected compensation and remuneration on both sides, would be candid and real and without the unmentioned yet present, cloudy calculation of commission percentages wafting in the air. In my career to date both as a candidate and a client of search firms, I have experienced both awful and awesome behaviour. When a candidate is treated as a commodity at whatever level of position in organisation the hiring process is for, the message being communicated is that my fee, my money and my material needs are more important than you are and you are simply a means to my end.

When a candidate is treated as a human being and is seen; when the attributes of love - time, conversation, explanation, communication, support and so on - are present, whatever the outcome of the process, you say to a candidate, 'I see you. You are human and you are much more than a means to my end.' When love is present from the beginning to the end of a hiring process; right from the thought and design of the roles and up to the go-to-market methodology and engagement of the candidate right through to the contracting and the first day of work, that process would be a process of discovery for all the parties involved. The outcome of it would enable the potential for the most successful of beginnings to the next season of life for organisation and individual.

INCLUSION IS WHAT MATTERS

The excitement I feel when I think about what it could mean in organisations to be accepted, genuinely accepted as a human being is indescribable. When a person knows that they can show up in the world as they are, all the energy used in hiding, managing, manipulating, excusing, stressing, pretending on the one hand, and on the other hand, all the energy wasted in curing, counselling, diagnosing will be directed towards the fulfilling of the purpose of the organisation. Difference would be welcome and genuinely celebrated even within groups who are different as exclusion is not the exclusive domain of the dominant group in organisation. I have seen women excluding women, black women excluding other black women, men excluding men and so many other different ways.

Whilst moving towards a culture of love would enable the provision of space for diversity in all aspects of the term, diversity in itself is not enough.

Once, I arrived at my place of work on my first day and as part of my induction process, I was to be introduced to the outgoing Head of Human Resources who had recently retired and was visiting the organisation again as part of his farewell process. I understood too that he was keen to spend some time with me in order to impart key points of knowledge accumulated from his many years of service and travel around the world on company business. The mistake however is that someone had failed to inform him that I was black and female. Or, indeed, had failed to remind me. As he strode into my office with confidence, all 6ft 4 inches or so of him, paying little attention to my waiting executive assistant who was herself waiting in line before him to have a quick word with me as soon as I hung up from my telephone call, he stumbled, almost fell forward, blinked rapidly as if to clear his vision, turned bright red in the face and could barely hide his surprise that someone different, black, female and 5ft 2 inches tall, had been hired into the organisation and into such a key role. He recovered, sat unsteadily in his seat because he could not retreat immediately to safety and in demonstration of the good social skills he had acquired over his life, proceeded to engage in very, very small talk with me. I played along, safe in the knowledge that he was no longer going to be a senior leader within my business.

I applaud and admire the work done across the world and in organisations of all backgrounds, industries and sizes to move forward the cause of equality and diversity. It makes my heart sing when I read and learn of women appointed into senior positions in local, international and global organisations, FTSE and Fortune companies with the power and influence to make a significant difference across the world.

It is encouraging to read of big symbolic and serious gestures to address inequality and to enable diversity being made through the appointment of people of minority backgrounds into roles responsible for the advancement of equality and diversity and inclusion in their organisations. It is a logical step to have someone from a minority group in organisation or with a minority background be the executive lead for the advancement of all minority groups in organisation. It sends a message of being taken seriously, firstly by the organisation and secondly, a message of encouragement and hope for the communities that the person represents, not only in how they look, but also in what they have the mandate to do. It is encouraging too and a demonstration of progress to read of senior business leaders of large international and global organisations lauding the economic benefit and commercial advantages of having diversity and particularly gender diversity in their organisations; consultancies too sharing data and trends that underpin the fact that diversity is good for business success and profitability.

In the United Kingdom, steps towards the reporting of the gender pay gap and in time, the reporting of ethnic and other minority group pay gaps will incentivise organisation leaders to take proactive steps to ensure all of their people are put on an equal footing in how they are remunerated and rewarded. In other parts of Europe and the USA, we read too of the flexibility of working introduced into organisations, the proactive promotion and recruitment of women into senior levels in organisation and the provision of flexible benefits to men too in recognition of their parenting rights and the role they may play in their own families. The plethora of initiatives too to support age diversity, the diversity of mental health issues, the emerging work on neuro diversity and a rejuvenation of attention on disability particularly in parts of the Western World signifies hope. After all, Rome was not built in one day.

Progress can, however, be faster. In the early nineties, I was a Head of Equal Opportunities in UK Manufacturing and all the issues discussed then that affected minority groups and how they could be resolved are the same issues I experience being discussed today, albeit a lot more eloquently. In addition, engagement levels in organisation reported in various ways and by various organisations continue to be inconsistent across the world and can be accelerated only when the focus is turned to love, unashamedly, fully accepting without condition, all of who you are and all of who I am love. It is a good and great to address issues and themes that are common to diverse groups of similar people. But if difference is the predominant focus, there could be more a risk of fragmentation and demarcation than the opportunity for unity, a coming together, and a working together with a shared purpose for the greater good of all and where the sum of all the parts is greater than the individual and the specific group from which that individual comes.

In fact, I would argue that a focus on love and the demonstration of all of its attributes would lead in time to the removal of labels and category for the representation of rights in organisation and the role of Head of Diversity and Inclusion would be replaced by a shared commitment, accountability and responsibility of all leaders to create and establish an environment and culture of working in which all of our people at whatever level, are free to be all of who they are without condition. That role could be replaced by a role of Chief Love and Inclusion Officer or Love and Inclusion Director, or Director of Belonging, Inclusion and Love or simply, Director of Love.

"I think in diversity, it helps a lot because people feel that they work in a culture where they feel they can be themselves.

They are not judged. I think it would be more fun; more laughs; People in our business are laughing all the time."

James Timpson

"And with regards to inclusion and diversity and difference, there would be a real feel and evidence that there is real respect for who we are and regardless of what our personal circumstances are, there would be no stigma or judgement as to whether anyone is brown, black, white, short or tall, thin or fat, there would be congruence and empathy with regards to from whence we came. There would be a valuing of each individual as they are and there would be evidence of this from staff to colleagues, to stakeholders to customers to the community. It would be everywhere. You would feel it and that sense of feeling would be so great. It would be powerful."

Ingrid Tennessee

"People spend so much energy trying to fit in and so when you are new to an environment where you are different, you are never quite comfortable in the new environment and there are games to be played and learned. I come from a working-class background and I don't quite have the etiquette that the modern organisation sometimes needs. When organisations open up their doors, they have more diversity at the ground floor level and then there is less diversity progressing upwards and I think that this is because people spend so much energy fitting in that they don't have much left for standing out."

Norman Pickavance

"The difference it can make is transformational. On employee engagement it goes without saying. But when we come to examine how we go beyond employee engagement to make and create that sense of belonging; it does all sorts of things. It means that it's easier to recruit the right people because actually you start to develop a reputation for just being a fantastic place to work."

Lawrence Hutter

"When it comes to engagement, people would be more motivated to give their best at the workplace. The community would be more important than the individual and with regards to inclusion there would be a proper understanding of the strength and weaknesses of individuals and a fair application of them."

Markus Hofmann

"We don't all start from the same start line in the race and it's so easy when by the luck of the draw, you find yourself in the clan or bunch of white, western, middle to upper class male - then you look at yourself and say why did you not make it through. So therefore, there is an ever growing consciousness that in the west, we want to build companies and commerce with the world and to do so we should have the world within these walls. Our walls. And to do so, we've tried for a while by saying 'here is the ad, the job is available to anyone' and that alone doesn't work. So whereas there is a kind of almost conflicting thing of open book justice for all, 100s of CVs came and after 30 - 40 years, the result is again the same - boys, western middle aged white men and now some women dominating the jobs, there is a consciousness now that we need to ignite true and genuine inclusion; to be the catalyst for something much greater and deeper and the routes in have to be thought through rather than simply saying 'well we did advertise the job'. For example in my company we are starting to put targets in and saying that at least 2% of our population which is 2000 from a 100,000 should be people with a disability and this is not about positive discrimination, it is about having a macro view vs a micro one."

John Mangan

PERFORMANCE COULD SOAR

If love were active and present in organisation, the difference it would make to performance and productivity would be immense and the difference this would in turn make to society would be astronomical. Our capacity as the human being to deliver extraordinary results is yet untapped because of all the current restraints we place on ourselves which are known and unknown. Even though our advancements are rapid and in the world of business and work we continually talk about how the only constant in life is change, which is true, what I also see is that the potential for more good and significant results in spite of the constant and fast change is significantly untapped; in fact, I believe that we currently experience only a trickle. The one and only wrench that can unleash the real potential of the human race is love.

You see when we were born, we came into the world without blemish and we only need to observe the interactions of children with each other to appreciate this. But, as we grew up over the years, our experiences imposed by others and self-imposed, some significantly emotional, edge us into places of comfort and familiarity, the safety of which manifest in different ways, some of which become detrimental to each other. I am not advocating that we all return to our childhood and participate in regression therapy. What I am advocating is that we together turn our attention to the most fundamental of human needs and gifts in the interest of what it can possibly unleash through the power of organisation. I asked the senior leaders I interviewed what they believed the difference love would make to organisational performance and productivity.

> "It would make a big difference. If you create an atmosphere of love, then people will start to do things for each other and for themselves and it will become self-perpetuating and of course what you really need to manage is the level of autonomy you give to people. You need to ensure that people are not then starting to compete for the wrong reasons. If you've got all your people thinking and acting in each other's best interest then it will impact productivity and it will impact engagement."

> **Steve Fox**

> "Love is fundamentally about human emotion and relationship and we want to be more humanistic in our businesses and organisation so the first effect should be if you're treating me as a human being then how am I going to react and therefore the first effects will be around my wellbeing, my mental state, my emotional state and then the connection from that into the more tangible outcomes of business such as productivity and creativity that we know are so important to the success of business today."

> **Peter Cheese**

> "It would impact motivation. If people were acting from a sense of vocation or their calling, then that's what gets you out of bed for in the morning. It's not a pay check. I realise that not all jobs are like this. But the sense that you are in some way following your calling and that you are able to live that out in the work that you do is the most powerful motivator. Helping people to find that in their work would be great. If you start from here, then it would change the purpose of performance

management and this is where the HR rule book needs to be rewritten because so often performance management is a control mechanism rather than it being an opportunity for people to realise the calling that they have and to realise it all the more effectively."

Norman Pickavance

"Love would have a massive and deep impact on employee engagement. It is about feeling that you belong. Ultimately if people are genuinely allowed to be themselves - their good selves - and have that safety of being validated and being okay, it gives them incredible potential to reach for the stars. And by extension, productivity improves. If you're good at sending love messages to your children for example, their energy is focused not on doubting whether they are good enough, their energy is focused on who they are, and your belief in them is so deeply established that you allow them to channel their energy into what they are trying to do and this is what the corporate world calls productivity and performance. Therefore, if your people are certain of how you feel about them and you have a culture that promotes this - when your people are encouraged, they will also encourage others. This is the effect of having a positive spiral effect. Productivity comes from ideas and ideas come from exchange and exchange comes from wanting things to improve and this is productivity."

John Mangan

"Love in organisation would make a massive difference. Ultimately people love being loved and all the things that that positive energy gives them. Jeff Bezos talks about customer obsession and that customers can be difficult and awkward, and it is the same love for your customers that can actually drive innovation in your business. If your customers really see that you care about them, that will drive a reciprocal behaviour that is good for you as an organisation and you could apply that to productivity and your own employees. When your own employees really feel that they are loved and are cared for, it becomes less about the money and more about they want to climb mountains for you."

Andrew Needham

"In terms of team performance, there would be a lot of care in the approach to the business. There would be excellent customer service. People would be very supportive also of each other; there would be a celebration and respect for each other in terms of each other's strengths and limitations and coaching for those with limitations. Because real love is about helping each other. And supporting them to be at the place to be where you are and if they are in a bad place, to empathise and to be non-judgemental. To also nurture and support in bad times."

Ingrid Tennessee

"The interesting one is about productivity and performance because if you get it wrong, it could go the other way. In another company years ago we were entering the Great Place to Work survey. We did it for 3 years on the run and our score went higher each year. In year 1 we made the top 30 and then the top 20 for 2 years afterwards and in fact over those 3 years, our performance went down. So the correlation was interesting. It became such a focus on how people felt about working there that we were more concerned about how happy everyone was than how well they were performing. There has to be a balance."

Neil Wilson

A FOCUS ON STRENGTHS

And in the world of performance management and development, love would make a difference on where our focus is placed, firstly as an organisation and most importantly as people. Objectives and goals set will be realistic and genuinely inclusive of the views and opinions of your people. Top down would be a notion of the past, the results of which would be the subject of business school case studies on how not to lead and love your people. They would be set, too, from a place of love that goes beyond the organisation's boundaries and in the knowledge that the decisions we make in life and in work can have both intended and unintended consequences in the positive and in the negative that reach far beyond our geographical boundaries.

There would be a desire to leverage and develop further the skills and capabilities that serve the individual and the organisation, with an emphasis on the "and". Strengths would be the nature of discussion as opposed to weaknesses and areas of improvement. Feedback will be given and delivered from a place of 'I want you to win' because when you win, we all win, and the organisation wins too. And of course, we know that when the organisation wins and wins with love at the root of its actions, the communities in which it exists and serves also win. The resulting ripple effect of then becomes all-encompassing and for the good of society.

Love in organisation would enable the opportunity for performance and career discussions to be a genuine and two-way exploration of what can be possible and in a way that meets the desired calling and purpose of both entities. They would be open and honest and conducted in an atmosphere of trust because what underpins that trust is a love so robust, it is entrenched in the DNA of the organisation of the knowledge of the attitude of love that underpins the entire process.

The removal of performance ratings across organisations, which thankfully has begun, will be rapid because of the appreciation that the human is more than a number and is far more complex than the ratings allow. The discussion around objectives and expectations not met will be held from a place of shared responsibility and ownership of what can be done in service of what is agreed. Across the table, the labels of boss and subordinate will become obsolete, because after all we are all leaders in organisation even though some leaders are required to provide leadership to other leaders. This does not however mean that we hide behind the structures we create. But even more important, we all are human and when love is present in discussion about performance and feedback, the discussion is conducted as human to human.

When love is present, the development of performance and the inclusion of your people, all of your people in the description of the behaviours and rules of engagement within the organisation, aside from the legalities required, would be paramount and a focus on the genuine inclusion of all would be prioritised over and above the time desired to conclude the exercise.

Norman shares two examples of what can happen when time is taken to involve all of your people.

> "When I was doing the merger of Swiss bank and UBS and rather than going out with a prescription of our performance management criteria, we actually ran facilitated workshops in every single location around the world and we asked people what mattered most to them and what they would like to see in performance management in the organisation. And because we listened and we'd gone out of our way to do so,

even though the answers we came up with may have been the answers we'd have come up with without the consultation, people felt valued and felt listened to and felt respected because they were involved in the creation of the future. We employed a loving approach that said we value you.

Another example is when I was at Morrisons. At Morrisons, they had taken over Safeway. And it had gone badly wrong. It was all over the newspapers, Chief Executive fired, new board members coming in and I was hired new in too. We did an employee opinion survey and what I did was I personally conducted small group sessions with about 1000 people in total and what I got out of that was people talking in language that related to them and their lives and sharing what mattered. Out of that comes the quirky things that you would not think were important but were desperately important to individuals. We ended up with six values and rather than telling people what they meant and should mean, we ran workshops again and this time for the entire workforce of about 130,000 people asking them what each of those values would mean for them. So if you take one of the values - 'great shop keeping', - we asked what does this mean for you, what it means is that it all looks nice and there's nothing on the floor and you can walk around easily - this was their contribution to those things that brought it alive, and in every single store, they identified one thing that they didn't think we were doing particularly well and everybody had a voice in that too and every store came up with their own action plan for that thing and suddenly that became the language in the organisation and when you have a common language you are able to talk about things. What happened here is that we went from a merger that failed to have a common language where we could talk about the issues on the ground so people started to feel good about themselves and with respect, listening, language, commitment."

Norman Pickavance

And he shares here an example of what can happen when some of your people are excluded, although unintentionally.

"At Grant Thornton, I was responsible for creating something called the vibrant economy. And one of the dimensions of that was working out how we would need to change our internal environment to support what we were trying to do with our clients. This idea was taken out of the book - shared enterprise. And so we changed our reward system and said that everybody will have a stake in the extra value that's created so it was like a step towards shared ownership. So we got all partners to vote for that and they did, 99% said yes, and we said we would introduce 3 things, sharing rewards, sharing ideas and sharing responsibility. When it came to sharing ideas, what we got lots of people involved, what could we do to make the strategic key imperatives come to life - so we asked everybody. In asking everybody, we created groups who would go out and facilitate that and in doing that, we bypassed the partners. So the partners, who had signed up to doing it and they knew what was going on were wondering when they would be asked and consulted - 'what about me?', so this bit of feeling part of it and when you position this in terms of love, you would involve everybody; they should have been asked for their views and what we get so wrong so many times, is that we miss steps because we want to do things quickly and because they had said yes, they said yes, we agree to what you're doing, we decided not to involve them. It would have taken another six months to involve them and to get their views but perhaps in the context of love, it would have been six months well spent."

Norman Pickavance

Career development discussions would cover the life of the individual at work and at home. After all they are the one and the same person. There would be a recognition of the fusion between work and home life and the benefit of erasing the still present separation between the two. Interests would be explored and the best roles in the best geographies, depending on the size of the organisation, that would best serve the organisation and individual would be explored. Organisation and company politics would be relegated because time would not be invested in the relentless upward career management and desperate efforts to adhere to the rules of the unseen clubs that must be obeyed in order to secure the most prized of roles.

"When we build trust and underpinned by love we can build a very strong relationship and a basis for success. Individually we also need to connect and you connect if you are able to share – when you are able to talk about the things you're going through at work or even at home and be able to do this knowing that your vulnerability will not be exploited. And the only thing that can bring us to that place of trust and genuine support is love. This will help us see each other as a unit rather than an individual within the team."

Sam Aiyere

"What is also important is allowing people to feel comfortable having conversations around their personal interests or personal fears in a way that isn't threatening. The classic route in the past for such conversations were limited to through a boss or through HR. Encouraging people to act as buddies or internal mentors or coaches in part for good succession planning, in part to allow people as many avenues as appropriate to them to stretch their thinking or how they are approaching problems or personal issues is a good thing."

Paul McNamara

And if in the event there is a belief and a conclusion that the skills, interests and capabilities of the individual are best served elsewhere, the manner in which this is handled would be in love and a mutual agreement that a parting of the ways at this time is in the best interest of all parties. Genuinely. If handled in love the monies spent on legal advice on departure would instead be diverted to the support of the individual in charting a different path as there will be no fear of recriminations and backlash of actions taken by sour individuals feeling hard done by or betrayed by an organisation they served for so long or gave so much of themselves to.

If the parting of ways, on the one hand, is a mutual one and the papers exchanged for signature are purely to comply with the employment law of the land, any monies provided to the departing individual to support their ongoing development, retraining and reskilling should not be determined by their level on the organisation structure or constrained by the status. It, instead, should be determined by the outcome of a conversation between individual and organisation conducted in love and the purpose of which being an investment in the future success of the individual and a demonstration of a legacy of contribution to community from the organisation.

MY WELLBEING AND HEALTH MATTER

Love in organisations would make a significant difference to the wellbeing of all of your employees, regardless of who they are because in love, employee wellbeing and health would be a priority. Your people at every level of the organisation and regardless of the nature of their role would feel, know and believe that their wellbeing was at the heart of those to whom they were accountable for their performance. They would know beyond lip service that their wellbeing was the organisation's wellbeing. This belief, feeling and knowledge will be underpinned by initiatives designed to support and promote their physical wellness, not only because of what they do but because of who they are. They would know that because they were more than a means to the end of the organisation, that their physical, mental and emotional fitness was a priority.

There would be an active demonstration of the belief that when you take care of your people, they take care of you and together you will take care of your communities and the very purpose that the organisation is there to serve, will be met and exceeded. When there is love, your levels of absence would be genuine and driven less by individuals finding creative ways to take a break from a job they feel reluctantly bound to, because of the economic benefit to their family and to those for whom they are responsible. When there is love, your people will be proactive in taking care of themselves because of the provision and education provided. The dreaded 'return to work interview' and conversation would be eagerly attended by all parties, if at its core was a discussion of support and help required and available to accelerate a return to the healthy integration of the returner at a pace and in a way that was mutually advantageous to all.

Issues traditionally seen to be taboo will be readily disclosed in the knowledge that support will be given free from the threat of stigma and unwelcome assumptions and conclusions. The variety of mental health challenges and the varying levels of complexity that they have will be simply that as people will freely seek the help and support that they need from loving leaders who in turn create an environment in which their people can feel accepted and accepting of themselves. The nature of conversation and dialogue around support and how to move forward will exude the attributes of psychological safety because both parties will be in no doubt as to the intention and the basis on which the conversation is being had.

Mentally your people will be stronger because they would be in an environment where 'no' is a welcomed word and an understood and embraced expression. Demands for documents, proposals, responses, board reports and other work deemed to further the objectives of the organisation and in deadlines that really are unreasonable would be actions of the past.

Calls made by desperate leaders under the apparent impossibility of a deadline, to team members on holiday or on training courses would be minimal and confined to times of real and genuine emergency. The number of repeated rewrites and multiple rehearsals before the all-important visits from headquarters and the amount of time taken to prepare for business and organisational reviews will be at a minimum because the focus will be on collaborative dialogue, shared problem solving, a shared purpose and a goal in furthering the success of all of your people. The focus in those meetings would be less on the theatre of performance driven by the various motives of the individuals in the meeting ranging from a desperation to be valued, to securing the next promotion, or even landing the biggest pay increase.

Flexible working would be genuinely that and not a 'tick box' exercise. It wouldn't be an organisation focused on its employer brand for selfish means and undermined by the accompanied introduction of employee monitoring and spying policies and actions by bosses untrusting of what members of their teams are doing in their own time. Comments made in innocence by leaders in positions of power will be taken as such. Innocent. Clarity where needed will be sought free of suspicion and wonder as to the real intention behind the requests. Feedback will be given because innocent comments can, at times, be delivered clumsily, in love and received in love.

The emotional wellbeing of self and others would be pursued and allowed to flourish. The expression of emotion and feeling in the workplace would be commonplace and welcome. There would be no eyebrows raised when grown men cry and time will be taken to check in with how you and your people are before the matters of the day are attended to. The difference love would make is that you and your leaders would be human and feel at liberty to operate and to relate at the human level because after all, that is who we all are. Human.

"Perhaps (idealistically) we would all behave differently… there are a number of things that would come out of that. Genuinely we could do away with a lot of the rules that we have about what people are supposed to do at work. We could start tearing up policies that regulate the way that we work and we really would reduce the more negative activity that relate to how we manage people at work. The bigger the organisation the more controls we seem to have and the more time managers can spend in those control activities and surely these would be much reduced."

Sally Cabrini

"I work in an organisation where we are only just learning to use love as an expression. We have been around for 150 years and the reason we've been around for 150 years is because people in this business love working here. They love the space that they're given. They work for a business that is trying to do the right thing. They love the people they work with and if somebody has got to go home because they have a problem then that's okay - somebody in the team will step in and help and will cover for them."

Tracey Killen

"I recently met a young engineer who was working on HS2 and I've watched him become increasingly stressed and tired. He's working for one of the engineering consultancies working on the HS2 project. He was weekly commuting from his home in the South East up to the West Midlands. Facing impossible deadlines, facing bosses who've made promises they couldn't keep who in turn were working for bosses who've made promises they couldn't keep and finally, one day, he told me, he was standing at the station about to catch his train and he just couldn't get on the train. He just couldn't. And he's now signed off work, a victim of stress, and one wonders - he's a young man in his early thirties - if all of his training as an engineer have now gone to waste because of the conditions in which we have made him work have now rendered him an absolute shadow of his former self. I think this is the negative example against which I would like to build some positive thought."

Mark Goyder

"If I had love pervading my organisation, I would have a satisfied, content, healthy, workforce where there is evidence of real happiness. We talk about work/life balance but when there is love in organisation, you would see people coming and looking and feeling glad to be here. They'll be working when they don't need to. Ensuring that the job gets done and not clock watching!"

Ingrid Tennessee

"If I was only allowed 4 dials that describe company performance one of them will have something to do with production, but the others would be all around how we are as human. For example, you may want to run a 100 metres and yes one of the dials may be how fast you can run but the rest of the dials would be how you are physically, how you are mentally, how determined you are and so on. The effort and attention is actually going into everything else. One's a product of the other and that's natural."

Andy Mitchell

"With regards to employee wellbeing, it would most definitely make a difference. What I observe is that we are the sort of organisation where people tend to work long hours, travel to all sorts of destination and, struggle with work/life balance. It's the nature of our business. Our work is often characterised as being urgent, complex and therefore quite intensive. I would observe that those people who are fulfilled in their work tend also to have more healthy and rounded lifestyles. Being fulfilled happy, confident, intellectually challenged day to day, loving what you do and who you do it with, I think that has a massive implication for wellbeing and health."

Lawrence Hutter

YOU HAVE MY ATTENTION

The quality of focus and attention you have on your own wellbeing and that of your people would be of a special and unique quality when infused with love. Let's turn our imagination to what would be possible in the engagement, loyalty and commitment of your people in an organisation where the active and operational attributes of love is present.

I wrote earlier that engagement levels across the world remain inconsistent and remain so in spite of the plethora of well-meaning initiatives and activities introduced by organisations and their leaders. My challenge here is the motive and the intention behind which initiatives to drive engagement upwards are more laden with an exclusive focus on the financial, more than would be admitted to, and less than on the human.

But when you have an organisation where the culture is one of unconditional acceptance of self and others as human, the beautiful full of all potential human that we are, the opportunity to unleash engagement levels become extraordinary. This is because your people will fall in love with themselves, their leaders, their organisation, its cause and the vicarious benefit is the spillage of this into community and eventually into society. Going above and beyond the basic requirements of the job description, if indeed there is one, would be the norm. Everyone in the organisation, from the Chair to the Chief Executive to the people who do the important job of welcoming visitors to the organisation will be aligned to the organisations purpose and will have an alignment based on love because of the assured belief that they are valued and their contribution counts.

When your people are engaged, you can ask more of them and they will be willing to give more. They would readily go that sometimes illusive extra mile and will do it willingly and with passion because they know who serves them and the results and energy created for the individual, the organisation and the communities it serves will be all the more benefitting.

> "If there was love in organisation - that is having a culture in organisation where people care about each other, they support each other, they are compassionate and they treat each other as human beings, the first effects that would be experienced are the effects of wellbeing and engagement - these are human responses to these behaviours. Then you would also have outcomes like increased loyalty and retention - because you're much more likely to stay in a place where people care about each other."
>
> **Peter Cheese**

"From a customer /client experience the opportunity for both you and your customers to love you back and the power to create very special moments is huge. For example at the weekend one of our vehicles was in an accident and what happened is that a member of the public stayed with the vehicle, made sure the driver was alright, phoned the branch - that member of the public was one of our customers. Another example - when one of our customers a mother came into the shop and her children were having a meltdown and the branch manager said to her, you shop in here every week, just take your shopping with you, no need to pay now and bring me in the cheque or cash tomorrow or when next you're in you can make up the difference. It is this type of behaviour, this type of love that has our customers loving us back. You cannot quantify it but we know and from our customers the letters of thanks we get regularly in our branches - that showing love to our customers delivers results for us. They make an individual difference and also we know that our customers then tell stories of their experiences to other people."

Naomi Gillies

"You will see people that would work hours that are not typically expected - people would work nights and weekends like as if they were the founding entrepreneur - no leaving, great hours, great ownership and open debate. Where someone can tell you that they think you're wrong, get excited about it and it's okay. And it doesn't matter what level you are in the company everybody has the opportunity to talk. There is no fear."

Andre Angel

"If you ask people the reason they join an organisation or the reason they stay in an organisation, you more often find at the top of their list that it is a good place to work. That is often short hand for them saying that they feel comfortable, they feel validated, that others care for them, more often than they are paid well or that they have mastery of a topic of they have authority or that they have status which are other indicators but much lower down as priorities for most people."

Paul McNamara

"It would make a big difference. If you create an atmosphere of love, then people will start to do things for each other and for themselves and it will become self-perpetuating and of course what you really need to manage is the level of autonomy you give to people. You need to ensure that people are not then starting to compete for the wrong reasons. If you've got all your people thinking and acting in each other's best interest then it will impact productivity and it will impact engagement."

Steve Fox

When your people are highly engaged, love their organisation, its purpose, its leaders and genuinely love each other. They genuinely accept each other and themselves as human beings unconditionally. The concept of change - driving change, executing change, imposing change - and all angles of change management will be simply a part of life. They instead will become a matter for addressing the ups and downs of organisational life, riding the waves of challenges, incomprehensible goals, winning on purpose and all the consequences that will arise from the choices that are made are embraced. Each and every person will see themselves as playing a key role in achieving the desired outcome and the success of the organisation. Moving forward and staying resilient in the face of adversity will be encouraged in self and also in others. There would be a spirit of helpfulness throughout the organisation, no one hiding behind the coat tails of another in the hope of sharing in the spoils of success for very little effort. When one is down, another steps in. There would be a welcome strength in vulnerability as people and leaders by example share their hopes and fears in uncertainty. After all, life is more than the job and being human in self and with others is more important than the financial gains and indeed it is this focus on the human and the self that will in itself lead to the success, the gain, the prosperity and the resilience of organisation because of the resilience of all of its people that is so very much desired.

> "Regarding change, it would make people think about the purpose of the change that is being done. Are you starting from a place of what matters most to people? It would mean that the human dimensions of the change process are better attended to up front rather than halfway through the change or at the end of the change. It will impact the way in which the change happens. It would also remove change as sort of a mechanistic approach and bring a more humanistic approach to change."
>
> **Sam Allen**

> "With regards to change management and implementation, people would be falling all over themselves to be part of the guiding coalition. They would want to be part of it. Kotter talks about having a vision and then having a guiding coalition. And a vision is no use if you don't have a guiding coalition to help make that vision a reality and as a leader that small team you may have around you, your management team who must have buy in and who must be supportive and visionary so that they need to promote this to everyone in the way they talk and

live it - if they have love, there would be easy quick wins and also sustained winning and progress. Team members would be volunteering to undertake tasks outside of their remits and they wouldn't be fearful of getting things wrong. Loyalty would be evident in the effective thinking that takes place. You'll see emerging leaders developing all over the place."

Ingrid Tennessee

"When it comes to change management - the way we drive change for ourselves - we are constantly changing and adapting. One of the things that's helpful for us and is a byproduct of the passion and belonging is that we don't consider leadership to be a privilege. We consider leadership to be a duty which we do alongside the real things that we are about which is serving our clients and looking after our people. When you see leadership as a duty and no one should be precious about it, then changing and adapting is a lot easier."

Lawrence Hutter

"Getting changes embedded into an organisation would be very different and people would show up differently at work and the other side of this is that if you love somebody you are supposed to care for them and so your expectation of how people might behave at work and the benefits that you would gain would be great and that means that you could reduce the rules and increase how you look after people better and give more focus to what really matters to an individual or to a group."

Sally Cabrini

"We all find change nervous or stressful in organisation but if you cared for your people, you would make sure that you did all you could to see them through that change. This should not be alien because we are all used to relationships and we all should know what love feels like and it can be comfortable and at times uncomfortable depending on the needs of your people."

Andy Mitchell

AN OUTBREAK OF TRUST!

The emergence of the value and importance of trust in organisation is one that cannot be denied. Reports in the local and international press plus various channels of media of organisations large and small, international and local, behaving badly and treating their clients, consumers and, indeed, employees with apparent disregard, are many. These bad behaviours can be seen and unseen and are present across industry and government all around the world. It is one aspect of humanity in which there is no discrimination or exclusion.

In organisation, the breakdown of trust emerges when expectations are not met; when what you said you will do, you do not do, when you deliberately and at times, non-deliberately, mislead others or their community. Trust breaks down when what you say in your fine and small print is not mentioned clearly in a contract of agreement, in the terms of engagement or exchange of goods and services and is therefore overlooked by a trusting or assuming eye until it's too late to renegotiate. There is a breakdown of trust too, when communication, particularly in times of anticipated change or uncertainty, is inconsistent or not forthcoming and yet your people see leaders and people of influence in your organisation walking purposefully into meeting rooms with doors shut, windows darkened, leaving them to their own conclusions and wild and exaggerated thoughts that are exchanged with others they in turn believe may be in the same boat as them and potentially facing the same predicament.

Trust breaks down when, in organisations, your leadership goes to the press or, indeed, goes internally to declare a line of action that is embraced, only to turn around and do the opposite without notice or explanation, demonstrating a lack of care for the impact on the hurt feelings and emotions of the individuals in the organisation whose hopes were raised as a result of the declaration. I could go on. I am sure you will have your own examples and some of them personal. And the issue with trust is that once it is broken, it becomes almost impossible to rebuild and would take a commitment from both sides and a willingness to forgive and to build again.

Now get this, if there is love in organisation, the kind of love that I am here writing and talking about; the one that says that you as a human being matter; that I as a human being matter; that the human being that we together serve matters, as does his and her family and loved ones, the communities in which they live and in which we operate, the societies that we serve - all matter, there would be an overflow and an outbreak of trust. It would be an outbreak, the intensity of which cannot be contained.

If love is present in organisation, the discussion of trust will be predominantly in the establishment of new relationships and motivated by a desire to understand, to know and to learn of the other parties' wishes, hopes, expectations and boundaries. If love were present in organisation, mistakes made and behaviours and actions executed that result in unintended consequences with egos and feelings hurt will be addressed through open dialogue, with a genuine desire to make things right and a ready willingness to forgive so that all may move forward for the benefit of the collective.

Feelings of fear will be aired and space given to talk about it, why it is there and how together it can be addressed and a feeling of safety and security for all can be instilled. If love were present in organisation the notion of goodwill be woven right throughout the fabric of the organisation and would permeate all aspects of the organisation's operation and life. Oversights would not be reciprocated with resentment and vengeance; feedback would be embraced as an indication of care and a genuine desire to see your colleagues win so that the organisation can win; mistakes would be great opportunities for learning and to try new things in order that creativity and innovation can flow; personal news about home and life would be shared openly without fear of reproach or and conversely the privacy of others will be respected - all from the basis of love. Your Chief Executive and all those in leadership positions in organisation will be viewed through the lens of human and indeed they would see themselves as such and see all of their people as such. As human - with heart, emotion, hopes wishes, dreams, needs and desires - like any other human.

If love were present in organisation and because of its active presence, an outbreak of trust, decisions would be made and executed at the speed of light. Adequate time will be invested to consider the impact of decisions and the consequences of choices made not just in the short term but also in the long term. The ripple of a decision made can extend beyond organisational boundaries to impact geographical locations and communities far beyond the immediate sight and scope of the organisation and the decision making leaders within it. Yet in love, required attention and consideration will be given because whilst the negative consequences of some decisions made in one country may not affect that decision maker, the reality is that someone somewhere, another human being, may be affected.

A human being without the ability to speak up or defend their position will be impacted and yet if love were present, decisions would be made for the sake of humanity and society and for that human being whose power, though may be minimal but whose quality of life remains still important. Organisations in which love is active and present will have leaders who think and feel contextually and systemically. They will know that the purpose they serve lies far above what they can see, feel, touch or hear. And when all consideration has been made to the direction of strategy, the actions agreed in order to implement the strategy will be executed seamlessly and fast.

In love, if decisions need to be revisited they will be based upon swaying and underpinning evidence and a consensus reached through clear and objective debate, the opinions of everyone who matters, regardless of their background or walk of life included. Behaviours demonstrated in instances of progress reviews will be done in love and not to undermine. Preparation will be optimum and proportionate to the nature of the meetings in which decisions and milestone reviews occur. The number of times subordinates are required to submit and resubmit papers for review ahead of key meetings will be kept at a minimum and will be deemed by all to be right and appropriate.

> "I also think that with love and trust, there's much more pace and accelerated decision making because there doesn't need to be a lot of debate about decisions. People are empowered and trusted to make the right decision according to their skills sets. People are trusted to do the relative jobs that they've been hired to do. You don't need to debate and discuss everything until every single member of the team has agreed."
>
> **Richard Gillies**

The active and operational presence of love in organisation means that business and team meetings of all sorts will be conducted in harmony, and against a mood of shared purpose and objectives, with room given to all to speak. The more silent will be encouraged to contribute or respected for who they are and in a way that they know their opinion does matter and who they are and how they choose to show up in service of the organisation counts. Low flying missiles of back biting, sniping, talking over each other and the logging of intellectual coconuts in the interest of one-upmanship will be unwelcome and appear foreign. Passive resistance or covert behaviours and campaigns to undo already agreed actions extinct and all because the dominant logic in the culture being one in which there exists an epidemic of trust set free by an underpinning of love and acceptance.

Disagreements, and there will be many, because out of debate and passionate dialogue emerges creativity and emotion, will be aired freely and without agenda resulting in immediate alignment and unity behind decisions made in favour of the greater good and the power of the collective. In an outbreak of trust rooted in unconditional love, allocation of resources will be effective, each leader whose region, country or part of the business willing to go without in favour of a colleagues region, market or area of responsibility and even at the expense of the short term gain of a healthy bonus payment because the long term gain is one in which the more or all colleagues win and the organisation thrives.

Shareholders would be educated and willing to maintain their shareholding on the basis of a higher need, the level and frequency of reporting and forecasting reduced in order to enable leaders and those responsible for delivering the return on their investments to focus on doing just that. Predictions would be honest and the criteria for success would go far beyond and above financial return, short term gains and quick fixes. In an outbreak of trust unleashed by the power of love, leaders in government organisations and those that determine governance and the rules of shareholding, large investments and ownership would work to ensure that investments where made honourably. They would insist that shareholding is held for minimum terms in order to allow organisations to breathe and pursue realistic yet ambitious targets. They would also introduce legislation that ensured international organisations behaved honourably and proactively in all the communities in which they served and operated.

Their treatment and attitude to our beautiful planet and its resources would be proactive and not the subject of crisis action and turn around attempts following public mistakes. And when mistakes are genuinely made, communications internally and externally of all that will be done to rectify them will be done not from a place of trying to save face, keep share prices up, maintaining investment, holding on to fat pay packages but more from a genuine remorse and a deep awareness of the risk to the established trust. They will be motivated only by love.

"The good news is that there is much more conversation about this. Many more people are tuned to the need to invest in trust-based relationships and to strive for longer term outcomes as well as short term results. Organisations are realising that a more rounded view of stakeholders - the obligations to community, to people more generally around work, which you can see in big initiatives around mental health, diversity and inclusion - is good for business. We are more thoughtful about it but still far from where we need to be. The danger is looking for easy solutions when comprehensive change is needed."

Paul McNamara

"Doing the right thing may mean making really tough decisions in the interest of the many rather than the few. We sometimes underestimate the complexity of change programmes. You also have to be ready to have the tough conversations maturely. You may have to sit down with a team and say "we have got too many layers, we are too complex, we have to change the way we are working and as a result of this some of our senior roles are going to disappear including some of you sitting in the room; however I want you to work with me in working through this challenge. We need to get the right answer, leaving your personal agendas to one side and then we'll have a separate conversation about what this all may mean for you - when we get there and when we know what the conclusion might mean for you'. And that is an interesting approach because turkeys and Christmas come to mind. But you have to be very upfront with people. There can be a lot of tears and tantrums in the beginning but then everyone calms down and says, 'okay we understand the question now, let's be professional, work our ways through this, get the outcome that's best for the business and so on'. Now this requires an awful lot of maturity". "We are not an overtly political organisation. If you have a very political organisation, you'll never get that trust because everyone's looking out for their own individual personal gain; looking out for themselves. If you lose the trust of your people in your organisation, I don't know how you'll get that back. If you have a culture of always looking over your shoulders, bearing bad news or always blaming and saying it's always somebody else's problem, that's a culture where there is no love at all. I guess I believe that love and trust go hand in hand."

Howard Kerr

"If love were really present we might see a shift in what the purpose of business is. On top of employee engagement, it would actually be what is the business designed to do. I'm inspired by the b-corps and the b-corp movement and I'm incredibly humbled to be in service to these businesses that are taking these quantum leaps.

Climate change is going to mean we will have to retool our total economy and the way we run business across the world significantly. We are going to need people to love and to care and this has got to be more than how we engage employees, we need to look at how we retool our whole way of thinking and the whole way in which we run businesses so that we are addressing climate change and we are looking at how we can deliver on the sustainable development goals. These are the sorts of levels and heights we need to reach.

We therefore need to focus on what we need to do to really make the change in the world that is needed. Business is a really powerful tool and we therefore need to figure out what the magic of love is and what it can really do and to release this in business. Business is a driver of change and the key to what can be done in the world to save our planet but it needs the right fuel and force and that fuel and force is love."

Charmian Love

6. LOVE AND THE BOTTOM LINE

....

MORE THAN ABOUT THE MONEY!

Yes I can be proudly described as idealist. And yes, I would say that the impact of love on the bottom line of an organisation should not be the focus of attention or the one dial that is examined in order to explore whether love can really make a difference in organisation. But indeed it can make a difference to the income and profit of an organisation. It certainly can.

Just think of the cost savings that can be made from reduced physical, mental and emotional health issues in organisation. Budget allocations to employee assistance services of all kinds would be reduced, potential problems anticipated freely and proactively addressed, and each person in organisation looking out for his or her neighbour and speaking up for themselves at the earliest signs of emergent issues.

Savings would also occur outside of the organisation as government, national and state institutions would also save money from the reduction in treatment bills for citizens and individuals with problems. Health insurance payments would be reduced too enabling us as individuals to save for other life enhancing or enjoyable living events. Local communities would have more grants to invest in community run activities for the benefit for all their members, contributing to the establishment of bonds and relationships of support that are increasingly so needed in them.

Can you imagine too the amount of cost savings that will be derived from a reduction in wastage of products and materials of all kinds? When there is love, the care and attention to detail that your people would apply in their work would be of a different quality. I cannot help but believe that the amount of food that is wasted across the world today would be much reduced and savings made redirected to enabling investments in the support of world food programmes and organisations that work to reduce the poverty.

Retailers of all kinds would work closely and in partnership with their suppliers to ensure that the love they have for their consumers and clients as human beings, the environment and the potential impact on human beings much further afield whom they don't see are taken into consideration. Agencies responsible for the establishment of quality standards would be given the latitude to apply a level of discretion in the disqualification of goods and products on items that perhaps may matter less to the end user or consumer.

For example, the appearance of labels on packaging. This is because the type of love that would be evident is a love that has a desire to leave a legacy and a loving footprint and impact that lasts beyond the tenure of the organisation's current teams and benefits human beings much beyond its borders. The World Food and Agricultural Organisation (FAO) reports that about a third of the food produced in the world for human consumption which is about 1.3 billion tons is wasted each year or gets lost. It also reports that each year, the food wasted in rich countries of the world which is about 222 million tons is almost as much as the total net food production of Sub-Saharan Africa of 230 million tons. Yet, we need not travel further than the next village, town or city to meet a hungry person.

It is wonderful to learn of organisations and there are many of them around the world, that are led and supported by people driven by love and compassion that are set up to help those who are currently disadvantaged but it does not stop the consideration of what can be possible if at the root of the wastage, love was the driver. The reduction in wastage would of course have a wonderful impact on our world and our climate contributing to the possibility of leaving a world behind in which our children and their children can live free from disease and natural disasters. When there is love and less of a focus on the financial return and more of a focus on the impact of actions on the human being, adequate care and attention would be given to the nature of the people that you employ and that your suppliers in turn employ. Where possible you would work closely and in collaboration to ensure that fairness, compassion, respect, kindness and love was the backdrop and driver to each and every decision that you both made along the critical chain and process of production.

Every decision made impacts a person either at the beginning of it or the middle of it in its execution, or at the end of it in its results. Money saved can be redirected to the investment in projects, and initiatives that support the long term or indeed provide environments and facilities that contribute to the wellbeing of your people and the provision of good work for the diverse groups of people in the communities in which your organisations reside. Money saved, enables money to be made.

The active and operational presence of love can also enable genuine organic financial growth. International consultancies, thought leaders, and commercial organisations wax lyrically now about the financial benefit and growth that can be derived from diverse workforces, leadership teams and boards and that is great. We have also the Global Goals for Sustainable Development set by world leaders who came together in 2015 with a desire to ensure a much better world for the human race by 2030 by agreeing 17 goals, which if achieved, would put an end to Poverty, Inequality and Climate Change.

This is exciting and is motivating. It restores hope and faith in our world leadership. But I do know and believe with all my heart that these goals will only be achieved and in the time frame established if consideration to the potential contribution of love, what it means, its implications and application was given. There are organisations today already demonstrating the attributes of love and its application that are growing and producing remarkable commercial returns and survival in increasingly competitive environments. Organisations like Timpson and The John Lewis/Waitrose Partnership come to mind.

"If we didn't have the culture we have, we will have gone bust. All of our competitors had a culture of professional management, a reliance on consultants' plans and they all have gone bust. We have just concentrated on what the colleagues in the business believe we need to do to support our customers and to do what's right by them and for the health of the business. We look after our people and we've survived and we are successful."

James Timpson

"What is interesting about the partnership is that we can do really difficult things and we can say to partners that this is really difficult but we're going to have to take those tough decisions and actions to really sustain our business otherwise we will be straining and won't be able to compete. The difference here is that although partners may think at an individual level, what has an impact is that what they are able to do at a collective level is to take the organisation's best interest to heart. I will put aside my individual view and will buy that at an organisational or collective level, this way forward is going to be for our good. It's the right thing to do. That's the Partnership's ownership model at its best. When you are able to put aside your own personal interest and in the best interest of the collective, this is an absolute expression of love and it's impacted our performance as a business and organisation positively."

Tracey Killen

And there are others too like the organisation mentioned by Mark Goyder-Buurtzog - in the Netherlands whose business model, Mark says, is not only breaking down the barriers to the presence of love in its organisation, it is a model that enables it to grow too.

"By contrast look at really effective business models like that of Buurtzog - a social enterprise company - set up in Holland by a former nurse. It has grown rapidly and is now become the largest provider of social and patient care in the home and has been voted the best company to work for in Holland. It has self-managed teams, very powerful training resources giving those teams to draw on and expert advice resources to those working in teams - so working in teams like that and a very different business model like this would help break down barriers to the presence of love in business."

Mark Goyder

Pedro Tarak introduces Guayaki, who is an organisation in South America he is also an investor in, that produces extraordinary results because of the attributes of love.

"My experience as a small investor is in holistic investments. I can tell you that the results are stunning! Take the example of Guayaki, yerba mate rainforest natural energy drinks. The statutory purpose of Guayaki is the regeneration of the South Atlantic Forest and the sense of community of its forest dwellers. In 2018 they attained approximately 60k hectares - circa over 200k acres, 1000 families returned to their own communities from urban slums and 600% increase in shareholder value. There you get a company that is holistic in its purpose and in its operations supporting humanity, the earth and the shareholders at the same time. It enables you to expand your loving dimensions simultaneously."

Pedro Tarak

The senior leaders I interviewed also reflected on the commercial impact that has and can be possible when the attributes of love in their business are active and operational.

"In my current business, I think the difference love would make is that love would drive productivity. I've had a lot of forgiveness in my business through quite a lot of change. So, the things I've got the business involved in now, on the face of it you would not have envisaged in a month of Sundays. This business looked like a dusty old business, ambling along, just living in the past and one resistant to change. But what I actually found was that the business was built on the idea of a positive attitude to things. Genetically it had evolved and its intrinsic underlying DNA allowed me to make changes without getting shot or falling over or exploding. This helped a lot. And I think the more that we can create the free flow and the opportunity for the people to be themselves and to bring themselves to work as they genuinely are and if we describe this as love in organisation, it is amazing what can be created and how expectations will be exceeded."

Mark Scanlon

"In our organisation's performance, I think what you would get a genuine care and alignment behind where the organisation is. There is a much more positive response to the organisation's performance even in the bad times. The organisation will rally with you as leaders. When you are really struggling, you need your workforce 110% behind you and this is where you really can tell and experience the impact of love in your organisation. It's not just about the good times, it is how your people respond when you hit the bad and really hard times. With love in the organisation, you get a loyalty - both from the individual and from the collective."

Naomi Gillies

"It would have a phenomenal impact. I think what I would see is a constant and sustained decrease in the evidence of unnecessary expenditure. There would be the evidence and care of our assets - so less wear and tear; people would treat the organisation's as if it were their own. They wouldn't spill tea and coffee and walk away and leave it. They wouldn't leave the computer on all night or leave the lights on all night. Because they'd be mindful, they'd be loving and be caring. Our resources would be maximised. We'd save so much. You wouldn't leave the fridge door open and walk away; leave the hot tap running and walk away; Savings equal profit and so if we maximised our resources it means that we would save more. We would regularly be in the black; We'd be surpassing our surplus and our profits."

Ingrid Tennessee

At the end of the day, it all boils down to your people, the love you demonstrate to them and also to yourself and the culture you work with them to establish - this is what will drive your financial performance and it can be extraordinary.

"As an example here is a story I was told by the then VP outside the USA of Microsoft who was based in Paris - two of his people came from Kosovo and when the Kosovo war was going on, they came to him to say how terrible the war in Kosovo was and wanted to know what Microsoft was going to do about it. Instead of saying 'you're software designers, go and design some software', he said to them 'well, go along and see what's happening in Kosovo and come back in a week to let me know what you want to do'. So, they came back and they said 'you have all of these displaced people, some of them have lost loved ones, some of them are seeing loved ones forced across the borders into Macedonia, and there are no records. What you've got is a bit of a database problem. We've designed a piece of software which we can use on the current generation of mobile phone. It will enable us to create records so people can start to have their identity restored and have documentation that means that they can start being allowed to come back home; it means that people can be tracked and traced and so on.' And that was developed by Microsoft and became the software that is, as I understand it, now used worldwide by the UN High Commissioner for Refugees. So there was a Chief Executive who responded to an expression of love by people in his business, opened the door for them to put that love into practice and from it, came an innovation that had a financial payback - though that was not the starting point."

Mark Goyder

"In a world where 80% of the value of organisations are intangible, what does that mean? It means that it's the ideas that come out of people's head, so therefore creating spaces where human beings can flourish becomes the pre-requisite for any organisation that's going to perform in the long run. The fact that we still only pay lip service to that is both shocking but also a massive opportunity for any organisation that chooses to really think deeply about changing the way it looks at things."

Norman Pickavance

"In one of my businesses, a private equity backed business, I had remortgaged my home to take part in the business to run it and to part own it and within 18 months we had doubled the value of the company. This is because of one really big contract with the government. And the only reason we won that contract was because of the people. And we were up against really big companies at the time. Though we were very small by comparison our approach was that we were just going to tell them what we will do for them, who we are and how we are. That point of difference was our people and what translated was our capability, our belief in the point that we cared, truly cared and our own belief in ourselves. That could not have been possible without love in the way that we are talking about it here. The contract win was the first of its kind it had been newly invented and they had to find new providers and that was us. It meant hard work. It meant some days, somebody putting their head around the door and asking of their team member - 'what can I do to help?' 'Do you want a cup of tea?' It also meant having fun together and enjoying the time we spent together. We demonstrated to our client too that we genuinely cared. It was also about demonstrating empathy and demonstrating that no problem was too small for us to deal with and we could not have had this attitude if we were not operating as a team in unison and helping each other."

Mark Scanlon

When organisations have challenges which they can and will do, because after all they are human, then it is inevitable that tough decisions must be made and may result in some of your people experiencing the outcome of those decisions in a way that hurts. They are human. What is important always is the motive in the persons and leaders behind those decisions and how those decisions are then carried out. We often talk in business and, indeed, more easily about the notion of 'tough love'. Yes, it may need to be a tough decision but it is one that can be made out of love and in service of a higher purpose and carried out with love for the persons that may be impacted.

"We've had a tough year in the UK for us and so we are creating a base line from where we can get stuck in and improve things. We have a lot of uncertainty around us in the political and economic context. My role as CEO is vision and culture. I'm progressively installing folks into their jobs and I know they'll do that well and my role above all is to just clarify that the vision and frame are as clear as they should be and constantly checking that the people are on that page. Secondly my role is also overseeing that the love factor is at the right level. Continuously. And making certain moves; moves are sometimes of ideas that we wish to put forward and they could also be defensive moves or attack moves - i.e. doing something really special for our market, our consumers, our customers - but also moves in which I may say of someone 'within the next two months, I want to see that person out of a role because it's contamination and it's not acceptable that they remain there' - that's like being a gardener. As a gardener, you're checking and pruning and adding and shifting and taking the time to see when the moment is right to make different interventions all of which must be from a place of my people and organisation first. I say therefore that it is absolutely massive - the role of love in the success and by extension in the bottom line of my business - it is absolutely massive. And if I get it right, I know I can dramatically improve the bottom line. I'm confident we can and we will and now is the time. This is our time."

John Mangan

And for the aspirational amongst the leaders I interviewed, the potential for what the active and operational presence of love can do in organisations including theirs is immense. I was encouraged and inspired by their responses. There is no doubt that all can see and believe in the potential that the power of the operational presence of love can bring to organisations including theirs, the challenge of course is always how to move forward and boldly into territory never before ventured into.

"Where love it is present it will have tremendous impact. It can unite people together for a common purpose. It means that there is happiness there is kindness and there is respect. That people care. Where it is authentic and is present in the behaviours and the actions that are taken and, in the leadership, it can have a very positive impact on the bottom line."

Sam Allen

"This is a difficult one because of the way many organisations are measured - we are measured purely on financial performance. It is difficult to go to your shareholders and say we are not going to be measured on our financial performance we want to be measured on harmony but actually this should have more of a focus because if you can get harmony, then financial performance will come."

Richard Eu

"I hope that love will have an impact. We are doing a lot of things at the moment and of course if we did them better the impact will be greater still. It is about helping people's personal states and well-being. Work is usually and should be the safest place to unload your issues. Therefore if you can make your work environment safe, your people can share problems about work safely and can also share about other parts of their lives. It doesn't matter where the problem stems from, we all suffer the consequences of it and therefore we all stand to gain from getting better at this."

Steve Fox

"The Church does have a bottom line. It is to fulfil the mandate that Jesus gave - the great commission - which is to make disciples that make disciples. That's the key performance indicator (KPI). If you go to the book of Acts, what it clearly shows is that in Antioch the people were first called Christians because they were exhibiting Christ's values in their behaviour; namely, love.

Secondly, we see in the first part of the book of Acts the rapid acceleration and growth of the church. Why was the Church growing? Of course the work of the Holy Spirit was evident and importantly, the fruit of the Holy Spirit were being also exhibited. What was evident is that people joined them because they saw what was happening and how this new community was living. They lived a life rooted and grounded in love. The whole essence of the apostolic church in the biblical sense is about transforming cultures. So, just as it did in the first century and still does today, love would have a positive impact even on the church as an organisation and our world today because it would reduce the tendency towards any selfishness, greed corruption, bullying, discrimination - all the factors that the church is not immune to."

Emmanuel Mbakwe

IN SUMMARY AND IN THE INTEREST OF HOPE

The difference love is making, can make, and will make in organisations, if allowed to flourish, is immense. Its potential to enable the success of all of your people, my people and our people in organisations, in community and in society, the world over is extraordinary. Its impact on the bottom line is only the starting point.

It is a shame that in the world of organisation, and the world generally, we have come to value the material and the financial the vantage of self over others much more than intangible, the immaterial and the non-financial, even though the latter is significantly more fulfilling of our human need and purpose. Let's think about it. Firstly, the impact on the less important. The operational power of love would have enough momentum to accelerate the earnings of global organisations who today would deem themselves successful on all levels far beyond their own wildest dreams. If global organisations were truly successful, a reduction in world poverty and the advancement of the resolution of climate change would be evident. Success would be increasingly defined not only by the upwards movement of the top and bottom line, the acquisition of market, but by the impact of actions on customers, clients, on the environment and most importantly on your people - what they say, what they feel, what they want and what they need.

When organisations, regardless of their size, have love in them, the net that is cast in order to attract people to their teams and jump on the train of their purpose would be cast wide and far. They would have an intense and genuine curiosity in the nature of the people who would be interested and eventually tempted to join them and align their own individual purpose with that of their hiring organisation. Each and every leader in that organisation would recognise the need and the beauty of leading from a place of love and the substantial benefits that go beyond standard productivity, and commercial gain that will be achieved. They would recognise, also, the potential that the experiences to be had by their new joiners and people could be some of the most enjoyable, most rewarding and fulfilling experiences that would come from connections that will be made. They would recognise, too, the life changing innovations in services, products, contributions and relationships that could be established not only for the outside world but also within the organisation itself.

There would be an establishment of good work - job design, playing to strengths, flexibility and flexible working - and opportunities for fathers and mothers alike regardless of marital status, or organisational status, plus forums virtual and real that enable easy communication and a sharing of ideas and practices; all the advantages of technology that can be possible, provided freely and without condition or the covert monitoring, one measure of constant checking replaced by another made less visible because of technology, yet as untrusting.

Strategic direction will be in line with purpose and a purpose that serves the greater good and the known legacy that can be created. Decisions would be made having fully considered all the options available and made with a willingness and a courage that may not appear logical in the short term but made wholly from a belief that in the long term the outcome will benefit the organisation, all of its people, the communities in which they live and the people whom they serve. All of the stakeholders would be aligned. Communication would be transparent, regular and without modification and given and received on the foundation of a genuinely shared agenda and purpose. Resources whether money, skills, or time, will be allocated on the basis of genuine need and service with one team member or divisional head or equivalent within the organisation willing to go without in order that the greater good may be served taking one for the team would be the norm.

Career planning and development discussions will be had on a basis of a focus on strengths and the maximising of those strengths and career wishes that produce a mutually beneficial outcome for the organisation and individual, knowing that when your people thrive and flourish your organisation will too. And, if when all options have been considered, there is an agreed parting of ways, it is done without resentment or regret and instead with a celebration and a recognition that there are times when in order to further thrive, a different environment and a different set of strengths would be required.

In organisations where love was evident, not only would the people be seen and treated as more than a means to an end, your people would also see themselves as more than the job. Their sense of identity will be not in what the job says, but in who they are as individuals, their own hopes and wishes and dreams intact and supported by a willingness and/or acceptance of the fact that there will be a time when a journey with one organisation ends and another starts, whatever that organisation may be. International moves and the compensation elements that accompany them will be discussed and decided on an individual basis and whilst of course, destination country employment laws must be respected, they will however not be used as an excuse and reason to deprive the individual of what can be made possible or to get a highly contributing individual for the lowest cost.

In organisations where unconditional love and acceptance was present, diversity and inclusion initiatives would be more about celebration of difference and uniqueness and less about compliance and avenues to raise a voice representative of a group within the organisation at risk of being forgotten or left behind. Each and every one of its people would be free of repression and able to express all of who they are and, in doing so, bring all of who they are to their work and all that work presents on a day to day basis because they would be operating consistently and continuously at their very best. The notion of absence would be one for historical case studies.

Marches and demonstrations and 'recognition' months would not be from the place of 'we want a voice', 'we must be accepted' and instead will be from a place of the wonderful world of difference. It is amazing how much more we continue to have debates of equality and inequality in all shapes and sizes across the world. And depending on the country and its demographic makeup, the debates centre around colour, social background, race, ethnicity, tribe, sexual orientation, gender, faith, class and so many other categories that I haven't mentioned whilst I applaud all that is being done today and appreciate the progress that has been made, I cannot help but imagine the awesome difference that love would most certainly make.

Unconscious bias and the notion of micro aggression will become relics of the past because a culture of love is one in which motive is fuelled by care, respect, kindness, patience, compassion, genuine interest and trust. And because there is trust, decisions made with and on behalf of others will be readily accepted and executed. Everyone from the top of the organisation to the bottom rejoicing and sharing in the outcome of success. Questions like 'where are you originally from?' would be out of genuine curiosity and an opportunity to build common ground.

The difference in compensation and monies earned between the top and bottom of the organisation will feel real, good and acceptable by all and the plethora of reports from various sources about the discontent with pay at senior levels in global organisations will reduce. Contentment will become part of how 'people just feel around here' in organisation. No one looking over their shoulder or across the meeting room real or imagined, in envy of how another person is treated, feeling unfairly done by. Meetings will be attended by the right persons and projects will be staffed by those who are most able to deliver without hint of favouritism, status or bias. Training and development would be continuous and consistent, love, of course would be on the agenda in its different guises.

The monies invested on productivity drives, wellbeing and engagement initiatives will be more about maintenance than about problem solving. Executive leadership teams and boards will be populated by diverse thinking and oriented individuals, the recruitment firms hired to support this will have leaders in them full of courage and able to genuinely challenge the stakeholder beyond lip service and free of the constraint of fear of losing a hefty commission. Candidates presented will be treated with love, care and respect and not as commodities or the means to increasing the commission bank. Candidates will be partnered all of the way, feedback given timely, honestly and supportively; no need to 'save face'. There will be an appreciation on all sides of the human behind each role and situation, because when love is present it allows you to be human and to see the human in others.

Suppliers big and small will be treated as genuine partners with payment terms agreed and set in understanding of the needs of the small versus the big, joint project and initiatives would be established in the interest of the prosperity of both parties, the people that within them and the communities they both serve.

We can and should dream big. Why not? When love is present in organisation, government monies spent in the areas of compliance and prevention will be redirected to the addressing of genuine world problems and maybe, just maybe the global goals for sustainable development will have an awesome chance of being met and exceeded by 2030.

Let's dream bigger still. When love is present in organisation maybe, just maybe, we would also see a reduction in the prospect of wars, boundary disputes, warring neighbours, be it across the garden fences or across the nation's borders, because an attribute and a value held in the privacy of one's home and life can spill into the relationships we have with others and at multiple levels. I can dream, but out of dreams can emerge the tangible, can't they?

When we say to ourselves, I am a different person at home to whom I am at work and I can compartmentalise my life, it is the first step to stress. The reality of life is that we are all of who we are at home and at work and in every aspect of our lives whether we choose to show it or not. Or indeed whether we choose to acknowledge it or not. In fact, it is one of the reasons, almost ninety percent of what we communicate is not what we actually say. It is who we are being. When we feel we must conceal or hide who we are because we are not welcome or we feel that we should conceal and hide who we are because others are undeserving or threatening, or may take advantage of our vulnerability, then the consequences of that withholding is a denial of others from seeing and experiencing our true selves and that true self is a good one. It inherently is.

"If as an organisation you have a purpose that goes beyond simply making money, then you've got to work on living that purpose too and being a role model."

Howard Kerr

7. LOVE AND LEADERSHIP TEAM EFFECTIVENESS

....

ANGRY PEOPLE

Two reasons why organisations fail to deliver their goals and objectives, live according to their purpose or meet the expectations they set for themselves and others is a) the dysfunctionality of the leadership teams within them and b) a leader who in spite of his or her capability is hand on heart unable to say that they have eliminated all dysfunctionality and have aligned and inspired their leadership team and organisation behind them. Very rarely, too, would a team's leader admit to the dysfunctionality that exists within his or her team or, indeed, organisation because of the implication it may have for their leadership style and behaviour and the behaviours they tolerate in others. It can be said that we get the behaviours we tolerate. We know, however of the power of an effective and high performing team. The heights they can have their organisation climb to, the energy they can generate and the opportunities they can uncover not only for their people, and all the stakeholders they serve but also for themselves as individuals. When an organisation is led by a leader and leadership teams that are walking in purpose, who know who they are as individuals and as teams, and who understand that no way is any one human being an island the results that organisation can achieve will be extraordinary. If we were able to quantify the amount of time spent by leadership teams debating and discussing the trivial, managing and guarding individual territory, individual team members making covert plans to ascend the organisational hierarchy at the expense of colleagues and engaging in activities and behaviours that undermine the progress of the organisation and ultimately themselves, it would be significant. Cost savings can be made not only through what you can see and count, they can be made by small tweaks and changes to behaviour and those tweaks and changes to behaviour when underpinned by love - an unconditional acceptance of self and of others - will be deep, far reaching, engaging of the wider organisation and long lasting.

The impact that a leadership team can have on the individuals within the team, the teams that they in turn lead, all of the people within their organisation, their families and their communities can be significant. Every behaviour has a ripple effect of consequences that are seen and eventually unseen but keep going on. An unseen consequence does not mean it doesn't exist. It just simply is unseen. It is very much like standing on the bank of a river or lake and throwing a pebble in and seeing the ripple effect that happens as the pebble makes contact with the surface. Eventually, the circle of ripples stops, you no longer see it, but the pebble remains.

When a leadership team is without love or the attributes of love are absent from their interaction with each other and how they go about delivering the goods and services promised and serving the people they lead, the reputation of their organisation can be jeopardised and social media platforms and forums soon become a place for their people to air frustrations, discontent, resentment and complaints. Leadership teams are role models and to aspire to be in one means a willingness to be one that people follow and who people look to for guidance. Now, we all are leaders. Whatever your position in organisation or in life, we all are leaders and we all have the capacity to have followership and leaders need to be led effectively and the greater the scope of responsibility, and the number of people for whom you are responsible the greater the impact that can be had.

A leader's mood can affect the mood of others; a whisper can sound like a trumpet call across the organisation; a suggestion can feel or sound like an order and a trial can feel like a decision. When a leadership team convenes in preparation for a business review of any type, be it of strategy, of talent or of brands and products, the people responsible for the delivery of documents and proposals, or evaluations at that review can feel like they're waiting for a life changing, career enhancing or limiting experience. Everything that happens or doesn't happen in organisation, every mood, every temperature, every atmosphere and energy is determined by the leadership team which in turn is a mirror of its team leader. Even in organisations that would be deemed progressive or further along the journey to embracing love as an organisational attribute and capability there would be those people who because of the nature of what they do, or the jobs they have within them, whose every movement, behaviour and style ripples through the organisation. The power and influence and impact of leadership teams and leaders cannot be underestimated. It has the ability to move mountains. It is all about and starts and ends with leadership.

"There's two ways of looking at this. One is we're all leaders. We're all just people. Yes, the more senior you are, the more power and influence you may have and the more impactful positively or negatively your behaviours are. But it would be really hard to create an environment of love if your leadership team didn't see all of themselves as leaders. For me it would be great when you're in a place where if someone is behaving in a way that isn't what we want to see it doesn't matter who you are, or how senior you are we will talk to you about it. The leadership team can certainly kill it. It has a disproportionate ability to damage. Secondly, there's a leadership piece which is about leading by example - and that's important - but we all have that obligation. If your senior people are not operating from a place of love it will be difficult to expect others around the organisation to do so."

Andy Mitchell

"In all successful situations that I've found myself in and where I've been part of or being part of leading, what I've experienced is that a very close small group of people who visibly are rooting for each other inspire large numbers. The numbers, the crowds of the teams, are totally conscious of what bonds, team spirit, affection, love, there is between these group of people - this leading executive team - and it inspires them and drives them; they want to belong to that and they themselves are further encouraged to interact effectively together.

I've also seen the opposite and seen the chaos, the unhappiness the lack of performance this can engender. The leadership team has a huge role to play on many things and it has a pivotal and key role to play in engendering love in organisation and it starts from within the team."

John Mangan

"I know from research I've seen on change management that if you've got trust, then you can accomplish a huge amount of things and if you don't' have trust, then you're in that world where dysfunctional behaviour happens, passive resistance happens, active resistance happens, and these are fundamental to organisational success. So when you have a sense of trust, it doesn't mean that change won't happen or that a difficult decision would never be made, what it would enable is a much more positive action and response in the business and the effectiveness of the team."

Peter Cheese

"The basic rule of thumb that I talk to people about is of like, respect and trust. And instead of 'like' why don't you put in love? With trust, it is one of the few and key pillars because if you can't trust that person in your team, then there's no point having a team. You won't be able to rely on their being accountable for what you think they'll get done. Respect on the other hand, is something about respect for their discipline and their profession and is also about respect for their purpose. Normally, the like aspect is about do you have to get along with that person. And I think that at times you don't have to because if the other two of trust and respect are in place, from a business perspective you can still get things done. Now, if love wasn't there, would the other two get you to the other side, probably, yes but I think it makes a much nicer environment and journey when love is present. I think 'like' can also work because it means that you have similar interests, you're happy to socialise with them outside of work, you can be civil to each other and you in the main enjoy being around them. Love I guess is much deeper and I guess to that if a team can love each other, there is the possibility that they can achieve significantly more together."

Charlie Wagstaff

THE MOST CRITICAL LEADERSHIP CAPABILITY

The impact leaders and leadership teams can have on the performance of their people is underpinned by neuroscientific research. In Neuroscience we learn that the part of our brains as human beings that we use in problem solving, creating and analysing issues, developing ideas and ways of working, that part of the brain called the Neo Cortex, functions at its best when we feel safe and secure in our environment. This is made more possible by our ability to have self-expression and to freely express our feelings, emotions, who we are with abandon and according to how we want to be. It doesn't take much persuasion to believe that the more you feel good about yourself and the more your people feel good about themselves and feel great, the more likely you and they are, to perform at your and their very best. Robert Plutchik, in his work "Emotion: a Psychoevolutionary Synthesis" (1980), talks about eight primary emotions - joy, trust, anticipation, surprise, fear, disgust, sadness and anger, that can be recognized in human beings. The emotions of joy and trust combined are akin to love. When these emotions are prevalent within a team and therefore within an organisation, the conditions for high performance and extraordinary results begin to come into place.

What, then, are those leadership capabilities and attributes that if present within a team and underpinned by love can motivate an organisation and its people to achieve the most extraordinary of results? There are seven in my view and are and illustrated in the diagram below. Whilst independently they are strong, when they work together and are fueled and underpinned by love, they are much stronger.

The first is **accountability.** When a team is accountable to each other and to others, it means that what is agreed is agreed and followed through. The expression 'my word is my bond' or 'our word is our bond' would have meaning and traction. The issue of contracts of agreement would be simply to comply with the law of the land and the requirements of governance. A promise would indeed be a promise and when oversights occur, there would be no denial or attempts to cover up. Systemic and consequential thinking would be commonplace, with careful consideration given to the impact on each other, other people and stakeholders, the environment, communities seen and unseen in the making of decisions and the choices of actions to pursue. Mistakes made would be an opportunity to learn, failure will be seen as just that and not an unwelcome attribute to assign to individuals. The allocation of resources within an organisation of effective leadership teams would be done on a needs basis - what is required to achieve the successful execution of strategy agreed for that location, or brand or territory.

> "In this team of 5 neat guys we had accountability to each other and to the organisation. Now the business grew to £3bn and the 5 neat guys were the heads of each of the divisions of the organisation. We had 100s of people employed we got to a point where I could look at somebody in the eyes and they could look me in the eyes and it was known without saying a word beforehand, what we were going to say. We had developed a culture that said - 'if I say I'm going to do something or if you say you're going to do something, we are depending on you to get that thing done.' If you cannot do it, even if you walked out of here saying you can do it, and afterwards you recognise you can't do it, come back and say 'I couldn't do it' and we'll take a step back and reconsider it. So there is a culture of accountability that evolved from that experience and has evolved with me in every company that I've established - tell me that you're going to do it, then do it, and if you find you can't do it after all, tell that to me too and we'll figure out a way to do it together or find an alternative solution."

Andre Angel

> "The team would be working well together and would work according to the strength of each of the individuals and apply themselves better as a collective. What they do will benefit people outside the organisation. We can look to Teal organisations like Patagonia as great examples."

Markus Hofmann

Accountability becomes significantly more powerful when the capability and attribute of **contribution** is also evident. It is contribution that enables the individuals in the team to play to their strengths and to encourage their team members to play to theirs too. When a leadership team is demonstrating contribution, it is one that leverages the strengths of others as individuals and the strengths of other teams within the organisation. Feedback is readily given and received. Forgiveness is given and experienced. Important meetings, conferences and away events are attended on a basis of relevance and not club membership. When leadership teams are operating from a place of contribution, giving experiences and time to each other and to members of each other's teams would be seen as an honour and a privilege. There would be active listening and full presence at team meetings regardless of what is on the agenda. Each person's hopes and wishes respected. A care and compassion for the wellbeing of each other and the collective would be priority. The development of people; mentoring and coaching and the investment of the all too precious time in each other's people would be a given. Nothing to be negotiated here. Scores on the dashboard would be milestone achievements progress for the whole team and not for the one. Reward and recognition would be a lonely place without teammates sharing in the accolade and the limelight. And because the leadership team is operating from a place of contribution, the organisation would be too. Reward and remuneration would be structured to recognize the value of the team and the power of collaboration; an acknowledgement that the sum of the parts is greater than the whole.

"For example, a really great project manager, who was an incredibly disciplined individual focussed on high quality delivery, started getting quite negative feedback from a client because he came across as being quite abrasive in his attitude. It was important that he understood that feedback from the client and that he was supported too. When the leadership team were made aware of the issue, we did not just leave it to his manager to sort it out. We made it a shared issue and supported his manager too and gave him lots of opportunities to have conversations - sideways, upwards - and in fact the very best conversation the individual had was with a director who was completely independent. It was really powerful just to say that I'm here for you. It turned out that individual had difficult circumstances outside work. We could have swapped the individual saying that the client did not like you, but I'm thrilled that we found out a more rounded view on the individual because we provided all the avenues for different conversations. The project manager now feels more engaged and more loyal to the business and in the longer term he will be better placed to help others because he is aware of the benefit of taking a more constructive and more human centred response."

Paul McNamara

Commitment is the ability and willingness to do what it takes to have your organisation and your team win. It is a demonstration of belief in what you are doing, why you are doing it and for whom you are doing it. When a leader is committed to his or her team and a leadership team is committed to their organisation, the flexibility of thinking is evident. There would be more than a few ways to reach the agreed desired outcome and when that desired outcome is one that serves the greater good of all, the energy, sense of urgency and the passion engaged would be tangible. No mountain would be too high to climb. Every single person in the organisation will feel included in the direction of travel; opinions will be genuinely sought and freely given. No offence taken when suggestions are not followed up because there is a confidence in the judgement of those given the space to lead and decide on behalf of the organisation. When an individual is committed to his or her team, it means that success is only experienced when the team is successful. It means that 'I am invested in your success and you are invested in mine'. It means too that in delivering what is necessary to be delivered to have all of the organisation successful, whatever it takes will be done to ensure that care and consideration is given to community, to the environment, to the quality of supply chain, to members of the organisation past, present and indeed future. It would be a team that recognised the importance and the value of legacy.

> "To me there are three things - firstly, there is tough decision making. If you are an organisation where you had mutual respect and love for your colleagues, you would make harder decisions because you would be able to have those conversations that you need to have without it feeling like you're just going to pull each other apart. Secondly, there would be a deeper understanding. You would know and have much deeper understanding about each other and because of this, you would get better value out of each other. This is about love and care and it means then that you are then likely to reach much better outcomes. Thirdly, it is about commitment. You would get a collective commitment because you would all feel that you are together making a difference and that you are part of the same thing. That collective commitment would make you genuinely feel that you are all part of the same organisation and you are all committed to the same things."
>
> **Naomi Gillies**

Responsibility is the capability and attribute that drives the desire to see all of the team win together and as individuals. It enables individuals within the team to provide ready support to each other without expectation of reciprocity, because the win for the organisation and all within it is what is most important. For individual leaders and the leadership team to be responsible, it means that the prospect of silo thinking is kept low. Knowledge and information is freely shared with each other and with each other's teams. In large organisations, leadership teams would easily and freely share information and knowledge across geographies and divisions without request or expectation other than a willingness to see each other win and to jointly celebrate in the success of each other. When leadership teams think, feel and act as jointly responsible for the achievement and execution of their organisation's strategy, the strategy becomes much more than an intellectual exercise. It becomes a cause, a journey, a goal whatever the size that simply must be delivered because the benefits for the individual means the benefits for the team.

> "It is all about relationships. People that love and care about each other can also fall out with each other. Balance is therefore really important. In my team, we talk a lot about collective leadership and the importance of taking on collective responsibility for all parts of the business. If something is going on with IT, the whole team will look at supporting our IT director. We take the time to understand each other and to strengthen our relationships. We look at the ability to listen. This is important. Seek to understand. Get to know each other."
>
> **Sam Allen**

Next is **authenticity.** Authenticity is the ability to be real and to be who you are. When a leader is real, able to reveal his or her vulnerability in the presence of others, by simply being who they are, they create an environment for others to be the same. Vulnerability takes courage and takes strength and it also shows a willingness to accept yourself and all your imperfections. Once upon a time, I attended a training workshop on an introduction to leadership. One of the most memorable tips I left with was the tutor saying that in order to have your people believe in you, it is important that they also know that you bleed. That you are imperfect and that you are human. Brene Brown has famously said that there is strength in vulnerability, and if you haven't watched her Ted Talk on this, I recommend that you do. When you are not being authentic or real, you may not realise it, but the members of your team and colleagues can spot it. We leak. There is something about being unreal and inauthentic that no matter how hard we try or convince ourselves that what we want to hide is hidden, it is impossible to. To be authentic and vulnerable though, we must also be authentic to ourselves and that is often the best place to start. When individuals within a leadership team are authentic and real with each other, it permeates right through their teams and to the wider organisation and spills out into their communities and into the relationships they have with their stakeholders, their clients, customers, and suppliers.

> "How many people, brilliant people, trying to do brave and interesting things would find themselves in a position where something they've tried hasn't quite worked out in the way that they expected? How many people could really feel that their sponsorship would be unshakable so that they can keep that sense of bravery and courage and their curiosity and their appetite to make a difference because somebody cares enough for them and that someone loves them enough to support them through the ups and the downs."
>
> **Tracey Killen**

"This soul and love dimension is opening minds to inclusion. It is opening minds to diversity of ages, of skin types, of religion, of sexuality of all walks of life and this is a good thing for organisation and for society. This is not just about bringing people in it's about allowing them to share without fear. Bringing in some softness in a hard world will allow so many people to breathe and not have to hide and if you get that out of the way and allow them to say 'I'm not judged here; I don't have to hide here' they can really give their energy to what they love and what is really needed of them because they're not burdened by having to hide. Too often in business we allow the head to make all decisions and don't allow the heart to have a say. I think in Leadership, if you allow without feeling awkward, your heart to have its role as well, it's crucial for success."

John Mangan

The attribute and capability of **trust** in a leadership team is the engine of effectiveness. Without trust a team will not function at its best. A breakdown of trust is an open door to dysfunction and the introduction of a leaky bucket through which money and time are wasted. When a leadership team is one who trusts and is trusted, there is a safety and a confidence that flows through the individuals and the organisation. The skill of second guessing becomes obsolete. Personal disclosure of fears, hopes, concerns, are made within the team without worry. Other teams and individuals with formal responsibility for people and employee experience in organisations where trust runs through will be seen as genuine support and refuge and not as spies sent from above to police what is being done or to monitor the extent to which policy and process are adhered to. Right from the front door and reception and all the way through its corridors, offices and communal areas - if the organisation was in a building - there would be an atmosphere of freshness. Virtual leadership teams and individual members who work in remote locations would have every confidence in themselves and in others to get on with the job at hand, a strong connection and bond still felt even when not in physical presence.

> "When we build trust and underpinned by love we can build a very strong relationship and a basis for success. Individually we also need to connect and you connect if you are able to share – when you are able to talk about the things you're going through at work or even at home and be able to do this knowing that your vulnerability will not be exploited. And the only thing that can bring us to that place of trust and genuine support is love. This will help us see each other as a unit rather than an individual within the team."
>
> **Sam Aiyere**

> "Love - is also about trust. Leaders need to feel trusted that they can be themselves. At the end of the day, it comes back to the boss, because people take their actions from the boss. I think allowing them to be themselves an encouraging them to love what they do, encouraging them to love their colleagues, encouraging then to be kind to their colleagues, encouraging them to help people who need help without having to go through a process or a budget - all of this would encourage them to love more."
>
> **James Timpson**

> "I know from research I've seen on change management that if you've got trust, then you can accomplish a huge amount of things and if you don't' have trust, then you're in that world where dysfunctional behaviour happens, passive

resistance happens, active resistance happens, and these are fundamental to organisational success. So when you have a sense of trust, it doesn't mean that change won't happen or that a difficult decision would never be made, what it would enable is a much more positive action and response in the business and the effectiveness of the team."

Peter Cheese

For any of the above attributes to flourish and thrive consistently and deeply, the presence of the most critical leadership capability must be present. It is the master of all capabilities. That capability and attribute is love. A team without love is one that would struggle to trust. When love is present in a team it means that each and every team member relates with each other first of all and consistently as human. When they see each other, they see the person behind the objective, the job, the action, the behaviour and at times the emotion. There would be a willingness to forgive and to move on. To jointly learn from mistakes. There would be a deep care and compassion for each other as humans. No one individual talking over another. Vengeance and resentments felt and experienced because of objectives not met as a result of one member's action would not rear their heads. When one team member is in trouble, all of the team is in trouble. Collaboration and helpfulness would be commonly experienced within the team and within the teams that they as individuals lead. The whole organisation would be a network and a hive of activity. When love underpins and is the foundation of all the above attributes, it gives room for a team of super humans to emerge. A team with a potential like no other. They would have a level of resilience and an ability to recover from setbacks that would be hard to replicate and that will be because love will be evident within them and in them. The love that is the greatest and most critical need; the love that is the greatest and most critical gift and capability of a human being, a leader and a leadership team.

"If you take love as a fundamental value, it means that you will do your colleagues no harm. The leader that is driven by love will seek the highest good of the other team members."

Emmanuel Mbakwe

"Love is making accommodation for one another in how we do things and so I think it would enable team effectiveness. What is also involved is a high degree of trust. And this is a huge risk - and when you have cause to distrust a member of the team, it can be dangerous for the team and for you. When trust is damaged, it can have a huge and ripple effect in the team and the damage can be long lasting. It's like being in a relationship or a marriage and you distrust your partner - everything is suspicious because you're looking for what's broken.

Trust and love to me therefore influence each other. It's difficult to love someone at work if they can't be trusted. You can't be second guessing each other in a team."

Mark Scanlon

UBUNTU RULES - TOGETHER WE CAN DREAM

The effectiveness of a leadership team in which love is present and with members who have the capability to genuinely love and be loved can be phenomenal. It would be a team of diverse individuals, diverse in their thinking, in their styles and in their preferences and bonded by love and acceptance. They would be united by shared values and motivated and excited by joint purpose and the prospect of the awesome implications of the extraordinary results they set out to achieve. In a leadership team where love is present, the notion of 'Ubuntu' which in the African language - Xhosa - means 'I am because we are' will be real. No individual within the team would see or even imagine any aspect of their success to be a result of their individual effort. Each and every achievement would be seen as because of the team and this would be 'team' in the widest sense. It would mean the organisation.

When a leadership team is a team in which love is existent, that team would be a line of one. Aligned and alignment is a description that would be used frequently by stakeholders inside and outside the organisation about them. Their team meetings would be places where real decisions are made and once made, all backdoors to the reopening of negotiations or for the sabotage of individuals by other members would be closed. There would not even be a sniff of an attempt to do that. It would not be in their vocabulary. In leadership teams where love was present, they would be led by team leaders intolerant of gossip or back biting no matter how strongly disguised as the seeking of counsel or advice. Veiled attempts to talk about each other, and particularly negatively, would be met with wisdom and an encouragement to confront or challenge with love in order that disputes and disagreements may be quickly settled.

Deviant behaviour and behaviours that break the agreed rules of engagement and put the health of the team and organisation at risk are quickly surfaced and expelled. The focus will be behaviour and not the person as after all, there is no room in a team in which there is love for discrimination, prejudice and bias of any kind.

"In teams love would show up in less competition. After I left corporate America and decided to build a business, to be 26 or 27 at the top of the ladder of a fortune 500 organisation and reporting directly to the CEO, I must have learned how to play the political game effectively. But when I left the corporation, I said I'm going to build a company that doesn't have any politics. But as soon as you have a 3rd person in the company, you have politics. So I had to learn how to try to eliminate politics by creating more of a united face of the group towards accomplishing the goals that we need or accomplishing the growth of the company. It is hard to do because people strive for roles, for positions, for equity, people want to compete and so the challenge is to make sure you sometimes play a game of 'stop listening' when they come to complain to you about somebody else, you ask them - 'did you talk to John about it?' - and if they say 'no', then you say 'go talk to John'."

Andre Angel

"I'm sure there are lots of bits of politics going on and I'm absolutely ruthless about getting rid of it. I hate it. I even have a sign on my office door saying no politics. There's a sign as you walk into the main office from the car park, saying please leave your politics in the car park. I think it makes a difference that we're a family business it also makes a big difference that the divisions don't compete with themselves, it also makes a big difference all the bonuses depend on how each of them does and it's all in one pot. We help each other out and all the bonuses in the business are shared."

James Timpson

"As a team, if there was more demonstrable love in the workplace you would see that they would care about each other. The more senior you get, the more isolated you get from your fellow senior leaders. I for example would like to a good relationship with my boss and the CFO and also good relationships with all the other colleagues. In HR you tend to be coach, support, mentor, listen to everybody's concerns, raise them on their behalf sometimes if they weren't brave enough. I think that those senior leaders of very big pyramids, often spend too much of their time leading that pyramid from the top of that pyramid instead of supporting and coaching their colleagues who might need help. In teams love would encourage more teamwork more support and caring for each other and would create a stronger bond between each team member."

Louise Fisher

"Whether you've got trust first and then love or love first then trust, the belief that you can rely on somebody and somebody has got your interests at heart and you trust that they are going to be clear and open and honest with you and if you're doing it wrong they'll tell you and if you're doing it right they'll support you - this is where proper discussions are had, where the right answer is more likely to be delivered in the course of action and decisions are made instead of shuffling along in avoidance because nobody wants to make a decision and because nobody wants to upset another, so the presence of love and trust in a team would certainly have the team be more effective."

Richard Gillies

HOW ABOUT US

When a leadership team is operating from a place of love and every single element of dysfunction is eliminated the rest of the organisation feels it, they see it, they hear it and they know it. Negative watercooler gossip and chat in all its guises and through all of its mediums become obsolete as individuals up and down the organisation free up their time and turn their attention solely to the business of having their organisation be successful. Suddenly, the time it takes to learn of decisions on proposals made and resources requested lessens. The concept of try, fail, fail fast, learn from it and start again will become embedded into the fabric of the organisation. Idea generation and ways to solve problem or bring new products and services to market will be diverse and inclusive and will not be the singular responsibility of a particular department or person. Hierarchy is simply the organisation chart as preparations for the Chief Executive's visits become joyful experiences and an opportunity to engage in dialogue at the highest level on the direction of the organisation, its approach to changes in the economic and social environment and an opportunity to show case and recognise the great work of colleagues.

When an organisation's leadership team is operating at its very best and as one, the leadership teams that they in turn lead will operate at their very best and as one thereby allowing unity, complete function, harmony, shared agendas and collaboration to permeate through the entire organisation. There will be a focus on strengths in every way at organisation, team and individual level; team meetings will last for exactly the time indicated on the agendas of the meetings notices; virtual conference calls will have all participants fully present and devoid of doodling participants making brief notes of the grocery shopping list; town hall meetings will be attended happily and without need for an edict of attendance from the chief executive's office, the point of them appreciated and welcomed by all.

Recognition events and kudos given to colleagues by colleagues will be met with genuine welcome, the culture of helpfulness, collaboration, kindness, compassion, forgiveness, love and trust permeating every sinew of every individual within the organisation. Attracting skills, knowledge, and all kinds of talent and capabilities becomes easier; labels used to describe people obsolete because no one will feel isolated or different or excluded in any way imaginable.

An organisation with an effective leadership team and effective leaders who walk in love and work in love is the organisation that we all deserve and must aspire to be and to be a part of. Actually, it becomes an organisation that people love and want for it to be successful because they'll know that when that organisation and all of its people are successful it means they are too.

> "There's a lot of evidence that says businesses that have endured for more than a couple of decades and have ultimately created value even in the narrowest of financial terms have been those which put a very strong emphasis on relationships and having a purpose beyond profit which means making a contribution that is broader. And so I would say the evidence is there already that if you want to create a lasting and enduring business that can adapt quickly then you've got to put relationship at the heart of it and if you want to have strong relationships then you've got to have love."
>
> **Mark Goyder**

8. MEASURING THE
IMPACT OF LOVE

....

THERE IS NO POINT talking about the difference love can make in organisation if we don't examine how that impact can be measured. No matter how honourable it is or how strong and deep the belief is that it is simply the right thing to do to encourage and actively seek to introduce a culture of love in organisation, it is also loving thing to do to explore how its impact can be measured. I haven't to date come across a specific instrument for the measurement of love in organisation and so later on in this chapter I offer you a simple tool that you can use in initiating a dialogue with your colleagues and teams in your organisation.

First, let's examine how we can measure the presence of love using our human senses.

WHAT YOU SEE

It will be difficult to smile, laugh and walk around with purpose in an organisation in which love is not present. When love is present and active, right from the greeting of the persons in reception, to the assistants who meet with you to take you to your meeting rooms, there will be smiles that instil in you a feeling of welcome. There will be a sense of pride in the appearance of the individuals and how they dress. When the active and operational presence of love in an organisation is present, you walk into an environment in which people smile, furrowed brows are few, when you visit a building and are greeted by people, the greeting is warm and welcoming regardless of your or their status or job title. You'll notice from organisational health surveys and indications, like absence levels and turnover, that your people want to be present and not because they have to. When absenteeism becomes inevitable which it sometimes is because we all are human, the reasons given will ring true and be true. You'll observes scrums and groups of people around the organisation or in down times gathering together to share precious time in each other's company, to solve problems or create new ways of doing. Depending on the nature of the organisation and the purpose it serves, you'll see the evidence of love in the treatment of its clients and customers and the feedback that is given about them. You'll read any organisational survey results and not just in the data sets, you'll read it in the verbatim comments made. On top of that, you'll also see the evidence in the participation numbers and percentages. Where there is little and I bravely say, where there is less than 50% participation in opinion and feedback surveys you ask your people to complete it can be an indication of an absence of the operational presence of love in your organisation.

> "We do surveys. We've not ever tried to put a quantitative measure around it. I wouldn't say to people - I love you 9.134% - it doesn't lend itself to that but what I do correlate is how people look like - the expressions they have - how they are feeling. Am I seeing and hearing the right conversations? What are their behaviours. When someone stumbles, do people come and help them?"

> **Andy Mitchell**

> "The indicators would be qualitative as well as quantitative. The culture and health of the organisation in terms of its ethos and its profits, the views of its employees - when you

look at staff surveys, you would see what they think of the organisation, they would be making genuine and real suggestions for improvement. It would be on their agenda to make things as best as they can be. They would respond so that the quality of their response would be effective. It would also be the satisfaction of our customers and our stakeholders. So when we survey them on the quality of our services, we would be getting excellent and outstanding across the board. When you look at the quality of the services offered and the way that the business is operating, you would see the quality and the care and the thoughtfulness behind everything - from the cleanliness of the furniture you sit down on, the clearness and sparkling feel of the windows that you look out of the products that are delivered and sent out. You wouldn't see any shabbiness in the wrapping of a parcel; there wouldn't be any shabbiness in the greeting of a customer; you would see it in the quality of the accommodation that we provide; my clients would be loving their homes, the paint on the walls would be warm and welcoming; the carpet will be clean and fresh, the staff would be excellent in greeting and they would be always looking for different ways of helping. So you would measure satisfaction."

Ingrid Tennessee

"Secondly, you can look at personal time management. The extent to which people are feeling able to leave the office early or arrive late or take their lunch. If you are in an environment where people are missing their lunch because they are too busy to just interact without an agenda. Too much busyness at the expense of interaction of communication - the random interactions that happen - you can watch that."

Paul McNamara

"In the USA because of the cost of healthcare there is data that now shows that focusing on human wellbeing is a better determinant of organisational performance than anything to do with employee engagement. So I would probably start with as a lead indicator, wellbeing statistics and data. And we know that there is a great deal of measurement about what would happen when people get sick and there are emerging measures of how healthy peoples' mental capacity is and I would explore those as early indicators of what is going on and this is not an employee opinion survey, it's about the quality of relationships I have with people and I suspect it would be much more qualitative. But having said that, we are at Tomorrow's Company involved in some innovative tech organisations that are looking at reinventing employee assistance around employee wellbeing so that you can provide people with the tools to self-diagnose what are the issues and concerns you may have, here are some activities you may wish to engage in to help you and it's all about creating a breadth and a richness. You can get early signal measurement."

Norman Pickavance

The current tools of engagement and employee satisfaction surveys can also be an indication and measurement of the presence of love. They can when effectively deployed and applied help you understand where your people are in terms of their loyalty to your organisation, the direction of your strategy and the level of confidence they have in the ability of the individuals placed in positions to execute that strategy. When the motive of using engagement surveys is genuine and the results given importance and attention, and the actions agreed followed through, they can be a great start to measuring the presence of love and to starting a dialogue around the facilitation of the introduction of love.

"Through employee satisfaction and engagement - is there a sense of belonging? Is there a sense of 'do I feel respected?' This would give you a feel of the mood of the organisation and the sentiment that is in there. We get some honest feedback that would enable us to focus on certain aspects in the business. An employee engagement survey is only an indication."

Howard Kerr

"One can also monitor engagement on a global basis if you're a big business - say a global company with different operating companies across the world. You can look at how employee engagement relates to business performance overall and I would hypothesise that in those where there is high performance, you have great leadership and have high employee engagement. Having that transparency would then provide a very good platform for leadership development."

Lawrence Hutter

"Measuring it has to be around employee reported outcomes. We would may be come up with employee engagement and employee experience measures. I would also want to measure it against the strategic objectives in the organisation. For example, the delivery of safe effective care – this an example of one our strategic objectives against which I could measure it. I would also be interested on the impact on our partners – their experience of us as reputation matters too."

Sam Allen

As you delve deeper still, you'll see the evidence of love and will be able to measure it through the speed of decision making and the speed by which you and your people recover from setbacks and unexpected challenges.

"Also you can see from results and fight backs - for example we had a brand this year that suffered for six months, so we said we would dig deep and find ways to see what we can do to salvage things and the team behind it really dug deep. What happened is that it surged in the last month and surged sufficiently enough to finish annually ahead of the market - it was like a fairy tale ending. So bounce back results would be a great measure of the presence of love because you can see the real efforts that the people make and see too from the spirit of the people working on the brand or problem if there is love in the air and if there is, the difference shows up in the quality of the results and the resilience and sheer determination that emerges."

John Mangan

"I may not necessarily use the love word overtly when I come to measure it, but what I would measure would be highly effective teams - implicitly working together and having a common sense of purpose. I would also measure the success of the organisation - because for love to truly flourish, you do need the organisation to be successful. There are tacit performance indicators that would demonstrate that this is working and they will be as important as indicators that you look to that confirm that the ship is turning around."

Richard Gillies

"There are some things around business decision making - the speed with which the right people come together and contribute in the right way, making better decisions. People would move quicker too - the control environments we live in, more people would do the right thing, therefore you could have less controls and restraints and be able to move things along quicker or get better decisions or be more successful in bidding for work or getting profitable work. Some of the measures would be on positive business measures like you would have now. It would be understanding what had changed and perhaps more focus on the qualitative. The business is there and still has to deliver its strategic goals - to meet the needs of its customers, to deliver profit to shareholders and so on - these have still got to be the measures of success but what would be different when love is in the organisation could be how those goals and objectives are met. It will be in the articulation of the "who" and the "how". You would experience a very different culture."

Sally Cabrini

The culture of love in your organisation will also be seen in the reports and comments made on social media platforms accessible to your people and available for the public to read and the more anonymous the opportunity for comment is, the stronger the potential for the indicators of love in your organisation can be seen.

"One of the good and convivial uses of social media technology has been something like Glassdoor. It would be perfectly possible to apply a Glassdoor approach for people to review how much love they encountered in their business. So, you could envisage a sort of love league table.

It would be capturing the lived experience of employees and indeed the lived experience of customers."

Mark Goyder

WHAT YOU HEAR

The nature of conversation in formal and informal settings, the energy and enthusiasm conveyed, will be evidence of the presence of love in organisation. There will be a structure of 'can do' and 'what is possible' versus all that may get in the say of moving forward with initiatives and ideas. The expression 'We' will be prevalent where it matters and where it doesn't matter because no one will be playing to an audience because the motive consistently and continuously is the good and success of the team, the organisation and the communities that it serves. Feedback will be commonplace and delivered through various and creative mediums and because in a culture in which love is present, feedback is experienced as a gift, the response 'thank you' will be heard, written and seen. In meetings the expression 'what do you think?', 'how can we help?', 'what have we learned?', 'what are we going to do differently?'; 'What's your view?' will be common and followed by active listening. The team leader choosing to go last in service of the team and to ensure that there is no hint of an influence of bias or "follow the leader" emerging. There will be a humility evident. A humility that is not an excuse for insecurity or a fear of failure or being spoken over, instead a humility that is evidence of a quiet confidence and assuredness born out of a shared agenda and purpose; a confidence that all are invested in each other's success and prosperity and that of their organisation.

"Also the kinds and types of conversation and personal dialogues that colleagues have - you'll be able to see it, witness it and also over hear it. Also the way that supervisions are conducted, you would see it in the notes, in the way that employees are rewarded - excellence would be acknowledged in the teams and for the individuals, not just from the leaders but also from each other. You would say the way in which targets are measured and what is put down as KPIs. We would be surpassing our targets. Complaints would be impacted and they would be lessened and dealt with quickly and effectively and our stakeholders would see that we were excellent at learning from our mistakes."

Ingrid Tennessee

WHAT YOU FEEL

How you feel and how your people feel; your experience and the experience of your people is an undeniable measurement of the presence of love in your organisation. If you wake up too many times with a feeling of dread at the thought of going into work or meeting up with colleagues then it is a result of one of two things. It is either time for you to move on because you are not walking in line with your God given purpose, or you are in an environment of working in which you are unable to thrive. When that meeting with your boss is one in which you are constantly seeking opportunities to avoid or postpone it or indeed you are spending an inappropriate length of time in preparing for it, anticipating all angles of attack and defence or combat, or trying to predict the mood in which he or she will be, then you are working in an environment in which you do not feel valued or accepted. If you are having personal challenges that you know may one day impact your work or your ability to work at your very best and yet not feel the need to share this with your boss, HR or colleagues, then you are in an environment in which you don't feel loved. When you raise your eyebrows and feel cynical at the mention of the apparently honourable organisation and team values and the jokes during coffee breaks are peppered with decisions about your colleagues which you join in with even when you feel that little bit uncomfortable, it is questionable that you are working with colleagues and team members with whom you feel accepted. How you feel and how your people feel; that intangible yet real experience is a key measurement and indicator of love and it takes leaders who walk in and with love to create and establish environments in which they and all of their people can feel free to be themselves.

"I'm a massive believer in happy accidents! I wouldn't measure it. When I see and hear things coming back to me that were kind of pushed out as an idea, but someone has picked up and run with it; Whether that's a business issue or something non business related or to do with the way people operate. It's what comes back to you. There has to be an element where you put in some effort in work and life becomes easier. Then of course it is also looking at the numbers. But it is a feeling for me more than a health check sheet. It would be a feeling of succeeding. A feeling of doing the right thing and a feeling of that being sustainable. And if all that comes together and works together, then it's having a feeling that this is all now coming together. So it is checking in with my intuition and my feeling about something. I guess it is emotion."

Mark Scanlon

"The way I will look at this is my experience of when people come to me and share with me and are open with me; and I can talk to them too and I can look them in the eye and share with them openly about what we are doing as an organisation and not keeping anything away from them. This is the first step – this is how you gain the trust of everybody."

Sam Aiyere

"Scheduling is one way to measure. After phases of work or projects delivered - simple things such as not forgetting to do a review - what has been learned? How did everyone feel about it? Personally and as a team? What has been good that should be replicated? What was not so good that should be corrected? Apart from the work output, how did each colleague experience their involvement? Has sufficient time been scheduled to have such reflections?"

Paul McNamara

Once upon a time, I worked in an organisation in which international travel was a core element of my role. During one of my overseas trips, I fell ill with a bad cold and signs of the flu which you could hear in my voice over the telephone. One day, I received a phone call from a supplier who did not realise I was out of the country and in our conversation, hearing the cold in my voice enquired about my wellbeing. I said I was sure I would get better very soon but was unsure as to whether I would be in the office the following Monday. A couple of days later and while still on my overseas trip, I received a call from my boss who had in the interim period had a call from this supplier and furious at being made to look like a bad boss, shouted at me and accused me of making her look bad and overworking me because I had told the supplier I was unwell with a cold and may not be going into work the following Monday. My boss believed and said this was me getting ready to give an untrue excuse for not going into work and was a personal let down. What you had here, therefore, was a situation in which one innocent conversation had with an unsuspecting third party who in turn relayed the content innocently with a stakeholder who, under massive stress, reacted in a fearful way. The entire exchange was an indication of an absence of love in operation in that organisation and certainly in that relationship because where there is no trust there cannot be love.

Some organisations choose to measure happiness because if your people are happy, they are likely to be more engaged and therefore more productive and do this in combination with the feeling their people and leaders experience across the organisation.

> "We don't measure love but we measure happiness. Principle one for us is about a happy worthwhile satisfying employment. This is what we measure and we measure this annually and also at other times when we want to. This

is about happiness, but I think that love drives happiness and happiness drives love. This goes out to circa 80,000 partners and some areas of the organisation will get 80 - 90% of turn out and other areas will get 30% engagement so it does vary in response but this is important to us because it helps us understand what areas of the organisation we need to pay a little more attention to. What we've never been able to do is monetise this, but there is a view that the monetary side doesn't matter because if this is part of our purpose, which is also about leaving the organisation better for the next generation, then that is what matters and it's not about the money. It is just the right thing to do."

Naomi Gillies

"Happy index is very important to us - we use this in our business. Also just going round the business, round the shops, me and my dad - going round the business, and you're spreading the love, spreading the culture, spreading the message. Leaders need to be seen and we take this seriously."

James Timpson

"Also by my own experience - I took my mum into a local Waitrose. Nobody knew who I was. My father who had been poorly for quite some time had not long passed away. My mum wasn't very well, battling grief and also clearly in the early stages of dementia. She was polarised by grief and also now having to live on her own after not having to do so for more than 65 years. The experience in the local store was like having a toddler go shopping with you and because she would drift off from time to time, I had her pushing a trolley to provide some type of anchor and orientation for her. Anyway, we were looking for a bandage as she'd hurt her knee and we were attended to by a young person - of not more than 20. He was so patient and nothing was too big or small for him and my mum must have asked him literally a version of the same question at least 8 times in 10 minutes and he kept humouring her and answering all her questions. Now where did he get that emotional maturity and the confidence to deal with my mother? - I felt so proud - because this was a Waitrose person; a person who had the care and gave the time to pay attention to my mother and not be frustrated or allow their frustration to show. I felt cared for. I felt loved."

Tracey Killen

What is clear though is there is and at least not to my own awareness, no known or widely used instrument available or applied to measure the impact of love in organisation and the more we talked and reflected on the value of love in organisation, the more the senior leaders I interviewed reflected on the value a measurement of love in organisation can present both in the ability to help break down the barriers and taboo of talking about love as well as the facilitation of a focus on the development of behaviours, capabilities and attributes of what is the biggest gift and need of the human being. And if this is the greatest gift and need why should it not be actively allowed to operate within the world of work which indeed is life too? It was inspiring and encouraging to listen to their thoughts.

"Things like customer and client experience, employee engagement - all of this can be measurable and will give you an indication; But they may not measure love in the context in which we are talking. But it is worth exploring. I think you could measure love - maybe you may need to create a measurement. You could create a love index; a measurement index. You could go and talk to your clients, your employees, your customers, your suppliers - and then explore what makes up a love measurement index. So you could definitely measure it and how much you attribute to your bottom line to that love measurement index on its own would take some working out but not impossible to do. First thing is to start somewhere with measurement.

You could look at creating a love measurement index with your employees - to understand how your employees feel about working here and working in your organisation. Think for example of the retention of your people and what they would say in conversations about you when they're with friends and around the table having a meal with their family."

Andrew Needham

"I don't think you could measure in isolation bottom line on productivity or engagement - they would all impact it but because you couldn't extract the exact contribution of love, you would have to measure it in isolation and create a measurement criteria and tool for it.

The kind of questions I would ask would be - does your organisation put you first? How high up the pecking order does your organisation put you? Does your organisation share the gains with you? Do you feel you have respect from your organisation? Are your thoughts and inputs respected? Are you treated fairly? Are you trusted? Are there any biases in this organisation - conscious or unconscious? And so on."

Louise Fisher

"These are questions that are never asked in any feedback form - 'do you feel that your colleagues love you? 'This would be most direct way to measure it. To ask the question directly.

An interesting notion is that often in business we have a system or systems that enable us to surface and talk about the bad things - for example harassment - but we less often have systems that enable us to surface and talk about the really good things in business and although this is becoming more possible, it would be great to see an increase in this."

Richard Eu

"It's the whole adage that what gets measured gets done and especially in a world where even though there is a shift, there's still a lot of scepticism out there. We need to be able to see the correlation between what we measure and business performance and overtime correlation can lead to causality too and then we're really saying something."

Peter Cheese

There is no point measuring the contribution of love to the success of your organisation and your work if you are not going to do something about it. At the same time, starting the journey of measurement can be challenging, will need the courage of a lion, and a willingness to take the first step.

Here is a simple tool with a set of questions that you may use in discussion with your team and in the gathering of thought ahead of a discussion. It is a sample of the Hofmann Organisational Love Indicator (HOLI).

Responses to the questions below will give an indication of the measure of the presence of love in your organisation and your work as experienced by you and by your people.

Hofmann Organisational Love Indicator (HOLI)			
		Yes/No	**Examples of how I know**
1	In relation to my boss	1. I feel and am valued 2. My contribution always counts 3. I am accepted for all of who I am 4. I can share all thoughts without judgement 5. I am given room to grow 6. I trust my boss and he/she trusts me 7. We work in and with love	
2	In relation to my colleagues	1. I feel and am valued 2. My contribution always counts 3. I am accepted for all of who I am 4. I can share all of my thoughts without judgement 5. We are invested in each other's success 6. We win and lose together 7. We work in and with love	
3	In relation to my own team and individuals within my team	1. Each person's contribution counts 2. I see and accept each person for all of who they are 3. I separate the behaviours I experience from who the person is 4. There is trust of and in all of my team - of me, me with them and with our colleagues 5. I am invested in the success of each individual within my team and of the team 6. I am all of who I am with my team 7. We work with and in love	

4	In relation to my organisation's suppliers	1. I see each person for all of who they are 2. I relate to each and every representative first as human 3. I know who they are as human beings 4. Our policies are written and implemented in the best interest of both parties 5. Our work is conducted with love always in relation to all of our suppliers 6. All reasons for rejection or termination of contracts are shared honestly 7. We are transparent in every aspect of our procurement process	
6	In relation to our clients and customers	1. I see each person for all of who they are 2. I relate to each and every client and customer first as human 3. Our ideas, innovations and ways of working are designed always in the best interest of our customers and clients 4. Our clients and customers know that we operate always from a love for them 5. All our decisions are made in the best interest of our customers and clients and the people they impact 6. Our clients and customers know that their feedback to us is valued 7. Our clients and customers know we care about and love them	

8	In relation to the environment	1. We demonstrate love in our treatment of our environment 2. All our decisions where relevant are made in the best interest of our environment 3. We encourage our suppliers and our clients to love the environments in which they operate 4. We know the impact of our operations on our environment 5. We educate our people about the impact of our actions on our environment 6. We celebrate the contribution of our people to the welfare of our environment 7. We are transparent with all of our stakeholders on how we treat our environment	
9	In relation to communities and people we impact and don't see (the global village called the world)	1. We know all of the communities that we impact even those we do not see 2. The representatives of the communities in which we operate know that we Love them and they Love us 3. We actively support the wellbeing - mental, physical, emotional - of the people in our communities without condition or expectation 4. We do not waste resources - food, energy, time - and celebrate milestone achievements in the reduction of wastage 5. We consistently think through the consequences of our actions on people in our organisation and across the world. 6. We provide employment opportunities where possible for the people in our local communities 7. We contribute to wellbeing programmes in our local communities	

10	In relation to my neighbour (the poor and the homeless)	1. We show love and compassion to the poor and homeless in our communities 2. We actively encourage the volunteering to causes and initiatives that support the wellbeing of our community 3. Our leadership proactively role model Love in action for people in our communities. 4. We encourage our people to proactively support local initiatives that impact the homeless and the poor 5. We contribute to the poor and homeless in our communities without expectation 6. We provide financial awareness and management programmes for all of our people 7. Our people know that they will be supported through personal challenges	
11	In relation to my organisation's purpose	1. My own life's purpose is aligned behind my organisation's purpose 2. I know the role my organisation plays in the fulfilment of my own purpose 3. I am able to operate at my very best all of the time 4. There is a culture of love - unconditional acceptance of the individual - here in my organisation 5. What is important to me is important also to my organisation 6. My wellbeing - emotionally, physically and mentally - is important to my organisation 7. My organisation is actively engaged with the implementation of the Sustainable Development Goals	

9. EXPERIENCING LOVE

....

THE POWER OF LOVE in all of its forms and ways we can imagine it to be can be overwhelming. It can be all consuming. It may also be indeed difficult to fully comprehend. This is one reason why broaching the subject in the context of work is one that is avoided in all of the most creative ways possible and all attempts to date to surface it as a genuine and real attribute and key to the unlocking of potential and performance in organisation and in humanity have not been sustained. Where do you start? With whom do you start? How do you begin the conversation? How will it come across? Will they say you've lost your marbles? Will they say you've lost your head? We have instead skirted around the edges and the peripherals, waiting for the first person to take that very brave step into the unknown world of how will they respond? How will they react? and 'how will I look'? The analogy that comes to mind is that of a group of walking adventurers in a forest finding themselves lost and coming to the front door of a beautiful old house full of character, set in the middle of a forest, the last place you would expect it to be. This beautiful old house has a beautiful wooden door behind which is a world of wonder and excitement and fulfilment where people thrive and because they thrive their organisations thrive and because their organisations thrive, their communities thrive and because communities thrive, society thrives. But they don't know it because no one dares to be the first to open the door.

LOVE BEGINS AT HOME

When you experience genuine and unconditional love at home and in your formative years, it sets a great foundation makes it just that little bit easier to speak freely about it during your mature years. When you experience love in your earlier years it also makes it easier to recognise, to see, to feel, to hear and to sense it in all of its forms and characteristics in your mature years. This is the reason why parenting is critical and the role of tutors and teachers in peoples' formative years is key to the quality of life and the attitudes and values we hold about ourselves and others later on.

One of the most enjoyable moments I had during the interviews I conducted with senior leaders was their reflection on their personal experiences of love in their home, early formative years and their personal lives. They also reflected on how this has influenced their outlook on life. I was inspired. I was encouraged. I felt special and I felt invited in. It helped me to understand how they in turn recognise it today and also how they demonstrate it in relation to others.

"As a person my first experience of love was at home. The tool kit of love comes from home. There are also people who build wonderful lives despite home. You can have people who have had terrible starts in life - in orphanages for example - and yet build a happy love filled life. But in many more harmonious and more standard cases, your tool kit comes from home. My subconscious use of my tool kit which came from home has been through all my interactions with my family and my friends and my work. It is about feeling happy to be me and being comfortable and feeling inspired and experiencing generosity. Because I've experienced generosity it's made it possible for me to also exercise generosity. Many things matter but above all what really matters is love. In the end, that's it. When you strip everything away, love is what really makes us go forward and also what makes us go upward and carries us. You wonder at times, when looking at myself and also around me at people who face extraordinary situations what carries people forward is love. Love is not limited to the partner you have in life. So many folks don't find that Mr or Mrs Right and still have wonderful lives. Love is in many different forms and can enter into life at different moments - e.g. a neighbour that becomes a lifelong friend. I've been extremely lucky to have two people - my parents who love each other deeply - but also loved us deeply and generously. We didn't belong to them they wanted us to fly and they continuously gave of their time and of their thoughts and of their energy to help us fly. With that you carry that and it becomes part of you and thankfully it is lovely to feel that effortlessly you can exercise it to others. Of course there is effort in love but it's great to be in a place where 80 - 90% of the love you give is virtually effortless and its' a lovely place to be."

John Mangan

"At home we all are affectionate and close. We are big on hugs. I have a happy marriage and am married to a man who's my best friend who I still love dearly one of the kindest and most interesting people I know and who's always got my back."

Tracey Killen

"I met my wife at university and as soon as I saw her, I knew I'd marry her although it took me about a year to convince her.

I like to think that I'm a person who likes love and is not afraid of it. My mother who sadly died a couple of years ago, was well known for being a very loving person and you sort of become that. It is part of who you are."

James Timpson

"Just like with your parents, it's not that they tell you that they love you it's when you get to actually spend time with them and it may not be a conscious thing at the time but you come out of spending time with your parents feeling better in some indescribable way or as a child feeling more confident in yourself. Happier. These are the manifestations of it. What's the one thing that as leaders you have too little of its time and what do you spend too little of doing - spending time with people. So it's an interesting reflection. To not underestimate the value of your presence with other people. When time is spent with me by people from whom I value it, this demonstrates love."

Norman Pickavance

"Of course from home, fantastic. I don't share everything at home because of the nature of my work and its confidentiality. What I share at home is a high level of what I am experiencing and the issues I face. My wife comforts me and she watches out for my state of mind. I know I can trust her and that she won't judge me. And of course, even if I do anything wrong, she would still say you've tried your best. In addition, I do have mentors outside that I can turn to. The one thing that I learned from one of my mentors was to take care of myself first. I really appreciate it when people are interested in my wellbeing.

In essence there should be no difference between love at home and love at work. When you know the people you are leading, when something is wrong, you should be able to pick it up. It is about having a pastoral responsibility here; it is about picking up the hidden messages and issues that may be underneath the surface."

Sam Aiyere

"One of the biggest measurements of knowing someone loves you is when you can be completely yourself and in being yourself, you know that people around you who laugh with you, hang out with you, do stuff with you - they just love you for being you. That's a very good feeling."

Andrew Needham

"Yes I have experienced love, unconditional love with my wife Judy with my two sons (32 &28), and with many close relatives including my sisters and my brother and it's contributed to how I lead my life today."

Lewis Doyle

"I was brought up in a very loving environment with wonderful parents. My father had a great public career and was a businessman and churchman and fully engaged in many parts of public life things. He was a loving disciplinarian. My mother who was brought up as a Quaker was a very gentle, strong, tranquil person. I've experienced the love of my parents - I am the youngest of 8 children and so to some considerable extent was brought up by my siblings and I feel to this day a wonderful sense of love and solidarity with them, I have been happily married for 39 years to a wonderful woman and have the joy of loving her and being loved by her and learning day by day and year by year, how this is something you have to work at. Then in friendship, I have some very strong and loving friends. And in the workplace, particular leaders I've worked with who I've felt believed in me and showed their love through helping me develop and challenging me to develop. I stopped being CEO at Tomorrow's Company over a year ago and felt a huge warmth and love from the people I've worked with through some really tough times where colleagues have stood by me and I've stood by them and we've been determined not to give up when things have been against us and believing that what we were doing has value and would make a difference - it's been a wonderful context for work."

Mark Goyder

My own background and formative years were infused with love. A rich, deep and intoxicating love. I am the youngest of five children born to parents who believed their entire life's purpose was to set their children up for a future and a world in which they can stand up on their own. My father was a University Professor of Chemistry and my mother was a seamstress who made the most beautiful of wedding dresses and children's clothes. My sisters and I lacked nothing to wear to all of the parties we went to. Both of my parents worked hard and diligently; often going without so that we may have. Hugs and cuddles were commonplace and being the last born, the hugs came not only from my parents but also from all of my brothers and sisters. I was a spoilt child. Spoilt with love and raised in an environment safe and secure in the knowledge of that love. I was blessed, too, by the teachers I had in kindergarten and primary school. I remember two – Mrs. Davies and Mrs. Adeniran - whose smiles, when I recall them, still fill me with warmth today. I remember that no question was too small or inconsequential for them. Those very early years provided a strong foundation on which I could stand as I progressed through the rough and challenging years of secondary school, and on which I still stand today.

LOVE CONTINUES THROUGH WORK

If you know who you really are and you are comfortable in that knowledge of who you are, why would you not be that same person at work? The idea that as you walk into 'work', be it a building or a virtual workspace, you shed one skin and image and grow another, or you reach into your briefcase or handbag for the most appropriate mask for the day and audience is false. When you are unable to be you, are who you are and to relate to others from that genuine and authentic place it makes it difficult for others to do the same with you. Constraints real and unreal take precedence and the very first grain of mistrust and conditionality come into play. You may say, "Well Yetunde, in organisation, we have different rules of engagement and it is impossible to demonstrate unconditional love. This is not your family and your loved ones; these are colleagues and there's a job to do. It's difficult to demonstrate unconditional love when you have employment contracts, shareholders, salary bands and bonuses and performance targets. How can you, with these conditions demonstrate unconditional love? This is work, not home!"

This is what I say in response. I say that it is challenging; it is not easy but that nothing great and extraordinary comes easy. What I say is that someone, somewhere, some human introduced and created the construct of organisation and work as we experience it today and it will be someone somewhere will challenge that status quo in the interest of advancement and the real purpose of work. That someone, somewhere can be you. Why not? Change, progress and transformation happens one conversation at a time; one action and one step at a time. All this requires is for the conversation to start. Now.

The future, however, is bright and is one that can be full of hope. Because today, when you take the time to genuinely reflect there will be times and maybe not many when you have experienced the attributes of love whether the word and expression love has been mentioned or not and as a result that experience has made a genuine positive impact on you. And why should this not? When it is likely that as human beings and with the advancement of technology and our knowledge, we will live much longer and therefore work in various guises much longer, why should we not have our working years be some of the best, most enjoyable and most loving years of our lives? My bold challenge to you is this - that the only obstacle to the full release of the potential of the operational and active presence of love in organisation is the human being. You and me.

Love is experienced today in work and by people at all levels and that experience is one that not only benefits them as individuals and leaders, it benefits those whom they in turn impact. The domino effect happens.

> "Latterly in my career, the line managers I've had who have all been completely different - have been driven by genuinely wanting to make me happy and feel loved in my role. They are polar extremes in terms of style but inherently what they've had is that they are just nice people. And therefore, when I've stopped working for them, it's felt like I'm grieving. There are 5 of them that I can think of and they all cared about me as an individual. They let me be myself. That makes me better at my job and also having had a son, they've put as much importance in that side of my life as they have done in my work."
>
> **Naomi Gillies**

> "I've experienced it in areas where people have helped me personally with how I can bring more of myself to work. When it is clear that people care, I am able to disclose personal thoughts that I may not have before disclosed in the business. Most powerfully, disclosing vulnerabilities brings authenticity and it also gives others a sense that they can open up too."
>
> **Paul McNamara**

> "This organisation has been very good to me. I have worked here for 29 years and a lot of what I have I owe to this

organisation. It's given me the opportunity and I'm sure that a lot of what I do and how I feel and how I behave today is a consequence of what the organisation has given me. I've received that investment, that affection from the organisation to be able to do what I'm doing now which will also mean that I'm able to pay it back or to move it on and at some point, I will pass the baton onto somebody else. It has given me that opportunity and it's given me that growth. I have no doubt that I'm a different person today than I was 25 or 30 years ago."

Steve Fox

"My first experience was of someone saying I'm not satisfied with what you're doing. That's an act of love because that person cared enough about me to take me aside to say, 'don't do that, you can do better' and it had a deep impact on me.

The best boss I had was a US based CEO. The whole level of interaction was pretty limited. I would see him face to face two to three times a year; we would speak once a month if that, but I felt completely supported and valued and empowered. I definitely felt that he had my best interest at heart and felt that he would listen and if I had a concern or an issue, he would take it on board. Also, I was used to him saying 'no, we're not going to do that' and that was absolutely fine too. Even in the best relationship you're going to have disagreements, someone's going to have to make a decision and that should not be a problem if the relationship is healthy. I trusted him and respected him. He was an inspirational role model to me in that regard and in terms of how I felt about working for him. It is something that I wanted other people to feel when working for me.

I remember too another situation I was told that the company was introducing a new layer of management as it grew. I was told that I was in line for that promotion. I had certain development points I was working on and I took on certain projects. Months later without any further discussion it was announced that my colleague had been promoted into the role that I had been earmarked for. That was a painful experience. I felt devalued. Even though I was promoted a few months later, that impact on me was huge. You learn from the good things and the experiences you have and you also learn from the negative. When someone makes you feel that bad, you never forget it."

Neil Wilson

"There are times when I go around the office and I talk to a lot of people and I'm very obviously there and present. Sometimes, when I'm not in a great place, people would pick it up and will say - 'are you alright? What's up?' It's just a human question. The most junior person in this company is just as likely to say to the CEO - 'what's up?' And there's a huge amount in there that says it is okay to treat anyone in this company simply as a human being and the fact that we may be at different ends of the hierarchy doesn't make that any less or more important. That means a lot because we all have down days and we all have worries and that's not an exclusive club."

Andy Mitchell

"The best expression of that to me has been where people have given me opportunity. That's where I've felt where I've worked hard, applied myself and on the basis of doing that I've had the opportunity to do it again. Where I've felt someone's backed me. No one's every told me that they love me at work but that's how I've felt it. I've felt that permission,

I've felt secure, the backing to go and do something even quite challenging.

Also beyond that, when I'm working with people and you just see the humanity coming out of people from time to time.

One lady - she'd been with the business I was once working in - who retired after circa 28 years. One day I sat down with her and I discovered that she lived in Italy and her husband worked with Olivetti and worked with organisations I could relate to from my childhood and we created such a bond and even though she's left the business now, she's like a mum to me. And that bond was created at work!"

Mark Scanlon

"My own experience stems from when I worked on a major growth focused consulting engagement. Two examples come to mind. The first was in 1997. It was about helping the company to grow. That business, which is a subsidiary of a global organisation was actually headed by a Christian. What was also interesting is the kind of people that formed the team. Although they were not all Christians, they had a high level of commitment to the cause and to one another. It was a very intense period, but the team members were very supportive of each other. You finish your own piece of work and then would go to a colleague to offer support and another pair of hands to help finish the work. The underlying principle there is that no team member's work is finished until we all finish. I learned a great deal during that project.

The second example I will give relates to when I worked on a big government programme in education. The whole team was a mixture of consultants and educators working on a culture transformation programme within the education system. Centred around children, young people and families, it was as if everyone who worked on that programme worked as if it was their life mission I would go as far as saying that it is probably the best team that I ever worked in. The main reason is the fact that I discovered that quite a lot of the people who worked on that programme as joint team members from the teaching profession were Christians or had been exposed to strong Christian teaching in there. I left the programme in 2008, yet we meet for reunions every year, which says something about the special connection that we had."

Emmanuel Mbakwe

"Most recently I've experienced it in the care that my boss my colleagues and my friends have extended to me because I've had a really difficult time. And their care and their time - from my boss asking me 'should you be here? Go home. Why are you here and not at home? And so on, and not doing that in a transactional way. My boss also hugs me. He'll just come and give me a hug. And ask me, 'how's mum?' He doesn't have a little checklist. I've experienced it very much as being treated as an individual and understanding my circumstances at this time. Not having someone reaching for a manual and saying - 'under bereavement, what does it say? What is the checklist I've got to cover?' It is the individual care approach. Asking me 'what do you need?' And by the way what one person needs may be different to another and it's important to understand that."

Tracey Killen

"Most notably when an individual might pull me aside and counsel me. When it wasn't necessary, when it wasn't requested by me but someone who took the time and cared enough and saw that they could make a contribution in a legitimate way. When they have given a piece of feedback or a suggestion or support.

I remember one day early in my career, going home and feeling that I was so unable to do my work and that I felt I needed to resign. I spoke to my parents and they said: 'well, you should go in and chat to the managing director. And I said: 'ah yes, good idea, he works late.'

So I got on my bike, as I lived not that far from the office and went in hoping to have a conversation with the boss that night - taking my parents' advice – but, interestingly, he had just left the building. I'd missed him. So I went home. I did not have a good night's sleep. The next morning, I went into work and I happened to bump into a friend in the lift who said 'you look dreadful. What's going on?' So we had a chat. He said to me - 'you'll be absolutely fine. No one has died. It is not a disaster. You'll be okay' and for some reason my mood was lifted.

It was a very small intervention, but it was from someone who demonstrated they cared. And what sticks in my mind is that a small thing, a thoughtful interaction, an insignificant comment, can have enormous impact. I did not resign as a consequence of that conversation in the lift. Two years later I told my boss what I'd intended to do and he said well if you'd come in to resign, I wouldn't have accepted. But I didn't know that at the time."

Paul McNamara

"The last phone call I had with my direct reports before I left my last company and corporate career was an international phone call with members of my team from different parts of the world - from the Latin Americas to the Philippines. I asked them to start sharing something positive so that we could end on a real high and everybody started sharing everything that they had achieved and it was all so positive and emotional that by the time it got to me, I was so emotional, I had to put the phone on mute whilst I sobbed and I realised that I cared very deeply about the people and that I was going to miss them. I was touched. I experienced love.

I also think back to an experience I had when I was at Forte hotels. I was in a team of 7 people defining the brand of Forte Post House hotels which had kicked off before I arrived at the company. It was the first hotel in the UK that had gone for a pricing policy of price per room and so we were creating this brand new British brand within the Forte brand and we were all excited, we helped each other out and I had such great affection. It was my first directorship, so excited to be doing business stuff and loved the people I worked with and these were great people doing great things together and they were treating me as an equal around the table, and this was probably the most pleasurable team I had worked in and although I've worked in others since, this was the first and so really had a huge impact on me. So in that environment I experienced it - it was given to me and I gave it back."

Louise Fisher

"At QinetiQ and at Coma where I worked for a period of time I was given significant autonomy to deliver for the business and within a broad remit. I felt trusted to deliver and I did."

Lewis Doyle

When you experience love you create the most memorable of experiences that impact your wellbeing, outlook and that of the people you impact in a positive way. And the more experiences of love and its attributes you have, the less impactful the negative experiences of life will be. Love can most certainly conquer all because genuine love when transmitted, is experienced as authentic, unconditional and without judgement. This does not mean that in the moment an action, albeit carried out in love, is experienced that feelings will not be hurt; egos bruised; and emotions scarred. It does not mean that. Sometimes tough love is experienced and particularly in the world of work and in organisations. The difference I am advocating is the place from which that action is coming; the ground on which that action is rooted.

IT STARTS WITH YOU AND ME

The ability to experience love in any form and especially when we are older or indeed at any stage in life, starts with how you see yourself. It starts with how I see me. Also your ability to genuinely experience love and in turn demonstrate it will come from how you see yourself and because of this, the love and care you also give to yourself. When you love and accept all of who you are, it becomes much easier to love and accept all of who another person is and to create an environment in which you can experience it for the good and benefit of all of your people and all of the people that they impact and others can experience it in your presence too.

"Ultimately along with love comes the first and most critical question of all - do you love yourself? And I must say yes, I do. I do love myself and I think that once that is established, we can ask, well what can we do with this? - and it can be great fun. Once you lift your head and say wow this is a pretty extraordinary gift and without running myself into the ground trying to take on the entire world's woes, I can decide to channel myself for good and encourage others to do the same - so if I say if I'm rooting for you and you're rooting for me and if that spirit of goodness is sponsored more deeply and widely across the world, it would improve this place. Because we have a big deep number of cynics that believe that for every good guy there's a bad guy and if you're not careful, you're going to get walked on and made to look a woos and it's upon us to be voices of the non-dark side particularly if we see the emergence of dangerous trends coming up in the world - talk around hate and so on - then we owe it to ourselves, to our people and to society to speak up."

John Mangan

"One of the biggest measurements of knowing someone loves you is when you can be completely yourself and in being yourself, you know that people around you who laugh with you, hang out with you, do stuff with you - they just love you for being you. That's a very good feeling."

Andrew Needham

You can demonstrate love to yourself by the things you give yourself permission to do and in so doing, know that you are setting an excellent example for others. If you can work flexibly and know that it will impact you and others positively, then give yourself permission to work flexibly; to go home that little bit early, to switch off the computer that little bit early; to join that team conference call from home and share it without fear or self-censure; to grab a day off to simply rest and do nothing. Accepting that you are not invincible and are imperfect is a great place to start and from that place are more able to include others in the home and tent of self-acceptance and imperfection and out of that all of you and all of them can and will thrive. That's experiencing love.

"I think that love can be experienced differently at work than at home. Particularly when you look at the more intimate relationships. So, for example if someone is very ill or has a mental illness – can they feel like they can bring their whole self to work? There is so much stigma in the workplace around mental health, so the presence of love would depend on the person's ability to show their vulnerability and feel that they can trust colleagues at work. For some people, it can hinder their ability to show their vulnerability.

Sometimes it can be quite painful to be loving – when you show your full authentic self. It will take time to introduce it into an organisation. You must be able to do it in a loving way too. There is an element of risk when you bring all of yourself into the workplace and there is a risk that people would reject you. It's very personal and it's very individual."

Sam Allen

"Sometimes I left my underpinning values from my personal life at home and just brought to work those learned behaviours probably constrained by function, constrained by organisation, a bit constrained by not coming from the perceived right background and so you tend to stick to the rules and not want to put a foot wrong. And then with hindsight, you realise that actually, if we all brought more of our genuine selves to work in a positive sense then that would be more beneficial, but you've got to feel safe to do that."

Sally Cabrini

As you journey up the road of self-acceptance, along that journey you notice and continue to gain from the deep and innate benefits of joy, a deep seated joy, the kind of joy that comes from your unconditional love for and acceptance of yourself. It gives you the freedom to connect with your own unique sense of purpose and contribution to the world and your organisation and in so doing. It frees you up genuinely to create an environment in which others can do the same. It also frees you up to demonstrate a love for and acceptance of others.

10. Demonstrating love

....

WHO YOU ARE BEING

You cannot help but be who you are. You are who you are and I am who I am and the problem we have in organisation and that leads to issues and challenges of all types, is the perceived and/or genuine inability to be ourselves. But even from that place of inconsistent and varying levels of acceptance, consciously or unconsciously that is generated by the perceived or genuine inability to be ourselves, the very nature of who we are as humans which includes the need to connect, to prosper and to have others prosper and which include acts of kindness, compassion, patience, self-restraint and discipline, inclusion, fairness, all these being some of the attributes of love still shine through. When these attributes are demonstrated and experienced, the impact on the giver can be as affirming as the impact on the recipient. It is the same impact that can be had in the world of work and organisation.

STICKS AND STONES

I learned in one of the very first management training workshops I attended in the early years of my career, that whatever words you uttered out of your mouth, the tone, volume and energy around them is what truly conveys the message you are sending. That, on top of the body language that accompanies your communication, is what really sends a message to the recipient and can be confirming or contradictory of what you say. Many organisations invest in communication training and coaching, preparing leaders at all levels for impact and effectiveness in front of various audiences from employee and colleague groups internally to stakeholders, shareholders and media externally. They are trained on hand gestures, the use of pause, eye contact, how to sit, how to stand, how to raise and lower the voice and so many other techniques which are great and wonderful. And when it is a formal and high stakes event, the words that are said are also carefully scrutinised to eliminate any hints of bias and misconception. The challenge is that these situations are often orchestrated, well known in advance and with ample time given to rehearse, prepare and anticipate. They are not the everyday life of work and organisation in which conversations and meetings both planned and unplanned happen. What is often forgotten is that words themselves have power and the conversations we have with others and with ourselves contain words. Some of the same words when said in a different language or understood in the native language of the recipient can have even more power than when heard in a second language. The combination of those words, especially when infused with emotion deliberately or non-deliberately conveyed, can have a piercing impact on the recipient or in other circumstances reveal your deepest most innermost beliefs and values to the person you are with.

Once upon a time I worked in an organisation where one of my roles included the recruitment and development of international high calibre people, and a key element of my role was having meetings with heads of departments on their resourcing needs in the short and long term. I remember one of those meetings in which the enthusiastic manager said to me, 'I'd really like to have some more people like the good Indians I already have in my team. When you have a good Indian, they can be really good'. As he said that, I raised my eyebrows and asked him 'Would you consider any good Nigerians too?' When what he had said dawned on him, he of course went bright red, coughed, spluttered and apologised. I let it go and chose to focus on the big picture with someone with whom I had a respectful and cordial relationship. The message was received in my question. My words also had power.

What we say and how we say it is a behaviour that is ingrained in us and although with the power of choice, practice and a genuine intention and motivation to change, we can change it. And some of that motivation to change or to reinforce what is good will come from taking the time to really understand your people and appreciating that not one cap fits all. When you demonstrate a genuine interest in another person and in who they say they are, it is a significant step in the direction of demonstrating love. Every person is individual. What you say to one person and that is welcome or accepted or not impacting, may be experienced differently and in an opposite way by another. It is remembering that not all people who have the same skin colour, or have the same age or any other similarity, think the same, feel the same and want the same things from life. Understanding what to say, how to say it and when to say and the impact it will have on your people as individuals requires the one common theme that the senior leaders I interviewed shared as they reflected in the ways they have in turn demonstrated love to others and that is the precious resource called time. It is a resource that is equally important to invest at home as it is in organisation and work.

"Sometimes I will have a particular project that I've been working on. My wife will have other projects – a few months ago she just wanted to say to me that she appreciated that what I was doing was important to me but that sometimes she would appreciate more of my involvement in what she was doing. It suddenly just dawned on me that what she was talking about was the importance of being present in relationship. It's all very well being dedicated to what you are doing but this reminded me that I needed to be better at positively making myself present in doing things together and planning other things and joint activities around the place. This is one little example of what I remember hearing my parents say about marriage - that it is something you constantly work at."

Mark Goyder

"Making conscious decisions on how you use your time can be an indication of love and it can be even in the small and mundane things. In the earlier days when I was in A&M and not long in the business and building the corporate practice which meant a lot of time outside of the office, even if there was no specific reason why I had to be in the office, I would always go into the office when I had time and I would always have my door open just because I wanted people to have the opportunity - whatever was on their mind - to just come and talk."

Lawrence Hutter

"The way I demonstrate love is that I take the time. What I do and particularly with my own management team, is I sit with them and I will go through not just the what but also the how. How are we doing? What would you like me to do more of? I saw this and I thought that - was I reading you wrong? or right? I would also spend time thinking about them - both as individuals and as a team. Also, when I talk to the organisation, I say look guys this is a great business and when things don't go well, I put my hand up. I would say what I regret but also try to encourage. To be honest. To say when I've made a mistake. It's not terminal. Being accessible and ensuring that people can see that."

Mark Scanlon

"In the same way as I've experienced it. It's been with an intention of being fair and as I reflect, I've extended less compassion as I've got more senior. People can be extremely demanding of your love and not necessarily return it and that sometimes can be quite tough so therefore there's been a bit of self-protection involved too, but sometimes, it's about ignoring that, that lack of reciprocity and persist because what does it cost you? It is about doing the right thing

For me there is home and there's work and I believe that if love is missing from one, then the other must supplement the one. For example, if you're going through a divorce, you are reliant on what love can give you at work, having to throw yourself into what you are doing day to day, so that you can have some semblance of the familiar and routine or structure in your life and that in a way is your work demonstrating love to you. The converse is also true. If you are going through a challenging time at work then love at home is what keeps you sane and gets you through it - for example, if you're made redundant you've got to have a support at home. I also learned at a very early age, that there are some people that require a lot of love and they can be quite demanding and selfish and therefore, as a leader at work you've got to learn to manage that and to protect yourself. To be able to love properly, you must also have self-care and take care of yourself."

Charlie Wagstaff

"I try to learn from what I've seen in others. I never treat individuals the same. Spending time to learn about new people. So for example, I have about 80 people in my team so every couple of weeks, I run a new starters lunch. We go out together about 6 of us and spend time getting to know each other. I never talk work but try to get to know the person as a person and give them the opportunity to get to know me as a person too. The key is never treating everybody the same. For example, a key individual in my team had been having a very tough time outside of work. My immediate reaction is to see to give him a couple of weeks off straight away, get him to go and focus on what is critically important at this moment without worrying about work. But in the conversation with him, he said to me - the worst thing you can do is to send me out of here and so I said to him, then you stay here. He said - because I need this stability; I need this normality and that was fine with me. But I also did reassure him and said that if at any time, you don't feel like you want to be here and you need to go, then you exit right and that was fine with him."

Naomi Gillies

WHAT YOU DO

Time is precious in every context we can think of or imagine. It is the one resource that has organisations stand or fall because it is the one resource that has the individuals that make up that organisation stand or fall. This is all because of how we invest the time and what we do with it that we have in life. The more the time we have available is used in demonstrating love through all the activities and tasks we carry out in the interest of our purpose and goals, the more we give room for the value of the active and operational presence of love to shine through. The types of things you can do are many and varied. They can also be influenced by your context and the purpose behind the interaction and the action and when the underpin is love the outcome will always be a good one. Sometimes you must have a difficult conversation and one with courage and good intent to support the individual.

"Also as a leader I've always tried to be tough, caring, honest and fair with my people, fighting for their rights upwards and outwards, I've never been shy of defending my team, wanting to nurture them, wanting to grow them and develop them as individuals. Also being honest when things weren't working out because I felt that was the caring thing to do. I remember years ago when I was at Grand Met talking to a guy who was clearly in the wrong job and treating him with respect and saying I know you were appointed before I joined the organisation, I believe you are in the wrong job but let me do everything I can to support you finding another role where you'd be happier and perform better. I did that from a caring nurturing perspective. It was tough but he was clearly shocked to have that feedback but was so grateful to have that conversation. Because it was honest and it was caring."

Louise Fisher

"What I've come to learn is that the biggest driver of success requires you to tap into the instincts and the preferences and the motivations of every individual. Sometimes this involves difficult decisions. I have, on a number of occasions, counselled people out of an organisation because the organisation was not a right fit for them. But such interventions need to be compassionate and dignified to be helpful to them and to the organisation and to help them understand that that was the right decision for them."

Paul McNamara

Other times you will want to give of yourself to demonstrate that you are a human being too. When as a leader you give of yourself, it's saying to your people that you care enough about them to show a little more of who you are

"I hope in everything I do, that I always remember to treat people as people and to be curious and not to assume that what's right for one person is right for another. There's stuff in what I do in my day job which is clearly about mobilising 80,000 people through the business and ensuring that they're in the shops at the right time and paid on time - I cannot get away from that. It comes with the job. But I always in everything I do, and in my own team want to be open, to share a lot to make sure that they just don't see me as the person who does this job and to know that I love dogs, I prefer gin to wine, or my idea of heaven on a Friday night is a copy of 'Hello' and a bar of chocolate.

I think it's important to give something more of yourself and to share who you are with others. Why would people give back to you, if you're not prepared to share some of who you are and what's important to you, so they understand you on a much more textured level?"

Tracey Killen

Taking the time to understand your people and each other including taking time away from the world of work together to relate as human beings will demonstrate that you care and that you and your people are more than the profit line on the bottom of the organisation's financial reports.

"At work, I've worked with people who have been here for years, I know them, I know their families, I know the highs and lows of their lives. We have a community and I feel part of that community. We have these thank you letters and thank you boards around the building where colleagues can share their thoughts and recognition. Now we took about 150 colleagues over to Malta a couple of years ago, and a couple met there and now they're engaged and they sent us - me and my wife

- a photo of them with a scan to show she's expecting a baby - now that to me is experiencing the love of a colleague - they didn't need to share that news with us but they chose to. That's amazing."

James Timpson

"A key part of my role is to develop others and this is fundamental to me as a leader and so if I believe in this then it leads me naturally down the path of wanting to really understand the people around me - their motivations, their needs, who they are people - what stresses and doesn't stress them, their family relationships and all of this demonstrates a sense of care and compassion."

Peter Cheese

The development of others and a genuine desire to see others win is a demonstration of love and when that desire remains present even when that success for others is unlikely to include you or determine your own success it is a demonstration of unconditional love.

"I mean it and I do a fair amount of demonstrating that I care. I walk around the office and take the time to speak to people. Also, that saying - 'if you really love something, you've got to be prepared to let it go' - rings true. In my business, we're going to have to go. It's the nature of our work at Tideway. So I try to do a fair amount of mentoring and coaching and quite often the best advice that people need is to be encouraged to leave and that's difficult when you're talking to one of your big hitters. You really do have to mean what you say. If the best thing for you to do now is to be somewhere else, then that's the only advice you can give and it has to be unqualified and unconditional."

Andy Mitchell

"I lead, raise and support leaders. I consider myself a leader of leaders, not just within the church space but also in the secular corporate environment. At a personal level I am committed to raising the next generation and at the family level, our house over the years has always been a refuge for people generally and especially young people. I remember years ago, when I was working on a consulting programme, we had to go through a process of trying to understand who we are and what makes us tick. We went through a battery of questions and there was one section where we had to articulate our personal vision. When I came to that section, even without thinking, I just wrote down, 'to help people become'. That's my personal vision – 'to help people become'. This is also the vision of the ministry that I lead and established back in 2013 which is to help people become all that God wants them to be. There is no greater joy than to see people realise their potential."

Emmanuel Mbakwe

Demonstrating love in organisation and indeed to others can be expressed in many ways and one underestimated way is silence. It is a willingness to be present, fully present with all your mind, body and thoughts with the person in front of you at that moment, whether that is someone in your family and values some of all of you or in your organisation who also values some of all of you there too.

"I'm always open. You can talk to me anytime. Anybody can talk to me. It doesn't matter who. A sales assistant - who may be very junior - can just come in and talk to me. It's about having an open ear and an open heart. Allowing people to come to me to raise issues but also know that I will not override the people immediately above them. It's respecting the fact that people just want you to listen and I make myself available for that."

Richard Eu

"The ability to listen is the biggest thing that you can do in the happiness and love space - having your ears open. If you have your ears open, you will hear what is going on. We have this agreed way of working in our organisation which is all about active listening - being in the room, being present, not turning up in the meeting and being on your iPad the whole meeting because if you do that, you can't learn what's going on. I remember one of my previous bosses - very senior person - in a meeting; he came in and he had a twisty and squeaky chair and he sat on it spinning around and making it squeak, so I grabbed the arm of the chair and said stop it. He looked at me and asked why. I said, you have people who are about to come in and present to us and you sitting on a spinning chair and spinning it around doesn't actually demonstrate that you're listening. He said 'but I am' and I said 'it doesn't look like it'. And he got it. It is important not just to listen, it is important too to demonstrate that you are listening. There is no way that you can demonstrate love if you don't listen and that by the way is everywhere. Not only at work but also outside of work and in all areas and stages of life."

Naomi Gillies

Life is real and the culture of any organisation in which there is a hierarchy real or perceived means that what individuals who are in leadership positions do, sends ripples right through the organisation. If you are at the top of your tree, your whisper will be heard loud. If you are therefore blessed to be in a senior position in your organisation's hierarchy, you have the opportunity to demonstrate love - a love that cares, that includes, that shares and that welcomes - in so many different ways that would serve both the recipients and you very well indeed.

"I also do awards. I do awards at the beginning of the year. We have four awards and one is from the Chief Executive and I do them around values. And I'm able to choose the person and the award for how people are. What surprises me is people and how absolutely over the moon they are. It doesn't matter who gets the award, I underestimate the effect it has on the individual and it is great to see."

Mark Scanlon

"Small acts of kindness. Making time for people. Listening. Recognition. I have a set of little cards in my desk and I have them ready to send them out to people. People that I spot that may need a bit of a lift or also to say thank you for things.

One of thing I've noticed is the ripple effect. I bought someone a mug. A small token. One of our nurses. I then noticed that in the hospital, under acts of kindness people started giving and getting mugs. We must be aware of the ripple effect. Something small can grant permission to others to do the same. When you do one thing, it can be paid back in multiples over ten times over to others!"

Sam Allen

WALKING THE TALK

All of this will however matter much less or not at all, if the intention from where you are coming and the motivation behind any of our actions is bereft of love or any of its attributes. It is the reason why actions that are experienced as loving and generous in one organisation may be experienced as ingenuine, manipulative and with suspicion in another. It therefore requires a willingness to be imperfect and a willingness to challenge yourself as an individual in the walk of love through your organisation. It is human to want to do well for yourself; it is human that others can irritate, frustrate and make us angry by their actions. It is therefore human that this can also show in our behaviours.

> "I've demonstrated to others by demonstrating those values that underpin love. I ask myself - have there been moments when I've put myself out there for other people? Have I been selfless? Have I been kind? Have I shown care for those people around me? In terms of what I've said and what I've done, have I shown that I valued the people around me because I respect them? Because I care for them? When you think about it, you demonstrate acts of love in everything you do. In every way, much more than you think - because you may not have started from a place where you say how do you define love but when you start to define it and you think about what love means to you, you realise that you, I, may do a lot of things during the day that demonstrate love."

> **Andrew Needham**

> "I've worked very hard to show those around me that I come from a place of love and that I offer genuineness and kindness. So what I do is that I offer myself and give of myself freely. I own my mistakes and I'm not reserved in apologising. I don't think that you can over apologise. As long as you do it in the right way and for the right reason and at the right time. I also listen. I listen and hear what my people have to say. When someone is new to the office, I get up and go to that person and I offer them a big smile and I make cups of tea for my colleagues if they've been in meetings for a long time. I try to do a variety of things that show I care. I reward my staff out of my own pocket. I bring gifts when I go on holiday. I write personalised cards to say thank you to people individually for what they've done for the company. At Christmas time, I sign a card and put

a lot of thought and I make sure that I personalise it to that specific individual and say why I've written it and I always put in one sentence at least to say why that person is special. If I go into the kitchen and if there are dirty dishes in the sink, I wash them. I do the most menial tasks. I don't do it because I want to show off, I do them because I genuinely care and I genuinely love. I also smile as often as I can."

Ingrid Tennessee

"A lot of times people show they care mainly for the brand or for the bottom line. In Leadership however, we should have compassion for those that have less; love for those that are struggling be they in our teams or not and we should reach out to them. In sincerity."

Sam Aiyere

"I think this is very difficult in a work context…. Perhaps as a foundation if you are disposed to be more open, you do start to see through your experience that there are many different ways to be successful and there are many different attitudes that are okay and can still get people where they want to get to. So, moving away from being rigid about how people do stuff is important. It needs to be easier to have genuine conversations focussing on being in this together and being clear that great contribution is not about seniority. I wish I'd known some of this 20 years ago - maybe I would have made different choices. Hindsight is a marvellous thing."

Sally Cabrini

THE OTHER 'F' WORD

One of the biggest ways in which unconditional love and acceptance can be demonstrated in life and organisations is in times of adversity, injured feelings and egos, mistakes that impact other people badly and in times of significant change and turbulence. When expectations are unmet, promises forgotten and agreements broken. That attribute of unconditional love that can be demonstrated is called forgiveness. Like love, it is another word that is so rarely used in organisation and yet so much an integral element of unconditional love. It is difficult to demonstrate love if you are unable to demonstrate forgiveness. Like love, it is often an attribute that is reserved for family and personal relationships but is one that is so needed to have flourish in organisation. Forgiveness is the ability to genuinely let things go, to believe in the good in the other person and to demonstrate that that other person is accepted for all of who they are. That they are not their behaviour. And especially in the rough and tumble of organisation life, where decisions are made hurriedly and people's wishes and opinions are left out without malice and feelings and emotions bruised the resentment that sets in and which in turn can lead eventually to organisational dysfunction comes from a place of unforgiveness though wrapped up in all kinds of management and corporate speak. Forgiveness means letting go, moving forward whilst learning from the pain or mistake, without being held hostage by it and this applies at organisation, team and individual levels. It applies in communities and I daresay, it applies too at national levels.

So if there is one attribute of love that you can start to demonstrate, the impact of which because it is an attribute of love, will be extraordinary, it is that attribute of forgiveness.

11. LOVE, ORGANISATION AND COMMUNITY

....

THE IMPACT ON YOUR wellbeing and the wellbeing of your people of giving back and demonstrating love unconditionally, in the communities in which you live and operate should not be underestimated. Scientific research as evident in several publications all over the world promote the benefits, emotionally, mentally and physically for the individual and therefore the organisation of supporting and helping others. The Harvard University Study of Adult Development which began in 1938 and still is ongoing today reveals that social and human connection, though not the only one, is a key factor in the experience of happiness and health in human beings. A way of enabling purposeful social interaction for your people is providing opportunities for them to contribute to the wellbeing and the prosperity of the communities in which they live and in which your organisation operates locally and internationally.

BENEFITS TO YOUR PEOPLE

There are many different and diverse programmes and initiatives that you and your people can get involved in to support your communities. When you do this, you give your people the opportunity to try new things safely and without huge risks, because they will be doing things they love and things that others want from them. This alone creates a positivity that is infectious and carries back into the workplace. There is a benefit too in the development of your people because of the skills they will acquire and return to the organisation. Their leadership capabilities of contribution, responsibility, accountability and love will grow. And on top of that, when your people feel great about themselves, they are more likely to perform better. This means that encouraging your people to contribute, to volunteer and to demonstrate love to the community will in turn contribute to their performance and productivity. The benefits do not however stop there. Volunteering and giving back which is the leadership attribute of contribution can also facilitate the elimination of dysfunction within teams and heal rift, distance and division between people. When a group of people from the same organisation are set a task of giving back and contribution on a community initiative or project, that becomes the focus and emerging will be an appreciation of where they are in life versus others, and the value of working together for the good and progress of others.

> "The social part of work is really important. Many relationships are established and nurtured in the office, the connections people have in sport activities or non-work interests with other colleagues is incredibly powerful. This fits very naturally into community efforts whether it is funding or supporting local initiatives. Giving time to broader priorities gives a much wider sense of purpose and achievement to a team whilst bringing great benefits to society."
>
> **Paul McNamara**

> "This is about being bespoke in your thinking and being in touch with what is going on in your community. What a community wants and believes in one area where you trade may be different to another area. So what people in your community want in High Holborn in the South East of

England would be different to what people in your community want in Willoughby which is in the North of England and it is paying attention to the specific needs of the people in your community that matters.

Also it is about appreciating that as an organisation, your community can really teach you something. We have a lot of partners who volunteer with The Samaritans for example and that takes a lot of skill. It develops your ability to listen and even though it is to help volunteer with them, the ability to listen is a key and much welcome skill in our organisation."

Naomi Gillies

When you enable and encourage your people to demonstrate love in their communities, your organisation becomes one that is not only a great place to work because of the vicarious benefit of your people feeling great about themselves, you also become more attractive in the eyes of others. People will want to work with you and for you and stakeholders will be working together to enable your success because your success would mean their success and the success of others and beyond the material, of the people that they in turn love and are responsible for.

"An organisation that operates from the basis of love will be a beacon. It will attract a following and the community will see it as a shining example of what is good and what is real community spiritedness. A happy workforce would mean happy families, and this would impact on the quality of life in the community and there would be a huge mutual respect between the community and the organisation. It would also mean happier kids at schools and you would have schools that have students who have aspirations to work for that organisation in the future."

Ingrid Tennessee

"At one level it is recognising what is the responsibility of an organisation - the responsibility of the organisation is having a duty of care to its people. Today we have the multiple stakeholder in the business and so it is not only the shareholder it is so much more than that. The stakeholder is the people who work for you, your customers, your suppliers, the environment and also the society and communities in which you work. These are really important dimensions. And business recognises that their responsibility impacts all those stakeholders. You can treat your supply chain with compassion; you can treat your communities in which you work with compassion and show that you want to be a responsible employer; you want to demonstrate that you can be inclusive no matter where your people come from - you want to encourage, to support you and to give opportunity. So today, being a responsible business is being one who understands all of its stakeholders and understands its role in terms of behaviour and actions towards all those communities. A single-minded focus on one particular stakeholder - i.e. the financial stakeholder drives all sorts of consequences and can lead to compromise on all other factors that are just as important.

Extending the notion of love and compassion beyond the four walls of organisation into community and society demonstrates that this is an organisation that understands its responsibility within and to its community and the society it serves."

Peter Cheese

BENEFITS TO YOUR COMMUNITIES

An organisation is the sum of all of its people and if it is your organisation, it is a sum of all of your people and that includes you. Contributing to community is simply contributing to the wellbeing and the progress of others be they individuals or organisations, and at the root of it is the willingness to do it for absolutely nothing in return. It is to do it because it's the right thing to do. Love is a human need and gift and should be given without condition, or with the covert intent to have your organisation be applauded in the press, with one blind eye turned in the direction of the significant sums of money that can be swept out of one country by irresponsible organisations and into another because of advantageous tax breaks. The demonstration of love to community is best experienced and dished with warmth and should be unconditional and without expectation, driven out of compassion, a care and a depth of desire to have your people simply be kind and loving. Individually and collectively.

"This is about having soul. Progressively people are saying I desperately need to be part of this place and in that regard, I want this place to be connected and real and I want this place to also be a player in society. I don't want this office to pollute or this factory to pollute. I want to feel that this office is usable for others and not just for work things. We have assets here - how can we share them? And once you start that journey and people at all levels can come up with ideas and if there's an openness and all are interacting and all interconnecting, then we'll find a way to be more and more into our society. Society is the people themselves and we are the society. Some of our people live nearby. It's really important that leading organisations are a new type of aristocracy that can set the tone and climate of opinion and attitude in the world. People will look what the leading companies are doing. We must be aware that we are looked at and that we can inspire both ways downwards and upwards and it's a privilege and it's a privilege to be used and leveraged for good things. Now you don't have to do it, but what a pity it would be if you didn't. It would be an incomplete story."

John Mangan

"It can impact hugely. If you take the example of Bourneville or Olivetti - Mr Olivetti built a town for the employees - you can see how it impacted their communities at the time. If you look at the concentration of wealth and you look at the disparity of that across the world, it's only getting worse and people are getting left behind and businesses are not taking the responsibility of what's around them. People do want to work. There's a dignity in labour and a dignity in doing a job. In the SE of England for example, we continue to increase the population and the infrastructure is creaking; the cost of living and property is going up. Imagine though, that if there was a different level of corporation tax in the North East and businesses were incentivised or themselves chose to support their communities- help the miners and the ship builders those who are redundant to get back to work and provide opportunity for dignity, the spirits of people in the community will go up. So in my view, love can influence an organisation's behaviour in community."

Mark Scanlon

"It will result in a recognition that we are all connected and that we all share in the fruits of our labours directly or indirectly. I think that one of the things that is causing the backlash with corporates in the world today is that they are sometimes unintentionally disconnected from the communities in which they live. If you're in a physical place the people that come and work for you in that place, that's what they identify with. And because of the way global tax works, the value of what's getting done somewhere is extracted out of that place and ends up registered somewhere else in the world that is completely unrelated to that and that's where they pay tax. And so at a very simple level, systems have been set up that allow people not to do that. So it's putting nothing back into that place. And this is not right."

Norman Pickavance

"Love is an extension of what we do and who are in The Partnership. And a lot of time organisations responsibility programmes are based on how much time is spent by their people with charities and in digging over gardens for people which is great - and there is more that can be done.

I believe though that a big organisation's primary responsibility in the community is to create employment and to create good work and through good work you offer people opportunities and by offering opportunities, people can stretch into space they didn't think they could stretch into and they can create income and wealth for their families and through that virtuous circle, they can begin to offer wealth and opportunities for their family and community that would not have been possible before or may not have had.

I remember well the behaviours in the past of organisations like Cadbury's and Unilever with Port Sunlight and I know that globalisation has made it more challenging today and there are huge geographics but ultimately it is about thinking and holding dear that in the local communities in which you operate, your primary responsibility is to create work.

So if you come back to the notion of love and care - that same love that you feel for the people in your organisation you absolutely must extend to the community in which you are based and the reason why you should do so is because that is where your employees live."

Tracey Killen

"I think it's a circular thing. If you work for an organisation that is clear about its purpose and its place in society and its social purpose, you're more likely to love that organisation. There is a wonderful example of once when I opened a refurbished Marks and Spencer's store and we had put Swift boxes for birds under the eaves because we don't put panel roofs on things anymore and so Swifts don't have anywhere to live and so in they come in from North Africa with nowhere to live. So we put up Swift boxes for them which in the context of a multimillion pound business a £35 per unit Swift box is attention only and there was a sales adviser who'd worked in that store for 15 years and she was part time and we did the opening and she came up to me as the director and that may well have taken some courage but she came up to me and out of all the things we did the one thing that she singled out was the swift boxes - she said to me 'I'd just like to say that I'm just so impressed with what we've done. I thought thank you very much - no mention of nice new fridges or the customer toilets - she said the bird boxes we've put up are just amazing and they say a lot about this organisation. I'm on holiday next week, but I'm going to come in everyday to monitor them and to see if we get occupancy and I'm so proud!" And what that kind of connectivity and connection with the brand and the company that she worked for would give you - I don't know. But I think it's priceless and can only be to the benefit of the company and how it's viewed by its community.

That sense of purpose, community and doing the right thing by your purpose and by your community - that sense is intrinsically linked with love."

Richard Gillies

It is clear that the impact of an organisation demonstrating love in its community can be significant for the organisation and the community. And when you think of international organisations, global organisations and the potential impact they can have in the communities in which their people live and in which they operate, the feeling of hope and excitement cannot help but be felt. It can break down barriers, promote cultural and cross-cultural understanding, deal with the negative effects of climate change and meet the basic needs of the poorest communities all over the world. A desire to help community will impact society and encourage way of working that drives collaboration and helpfulness between organisations as purpose, society and humanity become more important than profit and the bottom line. Competition lines become blurred as a mindset of win- win for us and for all starts to emerge. The World Economic Forum (WEF) in its published article 'Why the future of well-being isn't about money' in February 2019 states that even for governments around the world, if wellbeing was their main focus their resources would be allocated wisely and that by 2050 the impact on life expectancy and wellbeing of the human population will be much more affected positively by non-material factors than the material. The article says: "If human well-being is the main goal of governments, their resources would be more wisely spent based on what really matters most for human experience."

What I conclude from this is the important role too that government agencies as organisations can play in the demonstration of love to the communities in which the people they are responsible for, live. It is not only in the allocation of resources or in the nature of the big decisions that they make, it will be in the way they encourage the organisations that operate within their communities to behave responsibly and with love. When governments and the people who lead them and make the big decisions themselves summon the courage to walk in love then it makes it easier for others to do the same. Establishing the Global Goals for Sustainable Development is an excellent step and in the right direction and actively and proactively encouraging organisations of all sizes and leanings to adopt them would accelerate the impact they will have not only on community but also on society and indeed our world.

But as in all things, someone has got to take that first step or set the example so that others can follow and that someone can be you and me. Why not? When we think, really think of what is at stake and what love can truly and genuinely do, there is a possibility that moving now and doing this, can increase the likelihood of there being a beautiful world for our children and their children to live in, a world in which there possibly would be less war and conflict.

"I think it comes down to the personal example of the people at the top and in fact sacrifice - one of the most amazing demonstrations of love in business is the story of Tata and the Taj Mahal terrorist shootings. When I was in India some time ago, I talked to one of the HR Managers of the Taj Group and he told me that the Taj group of hotels have always recruited not from colleges so much as from out of the towns and townships outside the major conurbation. They invested 18 months in their training as opposed to the standard 3 months or so. In this training they emphasised that it is always the customer's interest that was put first. And there are these eyewitness accounts of survivors of that terrible night of November 26th, 2009 when the terrorists attacked there were these young kids - some of them just 18 and 19 gathering to help. They put their own lives at risks, they formed human chains, and some of them got shot, they kept their mobile phones on to communicate with the national security guard and so on. This was an example of sacrifice - an example of love from an organisation to its community and to society."

Mark Goyder

"It's significant. You have to build a business that, at its core, has to create that loving environment. So when you talk about your purpose and what you're trying to do, it has to be core to the business. The core of TangoTab is that when you eat a hungry person also eats. It was the reason we built the company. It is a commercial for-profit business - though its purpose is about creating a sustainable business model for scalability - our purpose for the business is much higher than making money. We support many non-profit businesses and we give back to the community. In the case of TangoTab, our purpose extends beyond money to be able to do what we want to do in the world, we need to be a successful and strong business. Also, when you embed the wellbeing and the welfare of others as core to the business, we find too that the business grows so much faster. In our case this is the experience."

Andre Angel

"When I set up HeadBox, my wife was very much involved with me for a short period of time early on, from the inception and one of the things that she influenced in those very early days was our social mission. She wanted HeadBox to put a stake in the ground around homelessness. It is so shocking that in London there's so much homelessness - when you come out of a tube, you're stepping over someone who doesn't have a roof over their head and we at HeadBox are in the business of space. We are making money from providing space to corporations who want really cool spaces and want to be able to find them and to book them really easily in that moment and at that time. So our social mission should also be about helping to provide space to people who don't have it. When we first started out, we were not able to do that but now we've set up a partnership with St. Mungo's and already I feel the power of thinking about homelessness and what can HeadBox do to help rid the UK and every city that HeadBox sets up in, of homelessness. That call to arms that our social mission is driving is very empowering and at the heart of it is love."

Andrew Needham

"For example, we've started a journey with Lancôme called write your future. It's helping girls across the world and here in the UK to overcome illiteracy. We are doing it with the National Literacy Trust. We want to help hundreds and hundreds of girls who currently cannot read to read - not because of what it's going to do for us but for what it will do for the world. It's because we care."

John Mangan

"Any organisation or community that is driven by love will be most effective. I refer to the first century Gospel church as an outstanding example. That's because love is transformational. It changes thinking, it changes attitudes and it transforms behaviour. It moves us and people from selfishness to selflessness; it moves us from competition to collaboration. That's because, as we read in 1st Corinthians 13, 'love never fails.'"

Emmanuel Mbakwe

An organisation is a person. It has a head; it has a heart and it has a gut. It can be healthy and it can be unhealthy and this can occur as a result of its own doing. Just like any other person. The good will or not that it has towards its people and if underpinned by love can impact a world far beyond its physical boundaries and geographies. The Domino effect is real and one person's action and therefore one organisation's action at any level can without care and love impact negatively the lives of others in parts of the world the names of which the people in that organisation can never pronounce. It is the reason why problems around child labour, modern day slavery, atrocities against the environment and at the hand of man and organisation occur. If love were present and its attributes allowed, nurtured and encouraged to flourish, the material and financial gain in organisations no matter their status will be significant and much more significant and beneficial for humanity would be the quality of the legacy they leave behind and in existence much long after they themselves has ceased to exist.

12. LOVE AND THE FUTURE OF WORK

....

ONE THING THAT WE KNOW about the future of anything at all is that it will involve change and a requirement to change and adapt; to grow and evolve and to continuously learn if we want to make the most of that future when it arrives. The future of work and, indeed, the future of anything can be anticipated with dread, fear and resistance or it can be anticipated with hope and excitement and an eagerness to experience the wonderful discoveries it contains. The leadership attribute of accountability comes to mind here because it means a willingness to stand by the choices that we make as the future beckons and the consequences, intended or not, that those choices may produce.

WHAT THE FUTURE HOLDS

The influence on the future of work and organisation of accelerated developments in technology, artificial intelligence and the emerging nature and forms these will take is significant. The concern and excitement plus the desire to ensure that the opportunities it brings are not missed is evidenced by the plethora of events, discussions, consultant articles, government bodies and organisations, profit and non-profit established and taking place across the world on local, national and global levels. This season is currently described by some people as the fourth industrial revolution.

The way work is conducted in and around organisations will be impacted as machines and robots take on some or all of certain jobs currently reserved for humans, with some industries being impacted more than others. On top of this, organisations are finding themselves comprising the most diverse in terms of age and generation demographics than ever before. People are living longer and working longer thanks to the advancements in medical and health technology. We learn, too, of the ageing and stabilising populations in the west and the youthful and expanding population in other parts of the world like Sub Saharan Africa. Artificial Intelligence, the availability and access to immense data that decision makers across different professions in industry and organisation, means that there is an ability to tailor and personalise services, goods and products to the end user that has exploded the notion of complexity to new and different dimensions. On the one hand there are mega malls, shopping centres, supermarkets and mega online retailers, supermarkets and shopping centres and on the other hand, there are personalised offers, combinations of offers produced for the individual. In the home there are intelligent machines too as appliances increasingly have the ability to detect and proactively offer what is needed for each inhabitant and individual in the home. Marketing language has evolved from shouting at the consumer and end user to a language of listening as customers and clients no longer visit the internet but indeed live there as global platforms of connection, learning and education, health improvement and diagnosis and goods acquisition of all kinds move to the virtual world. Indeed, I remember a time when a mobile phone was a public telephone box on the corner of a street with a coin slot that took different sized coins depending on whether my call was going to be local or international. I remember also a time when that mobile phone became much smaller than a telephone box but was a box the size of a small brief case lugged around by its proud looking owner. I am sure you can also go down memory lane.

The implications of the future of work on the world of work and organisation are varied and diverse depending on the industry you're currently working in, your propensity and willingness to reinvent yourself and learn different things and of course, your attitude and approach to change and uncertainty. The way we work is changing fast and will continue to change as technology allows for access to information, dialogue and collaborative working across geographies. It means that blended organisations will continue to emerge as a new type of independence and autonomy is afforded. Where we work is changing fast too as advances enable the opportunity for more flexible working and the ability to organise patterns and structures of work around the individual's life stages and wishes, thereby contributing to the advancements in equality, diversity and wellbeing. The way we learn is also fast changing with the emergence of different and varied technologies that enable immediate and instant learning, distance and virtual meeting places, classrooms and conference rooms with downloadable programmes and applications that enable learning on the go. Our clothes are also becoming intelligent as are our homes. Wristwatches double for compasses and compasses double as navigators, movie players and health monitors. The end of what advances in technology, artificial intelligence and the various formats and forms that emerge can do and will do are as far and wild as the imagination can produce. What I love about the technology in particular are the opportunities for the development, investment and management of relationships they afford. The ability for family members spread across the world to connect, to see each other and to laugh, talk and share stories with each other across time zones and geographies is beautiful. I currently live in the UK, my siblings in Nigeria, my nieces and nephews in the United States and my in-laws spread across Germany and Japan, and at the press of a few buttons, a couple of minutes waiting time, we can all be online.

"In the age of WhatsApp, you have a situation where my parents in law are pinging messages back and forth to my nine year old - a huge age gap - and they are relating quite nicely sending jokes and messages along with smileys - this is what technology is allowing us to do - linking us together and enabling us to relate and to express care and love across generations."

John Mangan

The rediscovery of childhood friends made years ago and the knock-on effects of this that technology and virtual platforms afford are priceless. Relationships of different kinds, platonic and romantic, common interest groups, communities and tribes all allowing a connection and a sharing and expression of perspective never before possible. And for the independent worker anywhere in the world looking for a buyer of their own unique goods, products and services, the world becomes a global village for them and a place to which they can communicate and market right from the privacy of their own home. In addition to that, the opportunity for new business ideas and emerging entrepreneurs to connect with investors in different parts of the world has made it possible for individuals to share their creations and ambitions with as wide and varied an audience as possible. Authors in one part of the world are able to find illustrators, publishers, editors and transcribers in other parts of the world, engage with them, commission them and produce the end product either with help or directly themselves. The number of options and the power of choice available to individuals and people in all stages of life and of all ages has exploded and will continue to do so; with no end in sight.

GIVE ME PATIENCE. NOW.

What has risen and continues to rise alongside the advancements in technology, AI, machine learning data accessibility and information sharing is the demand for access, response, feedback and delivery at lightning speed. Everything happens at the touch of a finger, the press of a button, a swipe to the left or right, a voice command and the movement or glance of an eye. Competition in all shapes and sizes now includes how fast, quick, brief and cheaply products, services and offerings can be delivered to the end user. Individual influencers across different media platforms can influence the growth or downfall of a brand or product at the stroke of a virtual pen and based on a very personal experience. And in the world of work and organisation the implications manifest themselves in virtual classrooms, bite sized learning, mobile applications to deliver messages on performance, employee opinions, quick tips and 'how to's' on wellbeing and personal health. These are also delivered through the same devices through which enormous files and documents containing reading material that must be mastered before virtual board meetings and conference rooms, emails from colleagues and superiors requesting confirmation and submission of proposals agreed are also transmitted. So the human being; that individual has a large cocktail of demands, personal aids and information portals to access and also is barraged with a plethora of pop-ups, covert and overt sales pitches from all kinds of consumer platforms, peddling products that his or her digital footprint have indicated will be welcome. At any time of the day or night. And in a world and industrial age where life is lived out loud for all to see and private lives, personal turmoils, celebrations and every experience that lies between pure joy and absolute despair that you can imagine can be accessible to strangers the potential for loneliness, stress, depression, anxiety and all things that draw down the energy of the individual increases. And these are human beings and individuals who are your colleagues, your consumers and customers, your clients your friends, your family, people in your community, your society and your world.

LOVE STILL COUNTS

What is so beautiful about humanity is that no matter what changes, developments, revolutions and evolutions happen around us, at our very core is who we are. We know that in the world of work, many of the jobs and roles that exist today will become extinct in the future. What we do not know is all the forms and shapes the jobs and roles of the future will have. They will emerge of course and organisations, whatever shapes they are in will have to be ready and adapt. The recognition of the human behind the machine is evident in the nature of the skills and capabilities various bodies, think tanks and international organisations are advocating as critical to our survival and ability to thrive as the future marches towards us.

According to the World Economic Forum (WEF), there are ten skills we will need as human beings to survive the rise of automation. In my view, six of the ten - complex problem solving, critical thinking, creativity, emotional intelligence, judgement and decision making and cognitive flexibility - will function consistently at their best when the individual is working in an environment in which he or she feels safe and secure and feels great about who they are. The other four - people management, service orientation, coordinating with others and negotiation - can only be really effective when carried out by individuals and leaders who in themselves feel secure, feel great about who they are, are operating from a place of acceptance and an intention of win-win.

This is why love counts and will continue to count. The greatest need and gift of the human being remains the same. And, the gift, need, and value of love in organisation to the individual, the team and to the organisation as a whole also remain the same. The world of science and neuroscience aided by advancements in technology, continues to confirm this. You also could argue that this is why there is today, a welcome and increasing, though not fast enough openness and willingness by influencers and leaders in organisation at all levels to explore the potential value of love and the difference it can bring. This is because with all the benefits, developments and advances for the human race the fourth industrial revolution and its successor may bring, alongside it can be significant disadvantages if we don't take care. And that care is the support that is put in place to enable members of our workforce and community to adapt to the new and different and to acquire different skills that enable their independence and continued ability to provide for themselves and those for whom they are responsible.

"One of the things is understanding the value that we all get from society of the fact that people do work, have valuable work and are able to work and the self-worth that comes from having a job, providing for yourself and your family. That is probably one of my underpinning and strongest values - that is if people have work, it enables them to earn money, it enables them to live their lives, support their children and this is where self-esteem can come from and that is really important. I don't think as a society we understand this or believe this or take it to our hearts as much as we should. That's the first challenge. People assume that an organisation will benefit from doing without their people without understanding what that means for us all as society.

Having said that, we cannot hold back the tide so there needs to be dialogue within an organisation that says while you can do that with technology - do you really want to? Is there really such a big benefit? And what would you lose by doing that?

The other thing is that we need to recognise that people do not have and will not have one type of work forever. So, we need to recognise that people can learn to do things differently no matter how old they are. My mum is in her nineties and very independent, 5 years ago, we went to her home at Christmas and she'd bought herself a tablet - which she wanted to have set up for her. Bear in mind that she never learned how to use a mobile phone. She has become increasingly hard of hearing and she wanted Facebook and email to be able to stay in touch – to keep connected. Now she stays in touch with all of us who live in all different places using this new technology. She learned because it was a real benefit to her! So, where people have a need they will adapt and we need to be ready to help them. What we should do and can do and if we had a more caring environment is to support people in upskilling themselves and helping them learn to do new things and without focusing on age. In a more "loving" environment, you would be thinking ahead and perhaps you wouldn't be so judgemental about who can re-train or learn new skills. You would assume that everyone can learn. You would also find that individuals would be willing to learn new things and to pick up new skills because at the heart of it in a more positive environment, they would feel more valued as human beings."

Sally Cabrini

"All of the indications are that the world of work in 10 years' time will be very different in many places. But I don't think all organisations will change - Entrepreneurial organisations with smaller numbers of people e.g. 100 or so may not need to change because in my experience these smaller organisations already feel like a family and are more agile and innovative. Technology investments can be made on a much smaller scale. These organisations are the heartland of the UK. Larger organisations who have to invest in technology to keep their costs down or to be ahead of the curve in terms of innovation and technology or to disrupt something would be impacted and they may need to reorganise. No, if a more caring feeling, leadership exists in an organisation then going through that transformation, and going through that change, their people would know much earlier on in the lifecycle of that company that 'gosh my job won't exist in five years' time and if I'm going to keep my job, my company's offering to reskill me now, because they care enough about me to help me prepare for the future and that might mean I have to go to night school, or it might mean I have to take a day off work to go and work somewhere else'. So it's the early engagement with people and explaining what will change; helping those people to feel comfortable about that change by demonstrating that you're investing in them now to be ready so that in five years' time, it isn't a load of redundancies, you would have eased your people into the new world, a new role a new way of working and have done that with respect and recognition for the values of your people, the contributions they've made and therefore you want to continue to grow them, to nurture them and to develop them. Now this needs forward thinking HR functions, forward thinking CEOs and forward-thinking CFOs to create the investment to do that."

Louise Fisher

"Technology can provide opportunities. We are not an organisation with a huge pyramid. Technology will however change certain things happen in a way that will challenge organisations - for example, audit - this will be an area that will be completely transformed by technology. As different parts of professional services become reshaped by technology, career paths will change and this will be an interesting challenge for business leaders to make sure that they can lead their organisations in a way that enables their people to adapt to the change and love will have a role to play here."

Lawrence Hutter

"This might end up being the only thing that's left. Let's be clear, Technology is going to make such a change in the world of work that we haven't seen or experienced yet. Therefore love may and will become more and more critical in the way we enable people to change to grow, to develop and do different things. I see too that there's less desire for material wealth and more desire for experience wealth and more of a sense of belonging and purpose and so on and this is where love and its importance will play a part."

Charlie Wagstaff

"Someone once told a story in a speech - before the industrial revolution, education systems were really based on our hands because the jobs were all about labour and were manual, so you would learn to be a farmer and you would learn from farmers how to grow. Then with the industrial revolution, we started to learn about jobs not really done through hands but with thinking – how to build machines, how to tinker with them and how to work them and the rise the service industry and then ultimately technology and how you think through programming. Our education systems therefore went from how we think about our hands to how we support and nurture the head and thinking about things. I think we are in the midst of the beginning of an epic revolution. Our education systems are going to have to change again. We will see robots doing so many more of the jobs we currently do and so what are we going to focus on is what robots cannot do. They cannot negotiate, they cannot build relationships, they can't be citizens or have that deep emotional connection, they cannot provide pastoral care and so for me that's the interesting thing. I hope we will see a move in our education systems to focus on our hearts because that's where we really need to encourage people to operate. So it's from hands to head to heart. And this is what I'm interested in seeing this in education systems and it will flow through to business. But in the interest of not being binary, yes we need to activate our hearts more, we cannot ignore the other powers we have which are in our hands and in our heads. It's like walking and chewing gum at the same time. We need to have hands, head and heart working together but what we really need to focus on now is how we enhance and harness the power of our hearts."

Charmian Love

And even through a change and transformation that an organisation's leadership may need to go through and at the same time, support and enable all of their people to go through the same change, ensuring a safe landing at their various outcomes, the application of technology can be deployed to great use at whatever stage of change the organisation is in.

"I think it's got a massive advantage. If people are just going to use tech and AI to take out the work that people do and replace what they do with process, then love has an opportunity and an advantage. If a computer says I love you - it doesn't mean much!

As technology and businesses change quickly, what we are finding is that old fashioned values of love, kindness, and sitting down and talking to someone has a bigger value. Because not many people do it anymore, so it differentiates you. Also, it feels good. People need to feel valued. They need to have that human contact."

James Timpson

It can support initiatives that focus on the wellbeing of individuals and demonstrate to your people that they are at the heart of everything you are and do.

"I think it's using the technology as much as possible and resources which support the advancement and implementation of a love based approach. If for example, as I'm sitting at my computer all day, it would be great to have a message that pops up and says 'Ingrid, have you taken a break today?' we sit at our laptops all the time and so you have adverts that pop up so wouldn't it be great that we had adverts that tuned into the wellbeing needs of your people. Maybe an advert that says, 'laugh group is starting now' and so on. Why not? It would be great too to be able to skype into short talks on teams and wellbeing, on leadership right there at your desk but in a way that serves each individual need."

Ingrid Tennessee

It can close gaps between individuals who are generations apart and at the same time working together, whilst building bridges in places where before these were absent.

"One of the implications of AI and technology is quite immediate - sharing and helping. Digital progress and evolutions have had the fantastic effect on one specific thing

- forcing entire generations to face into humanism. What's happening in the world is changing so fast and there is a generation that have grown up in this world and have only known lightning speed and people are realising that instead of being the traditional village elders who knew everything, those wanting to survive in today and tomorrow's world are having to bend over to their children and say can you help me and are having to engage in reverse mentoring. And in this upward mentoring, there is a re-joining of age and an erasing of age division and so the digital age is actually helping the younger generation have a teaching mentality and helping the older generation to come down from how big and important they are and to share, learn and do things together in a way that was not possible before."

John Mangan

Indeed, the future of work in organisation makes the value of love and what it can bring all the more important to our ability to thrive, to be future proof and to be resilient.

"It is super critical. A focus on a more loving approach is critical. We are seconding people to the Samaritans and I want for us to work with the Samaritans so that we can build for retail as an industry and for our business a really brilliant listening culture - because we are in a sector of 3 million people that will be 2 million people within a couple of years; because a lot of the jobs and basic work will be taken away due to AI and technology. We are being forced to cut our costs and there is no way out of it - this vice that we are gripped in. It is difficult for us to manage between the march of technology and the march of how people are choosing to shop. So all we know is that we are in a low pay, low skills sector, where we have got to find a way of developing more skilled and adaptive people, and are going to have to find ways of competing differently, we're going to have to be really light on our feet because all we really know is that life is going to be different. We haven't even figured out yet what those differences might look like and what they might be. We've got a lot of people in our sector who will be frightened and scared and unsure about what the future means and will be worried for their work. Although can't control the forces that we are operating in, we can choose to ensure as much care and as much information as possible is available to our people and make ourselves informed and informative. At the heart of this is the care and the love and the concern for all of our people. So, let's create a fantastic listening organisation. We should also be the sector that listens. We cannot fix lives, but we can create the space for listening. And we should be better at that than anybody else. The power of the individual is in being heard and in being heard you create and enable choice and control. This is a demonstration of love and its criticality to the future of work."

Tracey Killen

Love will be the one thing that differentiates one organisation from another and sets you apart from the competition and ensures that you survive this world of constant, rapid and uncertain change.

"I think that love should and will be the differentiator. As we move along with technology we become less and less human. But what differentiates us from the machine is emotion. A machine may be able to react in a certain way that looks like emotion, but living things are able to actually feel and express real emotion. So, as we move along and we talk about the skill sets that we need to survive and to cope with the fourth industrial revolution, it has to be to do with what and who we are as humans. The service industry for example, will develop even more - even though people can go and shop online - but it doesn't mean that you cut yourself off from human interaction. Therefore, skills that we will need to build for the future workforce will be skills that have to deal with human emotions and one of these emotions is love.

Companies that succeed in the future will be the ones that can tap into the human emotions and develop the organisation's ability to love rather than developing technical skills because everyone will have technical skills and have access to the same knowledge so the level at which you compete has to go into more the emotional side of things and the more creative side of things. In the past, the guy who knew how to read and write was way ahead! It was to do with knowledge. But as this gap is closing up, how you will differentiate yourself will be on connectivity - emotional connectivity and this is where love comes in."

Richard Eu

For love itself to be that differentiator which when allowed will be the biggest and most positively impactful organisation and leadership capability, it must itself be embodied by the individuals in leadership and positions of responsibility and decision making around the deployment and application of all that the future of technology and the fourth industrial revolution have to offer.

"I am convinced that not only AI, but also other technologies will develop regardless whatever we say or think. But technologic innovation is not enough to change our cultural paradigms and cultures. If at the same time we redesign the economy and the genetics of organisations, then I am confident technology will become an enabling tool for the good."

Pedro Tarak

"Areas like AI and machine learning can be used for good purposes and bad purposes. Just like broader technological, scientific and medical advances all need to be made in an ethical way. I would be concerned less by the emergence of AI, technology, machine learning, bitcoin etc. and will be much more concerned about the motivations and the care of the individuals who are experimenting inventing and adopting them. Technology and AI per se are then only going to reflect the care, the attention, the positive or not motives of the individuals who design them and use them."

Paul McNamara

"What we are going through is what people are calling the fourth industrial revolution and technology is moving and growing at such a pace that it is difficult to keep up and understand it let alone control it. This brings about many challenges and it also brings about many opportunities. The most important thing in all of this is that the future of work is human. The biggest danger with the future of work is that you've got to keep the human front and centre. At its most basic level is how you design jobs that are good for people. What is a good job? In the research we've done the most important determinant of seven major features of a good job - voice, using my skills and so forth, is that it's a job that fundamentally also supports my wellbeing. If this job is good for my wellbeing - my emotional, physical, mental wellbeing - then that's going to make me more engaged and productive. So when you think about love and compassion, the first order of effect will be on these human things - do I feel well, do I feel emotionally well? The future of work with all that is coming therefore means that we've to accelerate the ideas of humanity and the human at work to create a human centric work and world and not a machine centric world so that we can really get the benefit for humanity in the work place of technology where it can liberate us, give us other opportunities, help us work less and more efficiently and generate many positive outcomes. If however we don't design from that perspective, and if we don't influence the agenda from that perspective, who knows what the outcome would be?"

Peter Cheese

"We need to be rediscovering the human purposes of business. I believe it was Jack Ma, founder of Alibaba, who said that we have spent the last twenty years teaching people to behave like machines. Now we need to spend the next thirty years teaching machines to behave like people. We have a huge problem at the moment because actually people think business is part of the problem and not part of the solution. It would help if people saw the examples where businesses are showing that they are part of the solution. I do believe that there are many businesses which exist where love does flourish and people do treat each other decently but that is not the overwhelming impression that people get. I think love would contribute to the improvement in the trust that people feel in business; it would definitely reduce the issues of stress, burnout and issues of mental health that are worryingly damaging at the moment and ultimately it would contribute to greater engagement, productivity and greater financial success in the narrow sense as well - even with the impact of AI, technology and all that the future of work may bring."

Mark Goyder

"I think this is very timely - this work and discussion on love. When I also reflect on the issues to do with mental health which are rapidly emerging, I am wondering whether one of the reasons why there are so many issues, is because people don't understand love. Love is a mental state that provides security and it provides respect and understanding what's going on around you that you can leverage or use as appoint of reference. As a point of reference, love is an anchorage and so when it is not there and organisations don't provide that which they should, issues emerge. The opportunity therefore to find oneself and to accept who you are and to have a community or an environment that allows this is one that can be provided in an environment in which there is a culture of love."

Charlie Wagstaff

AGAIN IT STARTS WITH YOU AND ME

The future of work and organisation; the impact of the fourth industrial revolution and all that it brings with it can have a great and wonderful impact on the individual, the organisation, our communities, on society and our world. Technology and all its companions when used as a force for good can be the most liberating and freedom creating tools and process the human being has ever discovered. Whatever lens we choose to look through, at the very conception of everything of it lies a human mind and a human heart. An imagination, an idea, a thought. Its deployment and use will depend on our willingness to learn from our experiences of the past the world over including our mistakes and our successes. It will depend on our desire and drive to do things differently so that all not one or a few may benefit. It will require our willingness and our joint desire to put the survival of our very being and the world and environments we inhabit at the forefront of our decisions and the execution of those decisions. When at the root of all of this is love - the unconditional acceptance of all of who we are as human beings - and its attributes, we can be nothing but optimistic and enthused at what the future of work will contain. I am.

13. LOVE AS AN ORGANISATION CAPABILITY

....

To develop love as an organisation capability requires the integral development of your people as individuals and leaders, your leadership teams and the introduction of organisation wide and large scale interventions that lift the whole organisation onto a different platform, together. It would mean letting go of age old traditional ways of learning and training whilst taking forward with you the good things that came out of them. This which means letting go of the notion that everything old, traditional, or 'not invented here' is bad. It would also mean the willingness to be the pioneer and the organisation that goes first, leading the way for others to follow. Going first, means taking all the derision, flack and quite possibly, admiration for embarking on a journey that though challenging, will have the most extraordinary of results. Results that are fulfilling, rewarding, satisfying and all-encompassing for all of your people, all of their loved ones, in all of the communities you serve, in society and most certainly the world.

If you keep wondering why I do this all the time - i.e. mention all the time how love can have the most beautiful ripple effect - it is because I really, truly, very much believe it can.

BUILD YOUR HOUSE

To build a strong house the foundations you lay down must be strong and able to withstand the rest of the building that you construct, the walls that go up, the pillars that separate each room and the roof that covers it. Likewise, for a farmer to sow his or her seeds in order to reap a bumper harvest, the soil must be prepared, tilled, cultivated and fertile. Every aspect of what your organisation stands for must learn to and demonstrate love and in such a way that all of your people understand it, embrace it and experience it.

It is not unfeasible that the definition of love in one organisation may be different to another but the definition I want to offer you and that is simple, easy to understand and provides in my view the most impactful and greatest opportunity for making a significantly positive difference, is the one I offer you at the start of the beginning of this book. It is one that is free of any connotation that may be untoward or have an undertone of impropriety. Here it is:

Love is an unconditional acceptance of all of who I am as a human being and an unconditional acceptance of all of who you are - who others are and is therefore the ability to value myself and others, warts and all, for the beautiful human beings that we are and in so doing, enable myself and others to operate at our very best in the world.

A mistake that is often made in organisation is the assumption that a person is their behaviour and this in my view is one of the reasons why it is challenging to develop love as an organisation capability. It is seen and believed to be soft with no room for it in the world of work and organisation, where tough decisions need to be made and tough conversations need to be had from time to time. The reality however is that love is tough and the real, direct and honest conversations that need to happen across and up and down organisations never really happen because of the avoidance of the 'tough' and in at times and in ways that prevent real damage. The whole aspect of 'pay later pay more' then comes into play. Because avoiding a problem or a difficult conversation does not mean the problem goes away or the difficult issue is resolved. The acceptance of another person does not mean accepting bad behaviours or indeed behaviours that are contradictory and contrary to your organisation's values and purpose. It means being willing and able to be tough on the behaviour when it's out of line whilst remaining caring and respectful of the individual and allowing the fact that you view them as a human being to show through what you say and what you do. Once you have a universal definition of love and its attributes that work for you and your organisation, attributes such as compassion, kindness, forgiveness, trust, patience, discipline, encouragement and so on, it is embedding these into your organisational values as underpin your purpose in the world and developing behaviours simply described that will enable a clarity of understanding in your people and leaders at all levels.

"It starts with defining love. Then the definition would fit into values and behaviours that come from and feed into our idea of love. This is the first thing that could be done. We could then measure our values and behaviours against that - and think do we have enough love based values and behaviours in our organisation. I think many of our values and behaviours in HeadBox are love based but maybe we could do more. Then I think about our behaviours - what are those behaviours that can really demonstrate those love based, loved infused values and how well can those behaviours be demonstrated? Not only the behaviours but also the contexts the different contexts in which those love based behaviours can be demonstrated. After this, you could then think, how could we then measure its impact? And how would that flow through? We as an organisation could have a love based index - is there one that we could sign up to and share? And what would it say about us as an organisation when you think about what the younger generation is wanting from the organisations they work for this could be very powerful. But ultimately, it could be powerful for us regardless of the generations of employees because we all want to work in an environment where we can do something every day that is bigger than ourselves. We all want to be doing something that engenders that feeling. And when you talk about love, the very first thing I think about is about creating and doing and feeling a sense of something just greater than me. And there is something very powerful about that. It engenders a sense of purpose and there is something great about that - not just good - something great about it."

Andrew Needham

"I would bring them into a company manifesto and device reward and incentives around them and link them to progression - career progression too. I would openly bring things like generosity into what we recognise and applaud. So if we were deciding that love and facets of love are important, then I would encourage that we talked about it. Love as a word itself is so loaded so I would start with the facets of love and use love as the source to begin with and then over time, introduce the word love itself. I would not start with it in the first instance, I would use it and then migrate to it in time."

John Mangan

"Once you've defined the values, you need to then link those to the vision and strategic goals. Then make sure that you anchor those vales in the performance metrics, measures and the reward system. You then need to train people. What does it look like? That is where modelling comes in. Having done that, it's a question of monitor, reward accordingly and also let's celebrate and support good practice, because often people learn by seeing. What they see is what they will enact."

Emmanuel Mbakwe

"In the competency framework - having this as a value based framework rather than just simply competencies. I would also have it in our performance framework and meetings and encourage a dialogue about the impact of love - how are you kind and how are you receiving kindness. Making those powerful words a part of how we operate. Putting the words and what they mean in supervision and as agenda items; in training sessions within the organisation; In team meetings and in 121 sessions with the clients that we work with, in stakeholder surveys. Introducing these soft warm fuzzy words into our vocabulary so that we demystify it and also desensitise people to feeling a little awkward about this. So it is about changing the business speak to make it more heart driven; more heart speak."

Ingrid Tennessee

"Having a framework would really help – a framework that describes what love looks like in the workplace; what kindness look like and where there may be aspects of difference; a framework that describes what it means to demonstrate love to each other in the way we work together."

Sam Allen

"I'd measure it. I'd introduce a love survey every year. Webinars too. We do a lot of town halls in our organisation. So it would mean building it into our communication strategy. Also build it into your HR Strategy too.

I'd add the word love to your cultural values and to your value set, encourage love to be talked more openly and its construct, encourage a definition of what love would look like, we could ask our people what they would do to show love in its component parts for example, how would they romance their customers, their clients and their colleagues in a way that shows that they matter and they care. I would also look at introducing them into all aspects of L&D and into management training and development programmes too. How can we define it, how would we demonstrate it and so on. I would ask the questions particularly in our leadership programmes, around are we being parental in the love we show? And also how can our friendship love grow too - are we connecting? Are we finding commonality with our, peer set, our management teams, with our customers and clients? These are the sorts of things I would do."

Alan Price

How you define love and how you see it should then be embedded systemically and deliberately into every fabric, process and way of working in your organisation. And as you do this, the types of people you bring into your organisation should then mirror and have the capacity and capability to role model or in themselves develop love as a capability. Attracting and recruiting the right people, not in terms of face fitting but in terms of values and behaviours and a willingness to learn becomes critical.

"I'd start with recruiting the right type of people. Your recruitment is important in this. When I went for my assessment to become a director, it was as much about me as an individual and a human being as it was about my technical capability to do the role. Putting effort and thought into your recruitment process so that you can really maximise the chances of getting it right is important and in doing this, putting a focus on their values. The other point is the importance you place on the capability within the organisation. If you place no importance on it you will never develop the capability and so it has to be led from the top."

Naomi Gillies

And as your organisation grows giving your people an understanding of what leadership means to you and with you will be key, a value of which is to strongly embed the understanding that everyone in the organisation, regardless of level of status is a leader and must lead from the heart and with love. There should be no room for the abdication of responsibility to others. There will be people in leadership positions and who because of those positions have certain responsibilities particularly in relation to the needs and requirements of external stakeholders and investors. If recruitment and development interventions are aligned and reflect the attributes and values of love then it is likely that the individuals who occupy the stated positions of responsibility will demonstrate the behaviours of the organisation and use their status power and influence in service of the greater good of the organisation. Leadership in an organisation that therefore aims to develop love as an organisation capability can be defined as follows: *"Leadership is having the clarity of understanding of where you want to go, the knowledge of how you want to get here and the ability to,* **with love and without condition,** *mobilise people to follow you!"*

The introduction of organisation wide training and large scale interventions then also help to develop a culture of love and acceptance. The way you run conferences, town hall meetings and forums, where you run them and who attends all enable the development of love as an organisation capability. Can you imagine the collaborations, ideas, innovation and bonding that will emerge from an organisation wide event or if you're a large organisation, events where you have hundreds of your people at a time, a mix of levels and backgrounds and nations, celebrating, learning, doing, reflecting and sharing all at the same event?

Once upon a time, I had the opportunity whilst working in an organisation that wanted to create a significant shift and change in the behaviour of large numbers of its leadership cadre at different levels to facilitate the introduction of an intervention that would accelerate this. At short notice, we invited more than 300 of its people from across the world to fly into a European city for 4 days of training, action learning, problem solving, goal setting and resetting and planning. It was also held at the same time as the European football tournament which was a welcome side benefit for some. Now, the focus and the topic was about turnarounds, stemming the plunge in profits and margin and increased collaboration. We had four intensive days with colleagues and teams from around the world, pulling in the same direction, sharing views, ideas, practices and lessons learned whilst learning new ways of working together. The end of the four days had all leaving with concrete action plans agreed together and including where expert knowledge from other teams would be drawn. The end of the four days also saw all leaving with a wave of enthusiastic energy and uplift that spread right through the organisation. It was however short lived and very quickly swatted out by the day to day grunge of work in an organisation in which love and one of its core attributes of trust was at the time evident only in pockets. When I reflect on what happened, I wonder what difference love as the foundation of what we did could have made and how much more long lasting the energy will have been if love had been at the very core of all that we did, we said, learned, decided and then communicated.

Allowing all of your people to give feedback with love and training them all from the top to the bottom, to receive feedback with love will lift your entire organisation. There is no point having your senior people and people managers learn how to give and receive feedback in love and good intention if the people responsible for your front of office, back of office and security in buildings where existing, are unaware and unable. And if these responsibilities and duties are run by another organisation, it could be a great opportunity to create new and different ways of learning whilst facilitating an understanding of each other's agendas and purpose. If communication is key to the purpose of your organisation and it is important that all of your people can communicate effectively and through different channels of communication, then invest the money and ensure all of your people regardless of the nature of their roles are trained in communication, its impact and the value of communicating from a place of unconditional acceptance of others, which is love. If you are an organisation in which sales is a core organisational skill, training your people in the skills of negotiation should not be limited to only the individuals in your sales function. When coming from a place of love, consideration will be given to the potential benefit to the individual and the organisation of training people in other functions and professions in the skills of negotiation. The cost of doing this will far be outweighed by the benefit to the organisation that is seen and unseen and all the monies saved through the effective allocation of resources in other places because of the active presence of love would more than cover the expense. A culture of love in an organisation can only be a culture in which all of your people see themselves as leaders, thrive, feel great and perform at their very best. It would be a culture in which all of your people become resilient to the ups and downs of life and in turn will have your organisation withstand the challenges of life too.

"Organisations could put the effort in to understand the individuals that they have and not to assume that everyone is the same and that everyone has the same motivation, that everyone has the same career drivers and the more we understand that, the more we can guide them in the right direction and they feel that they are an individual that is valued rather than a cog in the wheel.

What really helps is a focus on coaching. That dynamic between a boss and an employee where it is clear that you are being listened to and that your ideas are important.

In my organisation we are working on developing empathy as a capability, which is an attribute of love, understanding what our people are all about and really developing our ability to coach others."

Neil Wilson

"We are doing this as an organisation. We've paused and said to ourselves, here we are, we are in this great business with a fantastic heritage and this wonderful purpose and principles that drive a rod of integrity right through our organisation. We're very blessed. We're very clear that we're an engine of social mobility and this is important to us. This is really powerful. But we've paused and said that in a world of turbulence have we paid enough attention to really making this real and present and do we need to do more to help sustain our business and our people just by reminding ourselves of who we are? Of why we chose to be here and to lead here rather than leading anywhere else? So we've decided that we haven't so in a kind of counter intuitive way, whilst the rest of the retail world is running around, we are investing significant time and money in the development and wellbeing of our people - giving them a week and the space to go and take care of themselves, to remind themselves of how brilliant they are; how talented and skilled they are; and why they're here, why the purpose of this business is the right purpose for them. And when you do things like this, you develop over time a capability across the organisation which is about love and is about caring. This is why I feel very blessed to work in this organisation."

Tracey Killen

EQUIP THE INDIVIDUAL AND SELF

Developing the individuals one at a time in organisation is key to developing love as an organisation capability. There is no point talking about what love is and what it means in your organisation if you are not prepared to develop the leadership and individuals within it and a great place to start is to encourage your leaders and individuals to view their own personal growth and development as integral to that of the organisation.

To develop love as an organisation capability, it is important to develop the individual within your organisation. Your leadership and management development initiatives should therefore have curriculum and content that develop and encourage the attributes of love in your people and in the people that lead them. The earlier you introduce this, breaking convention of grade and status related development, the better. Behaviour change and development is one of the most challenging to develop and is the reason why it continues to be the focus of development initiatives in organisations across the world.

"It would have to be through leadership development and incorporating the use of appreciative enquiry as a methodology. You cannot just say, starting on Monday, we're going to love each other! What we need to do is encourage each other to take time out to explore your own wellbeing, your team's wellbeing and what this would look like in the workplace together."

Sam Allen

"Everyone is promoted from within in our business. This is key. Then we also do lots of leadership development courses and it's not your typical power point - we talk - for example, we will enquire - why do we recruit on personality? We discuss not only on how we do things but also why we do them. We look for people who are simply enthusiastic, good and just want to get on. 10% of our colleagues are recruited from prison, we have people who have family in the business too."

James Timpson

"It is about Leadership. You can call it love or you can call it effective leadership and effective teams. Even though we've never said you need love in effective teams, but effective teams in my view must have an aspect of love in them. It therefore feels like leadership development and feels like experiential learning - and how you can get more people to experience what good looks like."

Richard Gillies

"You need to raise awareness at leadership level and across every level within an organisation. A culture of love is a culture of right behaviours. We should introduce a culture that focuses on the individual first and that says regardless of who you are or how you behave to me, I will show you love. My love to you is not based on how you relate to me. It is based on a culture of love, of discipline; a culture of excellence. It doesn't however mean that bad behaviour is tolerated. We can achieve this by coming together; consciously developing something as an entity that can then be rolled out and everybody will be involved in this."

Sam Aiyere

One significant way in which the attributes of love and acceptance can be developed in your people is enabling them to become more self-aware. When they are more self-aware they are able to more effectively learn about the beautiful attributes they have and the impact they have on others, intentionally and unintentionally. Developing the attributes of love and acceptance in your people is also about providing them with the tools and interventions that allow them to adjust and align in a way that would be enabling and supporting of them and of others. There are many tools and resources available to organisations and many of them free - for example simple conversation - that can be employed and made available for development. Some of the capabilities that together enable the development of love as a capability, that acceptance and unconditionally of self and others are the ability to listen through taking time out to have periods of sitting quietly without distraction or attention to anything other than self. Practices of mindfulness and meditation enable this. Retreats and time away spent in nature and outside buildings encourage perspective and freshness of thinking as are travel and exploration away from your normal day to day environment and context.

Giving the individual and yourself the tools and the permission to delve into the understanding who you are and what makes you tick can be liberating; asking probing questions about life and work and how they align with purpose, what you love, what you hate, what you enjoy, who makes you laugh and all types of questions, asked with an intent to genuinely listen without judgement and that includes listening to yourself as the individual without judgement is a great place to start. Understanding who you really are is the first step to full and unconditional self-acceptance and to creating an environment in which others around you can be encouraged to understand and to accept all of who they are. One tool that can be used in an exercise along these lines is the Vital Questions Framework which can be found in the book, Developing Inner Leadership: A pathway to wholeness by Ralph Lewis. There are in addition many tools that enable a basis of self-understanding - personality questionnaires, 360 feedback surveys, personal values identification, emotional intelligence assessments and so many others. It is simply a matter of finding the one that appeals most to you.

Some of the things that I've done, and I've seen others do in the world of work and life to develop themselves as individuals and leaders and deepen the capability for self-acceptance are as follows.

I invite you to try them to see which work for you. I only ask that when in time, you discover new ways of enabling self-acceptance in you and in your people and leaders, you share your insights and benefits with others in the spirit of contribution and without condition.

1. **Let go** - developing a muscle of letting go is one of the biggest things that I did. Resentment, vengeance and unforgiveness though not words or expressions that walk the corridors of work and organisation are emotions that very sneak up on us through our careers. The boss that didn't stand up for you; that promotion that you didn't get; the performance review that went pear shaped; the client that rejected the proposal; the strategy direction proposal the board declined; your exclusion from key business meetings; the budget increase that was promised, declined; the pay rise given to the undeserving team member, the list could go on and on and could themselves fill a book when gathered over many years of working with others. What happens when you don't let go is an accumulation of

unresolved issues that then cloud and inform negatively the way you relate to others and this is a road that leads to team and organisation dysfunction and for self, potential stress and depression.

2. **Embrace your strengths** - there is nothing more satisfying than knowing what you're good at and what you can excel at, focusing on this and leveraging them for your benefit and others. When you play to your strengths, you feel great, others around you feel great, you're open to ideas, feedback and contribution from others and you perform at your best. And when you are operating at your best, you are more inclined to emanate an energy that's infectious and encouraging of others around you to do the same. The icing on the cake is that all the developments and trends in the world of neuroscience and neuro leadership confirm this too.

3. **Time out** - investing time in yourself to read, learn, discover and try new ways of working and doing things that would be of benefit to your organisation or to yourself is satisfying. In the process you say to yourself subconsciously that you matter, and you dial up the leadership attribute of contribution to self and to others too. In taking time out you find yourself helping others and helpfulness is a human behaviour that enables happiness. When you are happy, your people are happy and the wellbeing in you and your organisation increases.

4. **Acts of kindness** - doing things, planned or spontaneously, that bring a smile to others affirm others and affirm you too. It demonstrates the appreciation that we all are human and in spite of the system of processes, stakeholder requirements, budgets, dealing with the competition, working out of go-to-market strategies, business development, organisation politics

good and bad, underneath all of those things, lies a heart in a human.

5. **Honour your agreements** - When I was growing up, my father always came home from work frustrated and disappointed when he'd attended a meeting in which a colleague or superior had agreed he or she would say or do something, only to find during the meeting that he was let down and left 'carrying the baby'. I remember, too, when at primary school in Lagos, Nigeria, my best friend, who had promised to secretly put an anonymous letter telling a boy in my class I had a crush on him inside his locker, when caught red handed by his best friend, immediately blabbed 'Yetunde sent me!' And in more recent years, I counselled colleagues who have felt thrown under a bus by their boss or colleagues when they needed them the most, meeting dates promised with one attendee simply not showing up and without prior notice. When you honour your agreements you make it easier for others to honour theirs. Even with themselves and the leadership attribute of accountability develops too.

6. **Sitting** - Simply sitting, quietly, upright in a chair, your gaze fixed on a spot in front of you, paying attention to your breathing and away from all distraction whilst paying attention to your heart beat starting from as little as two minutes a day, first thing in the morning, allows you to develop composure and over time the ability to respond, not react, to situations. Some people do various forms of meditation too. This is another resource that neuroscientists have found helps to improve brain function. Thanks to technology, there are apps that can also be downloaded on to your phone for you to listen to in order that you can practice your 'sitting' in transit.

7. **Journaling** - I never did journal before until I was asked to do so as part of a self-development programme I participated in. What I gained through journaling was the opportunity to reflect on the weeks and months I've had, my learning, my responses and what I would indeed do as a result of that learning. I also learned to record my achievements, the answers I'd received to prayers, times when I'd leveraged my strengths and the outcomes delivered as a result for me, my colleagues and my team. Whenever I experienced a disappointment I would look through my journal and remind myself of the many times I've succeeded and been happy.

8. **Making requests** - This is a lot easier said than done and some would say more challenging for women than for men to do. In my own experience, I've observed both men and women find it difficult to ask for what they want or make a request of a colleague and the more personal or self-benefitting the requirement, the more challenging it becomes to make that request. When you make requests and are willing to ask for what you want and underpinned by your why, you bring clarity to what you do and why you do it. When you make requests of colleagues and others it also becomes easier for them to make requests of you.

9. **Swat the critic** - To be able to demonstrate love and in an authentic way, our thoughts, our words, our values and our beliefs about others determine and control how we behave with them and to them. And no matter how hard we try, our behaviours betray our innermost thoughts. How you think affects what you do and to whom you do. Period. Therefore a great place to demonstrate love is to demonstrate love to self. Reprogramming what you think and about yourself and what you say to yourself is key. If you are a person whose words and internal dialogue is crowded and packed full of negativity, it

will be challenging to have an external dialogue packed full of positivity with others. This is not about being a motivational speaker and shouting phrases of encouragement from the stage at conferences, breakfast or lunchtime briefings or from the podium in town hall meetings. It is about the energy that permeates through your physiology when you come from a place of self-acceptance and the way you swat that inner critic is through the employment of repeated affirmations, self-encouraging words and the wisdom gained from a good mentor and peer support networks and exercise.

10. **Find your own purpose** - knowing who you are, why you are here and what you want to achieve in life and why is one of the keys to resilience and resilient living. An organisation full of individuals and leaders who know where they are headed in life is an organisation with purpose, with genuine vision and an ability to stand in the face of uncertainty and adversity. As leaders and individuals, when you are on purpose, it aids your recovery from setbacks and your ability to help others through their own setbacks. It enables you to tap into the depth of joy that lies within you. A joy that is fulfilling and independent of external circumstances. When you relate to others from a place of purpose, it gives you a sense of perspective that allows you to relate with the human being in front of you and not with their label, their status or their position on the organisation's status chart.

"On a personal level, it is figuring out what your vocation is and what is the voice, the inner voice—what is it saying to you? What is your calling and to discuss with someone the extent to which you are listening to that voice or not in what you are doing."

Norman Pickavance

Developing your individuals and leaders is one thing and providing them with the tools that help their self-understanding, awareness and acceptance is another. What is key too are the things you ask and encourage them to do which can be as simple as talking about the value of love in organisation, because the more love is talked about, the more you familiarise your people with its value, start the breakdown of barriers and accelerate its development as an organisation capability.

"It is absolutely essential to let the thought deeply, deeply sink in. Then it is talking about it. To get it out there. It needs to be talked about. Talking about it and with the right people first and maybe with their peers and with their management committees. Let it flow. Let some people in too - people that will provoke thought and debate around it and guide you in how to implement it. I deeply believe that this is going to be central to winning in the future and so we'd better start getting into this and more than superficially. Then another thing is walking the talk. If you have a value that is not linked to behaviours, then it's not a value. Values are only able to come to life through behaviour and people have to see you making effort to demonstrate what you say you believe. It is also ensuring that your people and the other leaders that you lead are also making steps and of course it's tending to the garden all the time."

John Mangan

"You encourage your leaders to behave in a more loving way by demonstrating it. You have to address issues in a very loving way and helping them understand that somebody might be in a different place to where they are. It is about looking at people from their own perspective. You cannot just teach someone this. You can send people on a training course and they'll enjoy it but by the time they come back, and the stress of business comes back, they'll forget all they've learned. So you'll have to demonstrate it. Now 20 years ago I wasn't like that but over time I've come to learn this."

Andre Angel

The power of role modelling and setting the right tone when you're in a position of responsibility and accountability for our organisation is one that can be leveraged too. There is only one way in which the rain falls.

"Now you must remember that not everyone buys into this. I do have some cynical people in my team and some very open people too. So what I do is seek every opportunity to register my leaders on different types of personal development programmes and programmes that look to self-care like mindfulness programmes too - for example the mindful leader. I've registered the company as a mindful organisation. I like to send them on love based leadership workshops and I also talk about it. I talk about love and kindness as a place from which we operate. I praise and encourage them and also encourage them to do the same with their own people and I empower them to do as much as possible to develop their own people even though we have limited resources. I also always talk about gratitude and talk about being grateful for what we have, our teams and the teams that serve us and for our clients and so on - if we did not have our landlords, we wouldn't have the buildings that we use. I'm always looking for all sorts of opportunities to talk about love in a real and tangible way."

Ingrid Tennessee

"I try to set the tone from the top. I try to set an example. The Chief Executive is only a symbol but the tone you set, the words you use, they set the mood for your teams and for the business. And then I observe how they, in their own way deliver a similar mood or behaviour and respect of their people. I recognise that everyone is managing different situations and they are all different personalities, but they are all starting from the same position - the direction and tone that is set by me as Chief Executive."

Howard Kerr

"It's got to be personal example. It's to make themselves accessible, to be vulnerable, to be visible and being willing to listen to people; put themselves out there. You'll find huge wisdom out in the business too. Admit mistakes and create a climate where others can make mistakes too - there are statements of 'I've got it wrong' that look like they've been drafted by lawyers and there are statements of 'I've got it wrong' that are genuine and from the heart - the latter is what is needed."

Mark Goyder

"Leaders demonstrating their appreciation is a very powerful tool. The saying of thanks. The acknowledgement of effort whether it has delivered great or not so great outcomes. The acknowledgement of intent when it is good is very powerful; to say I saw what you did and I assumed good intentions and then having a conversation about it is critical. The presumption of people's instinct to do good as opposed to a presumption of laziness or inattentiveness or indifference or stress, etc. Very few people really get up in the morning to do ill and yet they're often perceived to. I think appreciation and a presumption of good intent are really important to foster and should be modelled by senior leaders."

Paul McNamara

"You don't have to do big things to actually establish the presence of love and demonstrate care for one another. It is doing the simple things like once in a while just as leaders going and walking the shop floor; let people see your face; genuinely asking after the welfare of your people; making sure that you are sincere when you say hello. If it is genuine, people will respond appropriately. Ensuring that our doors are actually open sincerely. That people can actually come into your space without booking an appointment. And when they do book an appointment, ensuring that you genuinely give of your time. All this would go a long way in helping to establish a presence of love in the workplace."

Sam Aiyere

A core characteristic of organisation and, indeed, of life are the decisions and the choices we make on everything we do and how we do those things. We also make those decisions in different kinds of contexts, forums and situations and every single decision that we make, every single choice that is taken, has a consequence for others whether we see them or not. Whether it is a decision on a line of action, a strategic direction, market entry, product launches, target consumers or audiences and so on, on the one hand, or on the other, a decision on what to say to someone in response to a question, who to hire or not hire, who to promote, who to let go or to hold on to, for how long. It is in our decision making that we can most demonstrate the power of love in organisation, the value it can bring and the difference it can make to individual and organisation wellbeing, performance and prosperity.

A lot of time is often spent and invested in the tangible, external and sensing factors that influence decision making with less time on the internal and intangible. Therefore, more time can be given to the examination of intention and motive behind decisions made and the potential consequences that these can have so that these can be made in as full an awareness of the consequences, mitigating actions put in place to deal with unintended consequences as much as possible and the full reasons why articulated and understood.

Below is the Hofmann-PIICA model of alignment for individuals. It is a tool I designed to help with this and has been found useful by executives attending workshops I have run in developing love as a critical Leadership Capability. PIICA is **P**urpose, **I**mpact, **I**ntention, **C**onsequences and **A**ction.

The purpose of the tool is to facilitate your thinking and enhance the quality of your decision making by encouraging you to examine your genuine purpose and intent. It is self-explanatory and easy to use whilst allowing for increased rigour in the process of your decision making and ensures that what and how you do, and what you and how you say and to whom, are all in alignment with your genuine intentions. It has a visual diagram to demonstrate the flow and a supporting set of questions behind each of the stages.

A simple way in trying out the Hofmann-PIICA model is applying it to yourself - for example, you can think of different scenarios:

- » feedback you want to give
- » perhaps a request you want to make of your team, boss, colleague
- » maybe declining a request made of you
- » the job you're applying for
- » the unlikelihood of delivering on the numbers requested of you

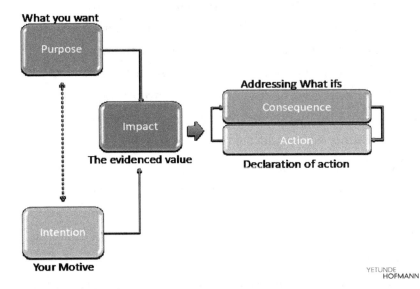

Hofmann-PIICA Model of alignment for individuals

Level	Possible Relevant Questions	Response Prompts
What you want — Purpose	1. What do you want to achieve? 2. Why do you want to do it? 3. How this plan/idea will affect the larger system you operate? 4. Who will this benefit?	1. The goal is to.... 2. The purpose is to .... 3. Implementing this idea is in in the service of the larger system vision to..... 4. It will benefit ....
Your motive — Intention	1. Where do you want this idea to get you/others in the future ? 2. Who do you want to be or be like in relation to making this idea reality ? 3. Why might someone object to this plan / idea? 4. What is my real intention?	1. This idea will lead to .... 2. I want to be .... 3. Someone might object to this plan if.. 4. My real intention is ...
The evidenced value — Impact	1. What are the benefits? 2. What is the outcome you want? 3. When do you expect to get them? 4. How do you know that you have them? 5. Is the action I am taking aligned with my real intention?	1. The beneficial effect of this will be... 2. The outcome I want is ... 3. The benefits can be expected when .... 4. An evidence of this benefits will be ...... 5. I am walking in alignment because ...
Addressing What ifs — Consequence	1. How will you know that the goal is achieved? 2. Where and when would you not want to implement this plan/ idea? 3. What positive gains are there in the present way of going things? 4. What are possible unintended consequences?	1. I will know the goal has been reached when.. 2. I would not want to implement this plan if.... 3. The present way of doing things.... 4. Possible unintended consequences are
Declaration of Action — Action	1. Now what are you really and specifically going to do? 2. What will be your ongoing feedback that you are moving toward/away from the goal? 3. What is currently needed or missing from the plan? 4. How can you preserve the positive gains of the "current way" when you implement the new idea 5. How can you avoid negative unintended consequences?	1. The steps to reach the goal involve.... 2. An effective ongoing feedback will be... 3. What is currently missing is...... 4. The positive gain will be preserved by.... 5. I can avoid possible consequence ... by ...

YETUNDE
HOFMANN

When you've landed on a scenario, try using the model. It would be helpful to write your answers down so you can reflect on them later. When you've completed the exercise, look back over what you've written and further reflect on the following:

» The adjustments you can make

» What you are learning about you and

» what you can do with that learning

Overtime and with practice, you will find that the considerations presented by the model become akin to you and integral to how you make your decisions.

GLUE YOUR TEAMS

In the early years of my career working in different organisations, I would often hear the phrases 'we must be a line of one' or 'I hope we are all aligned' expressed by my boss or the host or activator of a project team planning meeting, or team board presentation preparation meeting. In those days, I was the most junior in the room and invited by my own boss to take the notes and minutes of the meeting whilst learning about the business and giving me exposure to the senior people who were the gate keepers to my career advancement. I wondered why it was necessary to say this out loud as the minutes and actions were going to be circulated to everyone and they would have in the information required to progress agendas ahead of the follow on meetings planned. Over the years since then, I have come to appreciate that expressions like this are potential data points of the requirement to ensure that there is an atmosphere of trust, leadership and at its most fundamental, love in the organisation and in leadership teams. It is the glue that when present, keeps your team functional, engenders trust and enables synchrony.

Teamwork remains the most powerful and impactful way to effect change, drive innovation, solve problems and deliver results and the more attention that is paid to ensuring the team comprises complementary skills and capabilities, the more effective the team can be. The power of the team and team working is also the reason why the negative impact that a dysfunctional team can have in its organisation, whether the individuals in the team see and admit or not, is one that can tear the entire organisation apart and history is littered with examples of organisations large and small whose lives have been cut short and met an unsavoury end because of the impact of dysfunctional leadership teams. So imagine this, if a team that works well together can have so much potential to do great things within and for their organisation, and all that their organisation impacts, how much more extraordinary and amazing will their results be for all stakeholders, community and society, if their motive is driven by love, their interactions and the way they relate with each other, their decisions and all that they do is done against a backdrop of unconditional love. That acceptance of all of who they are as individuals, seeing themselves as the human being they all individually are and creating an atmosphere in which others around them individually and together can feel the same. Dysfunction will become a word consigned to the history books.

Therefore, although you can and must develop the individual and encourage the individual to develop him or herself, to really maximise the benefit for the organisation and accelerate the development of a culture of love, it is important that leadership teams and teams of all kinds that come together for specific projects and activities or are functional and hierarchical leadership teams develop themselves as a collective in order that they may travel furthest when they travel together.

There are many wonderful and helpful books that contain ideas and insights into what you can do to develop your team and many can be tailored to the nature and type of team you have, how long you have worked together, what you are trying to achieve, the tasks you have ahead of you and the culture in which you currently are operating.

If your destination is however love as an enabler, a backdrop and the glue and your motivation is the potential for yourselves as individuals, together and your entire organisation to make a significant difference in the world, you would together work to develop the capability to love and demonstrate love in what you do, for whom you do it and with whom.

The senior leaders I interviewed had their reflections on what leadership teams can do to develop love as a capability.

"They can start with respecting each other; being open and honest with each other; listening to each other - all simple things. It doesn't remove the need to have challenge but these are the really important things. If you haven't got those you are not likely to see love getting any further. These are the most fundamental things you want in a team and when a leadership team starts with this, it is easier to enable it through the rest of the organisation."

Steve Fox

"You can never underestimate the power of senior teams being really clear about what they value, understanding why they value it and then saying as a team - 'what do we need to shift in our behaviour for other people to believe that there's integrity in the choices that we make?' Then once you're clear on that, you can do all sorts of wonderful things and development interventions with your people around mind set and understanding themselves and so on. But the fundamentals have to be in place - and that is starting from the top team values and behaviours."

Tracey Killen

"I think that taking time out focusing on self, the team, on purpose and thinking about things like acts of kindness – how we care for each other, how we care for ourselves, how do we really promote and nurture this in the workplace. There should be an exploration of this, using various techniques and appreciative enquiry is one that I find works."

Sam Allen

"Stand back and understand your purpose as leaders and as an organisation. Reground yourself in what's important and if you understand purpose and all the things we've talked about and that you've got responsibilities to all these different stakeholders and communities and therefore you've got this core responsibility to your people, people that you employ and work for you, you start then to build the capability. If you just talk simply about love in the workplace it may lack context, but when you start to talk about purpose and responsibility then you create a context in which you can start to talk about love in the workplace in a meaningful way."

Peter Cheese

"There is a very nice quote that came out of the community recently which is about leadership that goes like this 'if your actions inspire others to dream more, to learn more, to do more and become more, then you are a leader'. I think that in order to do that, there's got to be a lot of love. I think it's important to inspire your people and in order to do this, you've got to understand and encourage them to learn from their environment and from others. And you've got to learn with them too. To do more is about if you understand what they are doing then you can have them do more and so therefore you as an individual and you as an organisation become more and you respond to your environment and not only do you become a leader, you learn to lead yourself too. You then also become more comfortable with yourself as an individual."

Charlie Wagstaff

"Bring your kids and your grand kids to work. Bring the people that it is obvious that you love. Bring them into the work place. This is breaking down the barriers between work and life. If you don't have kids, then bring those who are close to you or your aunt and uncle. Find places to bring the people that you love together and in the company of others at work. I suspect we'd all notice a difference. Your organisation will start developing love as a capability."

Charmian Love

Here are additional ideas that you can explore in developing love as a leadership team capability and as before, I invite you in love to try them out, feeling free to modify them as best works for your own team of unique and awesome individuals.

1. **Define your purpose** - This seems like common sense and should be par for the cause. There, however, are still so many leadership teams and at all levels in organisation that don't know and/or haven't defined their purpose. And if individually they know, they haven't together agreed it and aligned behind it. Defining your purpose gives you the opportunity to engage in discussion about it and along with why that's your chosen and agreed purpose as a leadership team. And when that purpose whatever it is, is infused by love and all of its attributes, it becomes one that inspires you, your team, all of your organisation, the communities you serve and live and the stakeholders that what to be a part of it.

2. **Invest in each other** - When you genuinely care about each other and as human beings, it is a knowing that flows through the team and an unspoken acceptance and belief that one person's success, wins and losses is the team's success, wins and losses. Investing in each other means taking the time out from the day to day activities of life and work to understand

and get to know each other as humans; to share your beliefs, values, hopes, wishes, likes and dislikes, fears, personal battles and triumphs, whilst respecting the personal space of each individual, appreciating that people come at life in different ways and at different speeds. Investing in each other is also creating space to share how each individual sees their own purpose in life and beyond the organisation, why they are here and how their purpose aligns behind the team's purpose.

3. **Invest in your collaborative leadership** - the leadership capabilities that flow from love are as critical to a team as they are to the individual and when they are operating within a team that is glued and in harmony it lays the ground for a culture of love. The speed of change in culture and organisation transformation of a team and teams that invest in their development together is more impactful in my view than the still common singular development that happens today.

4. **Play to your strengths** - Investing in your collaborative leadership will yield higher returns when you play to your strengths as a team by leveraging the individual strengths within the team for the benefit of the team's purpose and goals and for the organisation. And as in for the individual, a team that feels great about itself, creates an atmosphere of love and belonging within it, is a team that supports and challenges each other in equal measure and consistently performs at its very best. You become a team everyone wants to be associated with.

5. **Agree the rules of engagement** - Every team and organisation has rules by which it plays. It just may not have articulated it. Simple things like the structure of your meetings, the length of time given to certain types of agenda items, starting on time, ending on time, who stands in for who and for what, phones

off, language used and so on. The simplest of agreements can at times have the biggest impact on the ability of a team to operate at its best. And there may be more substantive rules of engagement too - for example, the stopping of a conversation or meeting when it strays into gossip; the undoing of decisions and agreements when not all of the team members are present; the nature of and what is communicated outside the team and by whom.

6. **State permissions and deletions** - The reason why I've separated this from the rules of engagement is in the interest of inclusion. When there is a dominant culture and way of thinking and looking at the world and often unnoticed, rules of engagement can be at risk of omitting something that may be important to a member of the team who may be uncomfortable in speaking up and requesting that a particular idea be included in the rules of engagement. Taking the time to focus on permissions and deletions, paves the way and encourages all of the team and in growing acceptance of all of who they are, to state what permissions and deletions should be considered for inclusion in the team's rules of engagement.

7. **Take time to sit together** - Starting your meetings with a short period of time sitting together in silence for two minutes; no distractions, eyes closed if that makes you more comfortable, gathering your thoughts and being present will contribute to the quality and effectiveness of your meeting. It gives you the time to calm down, to focus and to become truly aware of the other people in the room and yourself.

8. **Check in, check out** - Not every team has the luxury or the money to invest in quality time out to develop themselves but if over time, you choose to focus on who you all are as individuals, you are more able to tune into the needs of each other, what

matters most and what gets the best out of each other. Checking in with each other on multiple levels at the start of each meeting helps you in knowing each other. How are you? In work terms and in life terms? Two simple questions that you can ask and you can set a time limit too. No more than 2 minutes each per person and in that two minutes when it becomes a team habit, you can learn so much about each other and what can be done inside and outside the walls of organisation to enable the success of the individual and the team.

9. **Solve a problem together** - This may seem like a non-issue. After all, isn't this what teams are for? And I would say yes too. The issue though is that often, teams come together with reports and challenges stemming from their own area of responsibility and accountability as defined by the organisation and indeed by their own professional capabilities. They work on strategy and many times top down without including all the people that genuinely need to contribute and they execute from within their own tents. Solving a problem together would mean jointly delivering on a project together or coming together as a team to address an organisation wide issue and from an organisation first, team second and me third perspective. It would mean sometimes engaging in built for purpose business games to learn how each other operate in different situations and jointly reflecting on learnings had from mistakes made and victories won. Doing this regularly will be like oiling the wheel of a rusty bolt. The more it's oiled the easier it becomes to twist.

10. **Talk about Love** - One of the biggest barriers to unleashing the power and potential of love in organisation is the awkwardness that can accompany talking about it. But when you examine what it could really mean in the context of your purpose as an organisation and as a team, what it means to you personally

and how it would show up if it were present in what you do, how you do it, what and how you say things, the way you relate with each other and others in the wider organisation, how it would influence major decisions it becomes the right thing to do. A team working and walking in love is a team of courage, a team with ambition and a team that can achieve the extraordinary together.

11. **Learn and tell stories** - The power of storytelling should not be underestimated. Learn the art of telling stories; powerful stories that have a beginning, middle and an end; an end with learning, insight hope and a future and one that takes the listener with you and instils in them a hope too. Share your stories with each other and with your people having your learning and purpose at the heart of it, the implications for the organisation and what you all are there to do and when your stories are told from a team perspective and rooted in Love with all its attributes, the sense of belonging, energy and drive to go out and conquer the world that is evoked within not only the storyteller but also within the listener will be huge. Storytelling not only inspires, it unifies, it engages and when rooted in Love it compels others to act and to act with love.

A great way of developing the glue and becoming a team that works and walks with love is together when making decision applying and using the Hofmann-PIICA model to check yourselves and test the efficacy of your decision making. I designed the tool also for use by teams and is my gift to you. Here it is along with a set of questions that help you in navigating simply and easily round it. Overtime, you will find that your own questions also emerge.

Hofmann-PIICA Model of alignment for teams

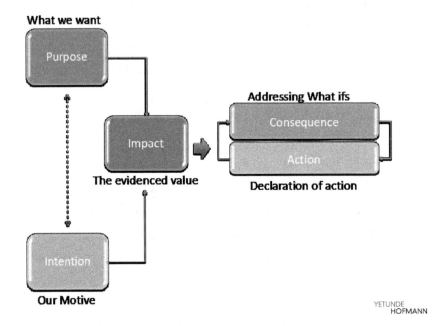

Hofmann-PIICA Model of alignment for teams

Level	Possible Relevant Questions	Response Prompts
What we want Purpose	1.What do we want to achieve? 2. Why do we want to do it 3.How will this plan/idea will affect the larger system we operate in? 4.Who will we impact?	1.Our goal is to.... 2.Our purpose is to ... 3.Implementing this idea is in in the service of the larger system vision to..... 4.All the stakeholders we will impact are ...
Our motive Intention	1.Where do we want this idea to get us/others in the future ? 2.Who do we want to be or be like in relation to making this idea reality ? 3.Why might someone object to this plan / idea? 4.What is our real intention?	1. This idea will lead to .... 2. We want to be .... 3. Someone might object to this plan if.. 4. Our real intention is ...
The evidenced value Impact	1.What are the benefits? 2.What is the outcome we want? 3.When do we expect to get them? 4.How do we know that we have them? 5.Is the action we are taking aligned with our real intentions?	1.The beneficial effect of this will be... 2.The outcome we want is ... 3.The benefits can be expected when .... 4.An evidence of this benefits will be ...... 5.We are walking in alignment because ...
Addressing What ifs Consequence	1.How will we know that the goal is achieved? 2.Where and when would we not want to implement this plan/idea? 3.What positive gains are there in the present way of going things? 4.What are possible unintended consequences?	1.We will know the goal has been reached when.. 2. We would not want to implement this plan if.... 3.The present way of doing things.... 4.Possible unintended consequences are
Declaration of Action Action	1.Now what are we really and specifically going to do? 2.What will be our ongoing feedback that we are moving toward/away from the goal? 3.What is currently needed or missing from the plan? 4.How can we preserve the positive gains of the "current way" when we implement the new idea 5.How can we avoid negative unintended consequences?	1. The steps to reach the goal involve.... 2. An effective ongoing feedback will be... 3. What is currently missing is...... 4. The positive gain will be preserved by.... 5. We can avoid possible consequences ... by

The first step to transforming lives and life is always one taken by an individual and/or a team with a purpose, a vision and a deeply held desire to make a difference and when that difference is about a force for the good of the human being, that desire can be motivated only by love. But what it does require, is the courage and the willingness to raise your head above the parapet, because you matter and you know that others matter too.

14. Looking forward

························

THE TOPIC OF LOVE is one that evokes all kinds of reactions and responses in people and is one that will always create an opportunity for reflection to different depths and in different ways. I for one experienced the love that says 'you matter' in the time that each of the leaders I interviewed invested with me, not one of them looking at their watch, cutting our time short or requesting for a repeated edit and re-edit of their quotes.

IT GETS EASIER AND THAT'S GOOD

What I did experience with some of them however was the gradual comfort and embracing of the notion of love, what it can bring to the world and the difference it can make, as we progressed through the questions I asked.

> "When I first heard about this, I thought blimey, love in organisation, you'd just about get away with it in this organisation for all the reasons we've discussed. Engagement in itself can be mechanistic. Love is way more fundamental. It is important. A lot of organisations and people will struggle with it but that is not a reason not to go for it and to start the discussion of its value."
>
> **Andy Mitchell**

> "I suppose I don't feel particularly comfortable with the use of the expression of love in the workplace. People don't

usually apply the word in the workplace unless you're doing something you shouldn't. But I think however, that the more it is normalised and the explanation and context is made clear, people and I too can get comfortable with it over time. It is about being clear about definition, what it means and the difference it would make."

Richard Gillies

"The whole discussion about love is fascinating in the business context. I want to ensure that the business has a proper engagement on the bigger issues around business rather than just the commercial success. What are we here to do other than the numbers we have achieved? What is the footprint we want to have and to leave behind? What it is that we want to do really well? If love is about purpose and it is about the human and the individual and having a collective purpose then stakeholders all around, not just your employees but also your clients, your investors, your customers, consumer groups, regulators, NGOs, government, etc - will see you as a respectful and purposeful organisation which will overtime acquire their love ... you see I'm using the word already!!

I guess the more familiar you become and are with using love in terminology, it and the more you use it and are willing to use it the easier it will be."

Howard Kerr

"Using the actual language of love in organisation and saying the word love is not an easy thing to do in construction. It's the nature of the industry. We don't use it in this context but it actually is an extreme version of enthusiasm and affection and support and relationship. There's nothing wrong with it. Yet we use the word in other places where it has the same meaning but not in the corporate world. But if you give people help with a good definition and give them the permission to use it - which is where leadership comes in - then there is potential for it to be more commonplace and welcome in organisation."

Steve Fox

There is certainly no getting away from the fact that introducing love into organisation will be challenging. It is certain that it will demand courage, ambition and a sense of purpose beyond self to even contemplate doing so. But there is a risk of lost opportunity if we don't.

"I think that there is a looming threat that because of the lack of love in our current discourse about economics, we are blind to the fact that what we're doing is a threat to the quality of human life, and there is not enough dialogue about what it is to be human, and what it means to be able to contribute to the communities of which you are a part of, genuinely."

Norman Pickavance

"We have talked about love. Love is very powerful. It is powerful in the home and it is powerful also at work. It is all things. Love is God. It is for learning as a leader and I'm a leader at home and I'm a leader at work. I need to learn, to listen, to forgive, to be forgiven. It is important to know that I'm imperfect. I don't know everything. There is very little difference between this and at work. We need to listen. To apologise when we get things wrong. We need to forgive.

We need to help people to become the people who God wants them to be. Of course, we want the organisation to thrive, to declare profits and all that, but it shouldn't be at the expense of the lives of those working for the company. It is powerful. Very powerful - if expressed in the way God wants us to express it."

Sam Aiyere

"In its true sense, you lose control when you think of the pure sense of Love. It is a putting aside of personal constraints. The phrase of losing your senses in an intense love or hate situation, it is the mind shutting down to some other motivation or some other force. It is powerful and compelling. If the success of a workplace or a person in their career or a profession is truly about passion, dedication to an outcome that is positive, then it is an accurate motivation to use."

Paul McNamara

"It's very important that certain values are seeded in world companies before they get too powerful through their economic influence so that we have got to seed in this world goodness and love as an umbrella theme has got to be pushed very hard so that as the world advances, we are not just pouring profit into the hands of a smaller and smaller number of people so as leaders are saying I came up with this new idea and are looking at executing the ideas driven by the love of this world and if we can ensure that just like people are voted into government that the leaders and people that are promoted into leading powerful companies have soul and a consciousness of love within them then that in itself would be a massive contribution to the future of the world."

John Mangan

And as we looked forward to the future and contemplated the 'so now what', some of my leaders reflected on what our conversation had stirred up in them and what this means for their own Leadership.

"I believe that there is so much that we can do as leaders. As leaders we impact so many lives Yetunde. As I'm getting a little more experienced in my role, I want more than anything else to be the difference. I want my legacy to be love based leadership. I want people to remember me as Ingrid cared. She really cared about what she did, about what she said and about how I felt. I want my workforce when they remember me to say 'Ingrid always had an interest in me and she always made the mundane extraordinary. She took what was of interest to me and made it her interest and that ultimately progressed this organisation.' Because people don't work for organisations, they work for their leaders."

Ingrid Tennessee

"Love is the only thing that matters at the end of the day. When everything is finished and you are ready to die, honestly how many billions of dollars you've made; how many cars you've driven or how much of a good life you've lived will make no difference if you don't have those who love you. There is an Arabic saying or statement that I've learned that says that' even the garden of Eden, without people should not be stepped in'. That means that life is not worth it if you don't have people who love you with you. It's not about what you have in life but who you have in life that's with you and that loves and supports you. When I created wealth the very first thing I wanted to do was to share it. I wanted to help others. Without people and without love, nothing is meaningful. Love is the base of everything. And once we all recognise it and a lot of people don't - maybe because of upbringing or being in difficult situations - but once we all recognise it and see it, the world would be a better place. It is the very basis of who we are as human beings."

Andre Angel

And others of my leaders reflected on what it means for the professions they represent and the nature of work that they themselves engage in and want to do in the world.

"I think that the next phase of economic innovation is international triple impact trade. How can we ensure the flow of love into international trade deals? How can we count on export/import contracts that enables love at different levels among societies? How to innovate international trade that creates integrated value? Will we have an impact globalisation phase in the coming years? Will the next free trade agreements have a triple impact approach?"

Pedro Tarak

"This is an incredible time of opportunity and coming back to our own profession, HR, we've got a profound role, a really profound role because if HR is what it is, it is about the people in organisation and so we have a particular responsibility for it and we've also got to recognise and own up to the fact that some of the things we've done as a profession have dehumanised work. We've been driven by efficiencies and processes and rules and to be honest this doesn't get the best out of people, and it doesn't get humanity into work. They are barriers to love and compassion because we create too many rules! Then you have all the unintended consequences. We have to shift that paradigm - the belief in an organisation that people are there to be controlled - to one that says people are there to be enabled to be supported and to be empowered.

HR has therefore got to move away from that very rule and policy based way of thinking to one that is about the real fundamentals of understanding people and what drives people's behaviours, why they do the things they do; and we've got to anchor things much more in the evidences we find in the areas of psychology and behavioural science. When we think about behavioural science and what motivates people and how you connect with them what we find is giving us a fascinating and deeper understanding of how the human being works and in this place, we will have the justification for the presence of love and also compassion in business."

Peter Cheese

"I think that organisations are not the prime instrument for a love-filled, love-driven world. It's the church. That is because the church is God's singular instrument of redemption in our world. I am very clear and convinced about that. So, one of the things that I think needs to happen, is that we begin to support church and church leaders in terms of how they can operationalise this whole principle of love. Now you may say that this is what church is all about but I believe we still have some way to go."

Emmanuel Mbakwe

"I would like to emphasise that I'd love people to look at business through fresh eyes. I'd love people to look at business with an eye to its potential rather than the stereotype and the track record of the businesses we read the most about. I'd love people to approach business in the spirit of abundance and I'd love people to think that actually a business is a place which brings people together; which is capable of unifying them to work towards a common purpose whatever their differences

-gender or political view, ethnic origin, upbringing, previous experience and so on. Business has at its best this wonderful unifying power when well led and I think while we are living in a very difficult disillusioned time and I'd love people to accentuate instead, the potential in business to embody the very best of what it is to be human."

Mark Goyder

What I learned from all these interviews is that even though we live in a world in which love is currently not seen in the main, to be part of organisation, it is supremely part of who we are. It is our greatest gift and it is our greatest need as human being. I learned with the help of my interviewers that if we fail to recognise this, we may fail to tap into the beauty of human that lies within us and the potential to create a world in which our future can more safely inhabit.

"My fear is that we will continue to see more individualistic and more commercial and more short-term instincts and actions. More obeying rules. More doing the "right thing" rather than the "loving thing", the "caring thing". But at some point, the pendulum has to swing back because it is not sustaining. If there isn't equilibrium in society, it corrects. It will have to."

Paul McNamara

"I think one of the things we have to find is a way of having this conversation. A conversation for enabling people to open up their hearts to what they really feel is a difficult thing to do. Whilst we are talking about love, I don't think necessarily it's easy for people to go from where they are to directly be open about the topic. So finding other ways of engaging in this dialogue and coming at it tangently where necessary, will be important."

Norman Pickavance

"You are on a good track and are on a courageous track. When we started the interview I was uncomfortable and by the end of our interview, I am much more comfortable and it does make you reflect - why would I be uncomfortable talking about something that is so integral to life and fundamental to who I am and who we are as human beings? So I think establishing a fact is a role that you've decided to tackle - the fact that love has its place in the workplace and it has its place in business. And yes it does. It's key. There is a taboo at the moment but it's one that can be and will be broken down in time. In ten years' time I can imagine a time when people will be talking about love in business in a very standard way - and talking about the love factor in organisations without anyone batting an eye lid."

John Mangan

By the end of my time with them, I left with a spring in my step, a hope and an anticipation. I left with a hope and a belief that one day, many organisations the world over will be talking not only about love and the significant value it can bring that lies beyond engagement, they will proactively be implementing, introducing, nurturing and developing within themselves and all of their people the attributes that enable a culture in which we all can and will thrive.

I am optimistic about the future of love in organisation. The developments in the world of tech and AI and all things pointing forward fill me with excitement. As machine invades the space of head and hands, increasingly the only place we can march toward with confidence and a sense of safety and solace, is the heart and in that place lies love.

We currently and for all kinds of reason fill this inevitable space and destination with alternatives that give us more comfort - happiness, compassion, care, vulnerability, kindness, trust and - alternatives that are beautiful and are all attributes of the one word we are less comfortable using. That word is love. But there is only one direction we are headed in and that direction is love. The future of work is certainly human. It is one in which that greatest need and gift and therefore our most critical leadership capability will be most required for our very survival and also our ability to thrive.

As I conclude our conversation, my own reflection is that whilst I do not know today where this journey to start the conversation about the value of love in organisation will lead me and you, what I do know and hope, is that I have planted a seed and opened the door to a deeper and more meaningful dialogue which in turn may result in action. If it does, then, maybe, just maybe, there would come a day when different organisations the world over, will be competing in love, to examine which amongst them demonstrate the most love to self, to others, the communities in which they live and indeed, to society.

Let's have the conversation.

ACKNOWLEDGEMENTS AND GRATITUDE

....

THERE ARE PEOPLE who have directly and indirectly impacted my views and contributed the writing of this book. People who have taken the time to sit with me and share their views, their hopes their vulnerabilities. I want to thank you all for your time, for your insight and indeed for your willingness to think aloud with me.

I want to say a big thank you to:

Andrew Needham - Chief Executive at HeadBox

Paul McNamara - Chief Executive at EValue

Samantha Allen - Chief Executive at Sussex Partnership NHS Foundation Trust

Lawrence Hutter - Managing Director, European Corporate Transformation Services, Alvarez & Marsal

Mark Scanlon - Chief Executive at Tenet Group (Chief Executive at Personal Group at time of interview)

Norman Pickavance - Chief Executive at Tomorrow's Company

Steve Fox - Chief Executive at BAM Nuttall Ltd

Jackie Bligh - Chief Executive at Worthing Homes

Howard Kerr - Chief Executive at BSI Group

Mark Nichols - Chief Executive at Xeros Technology Group

Ingrid Tennessee - Chief Executive at Quo Vadis Trust

Mark Goyder - Founder and Trustee, Tomorrow's Company

Charlie Wagstaff - Co-Founder, MD and Board Mentor at Criticaleye

Tracey Killen - Director of Personnel at John Lewis Partnership

Peter Cheese - Chief Executive at the Chartered Institute of Personnel and Development (CIPD)

Neil Wilson - Chief Executive Officer at Stanton House

Andre Angel - Founder and Chief Executive of TangoTab and speaks *English, Arabic, Hebrew, Italian, Spanish, German, French and Catalan*

Graeme Cook - Group HR Director at Keller

Richard Gillies - Chief Operating Officer at Simplyhealth

Pedro Tarak - Co-Founder of Sistema B. of Emprendia and Investor in Guayaki and Quinto Impacto

Paul Cardoen - Former Chief Executive Officer at FBN Bank UK Limited

Richard Eu - Chairman, Eu Yan Sang International Ltd

James Timpson - Chief Executive at Timpson Group

Martin McCourt - Non-Executive Director and Investor in a portfolio of companies; Chair of the Board at Glen Dimplex and Learning Curve Group and HeadBox at the time of interview

Lewis Doyle - Non-Executive Board Director Sussex Partnership NHS Foundation Trust, Pension Trustee and SMF. Board Advisor

Mark Reynolds - Chief Executive Officer at Mace

Alan Price - Chief Operating Officer, Peninsula Group and Chief Executive at BrightHR

Martin Bunge - Organisational Development and Sustainability at Emprendia

Sam Aiyere - Chief Executive Officer at FBN Bank UK Ltd (Chief Financial Officer at FBN Bank UK Ltd at time of interview)

Markus Hofmann - Chief Executive at 1st Crack and co-Founder of The Enjoyable Life Series

Naomi Gillies - Director of Retail Change at Waitrose

Emmanuel Mbakwe - Apostolic Leader, Pastor, Business Advisor, Leadership Coach and Mentor

David Allen - Chief Executive at Wates Group

Louise Fisher - Chair at the Chartered Institute of Personnel and Development (CIPD)

Charmian Love - Chair and Co-Founder B Lab UK

John Mangan - Managing Director Luxury Division, UK and Ireland at L'Oreal

Sally Boucher Cabrini - Director of Transformation, IT and People at Interserve

Andy Mitchell - Chief Executive Officer at Thames Tideway Tunnel

Mark Thurston - Chief Executive at High Speed 2 Ltd

I am thankful to Kevin Money whose willingness to work with me and co-deliver workshops on Love as a critical leadership capability meant so much as did his patience and sense of humour. It was a joy to jointly write with him our paper on Love.

I am full of gratitude to Markus who read through my entire manuscript to remove any duplications and Ross who in spite of his very busy schedule and work agenda, made the time to go through it too and at short notice. I was encouraged and cheered on by Martin Butler - author of *It's Not About Us: It's All About Them* and *The Art of Being Chosen* - who shared his insights and experiences from writing;

He also would not let me step away. I am grateful and thankful for the support of my family and friends - Sis, Ade, Yemi, Bodun, Beni, Nick, Theo, Massimo and Shanthi - all these wonderful people, thank you.

To Sam Collins - whose simple and loving introductory email, connected me to my publishers - thank you.

A huge thank you too, to my publishers - Authors Place Press - who chose to believe in an ambitious and yet inexperienced writer because of the potential they saw in me and the belief they had in the message I want to share with you.

Finally, I want to say how grateful I am for my life and career experiences; all the people that have journeyed with me through some or all of the years because without them and their contribution to my development and growth I will not be where I am today. To all of them, thank you.

CPSIA information can be obtained
at www.ICGtesting.com
Printed in the USA
LVHW082134300420
654542LV00030B/2143